Theoretical Foundations of Learning and Teaching

Theoretical Foundations of Learning and Teaching

M. DANIEL SMITH

University of New Hampshire

XEROX COLLEGE PUBLISHING

Waltham, Massachusetts · Toronto

CONSULTING EDITOR

John I. Goodlad
*University of California, Los Angeles
and Institute for Development of
Educational Activities, Inc.*

Foreword

Scholars in such fields as psychology, sociology, economics, anthropology, and political science are giving increased attention to educational phenomena. In time, their research will produce understandings which will enable human beings to intervene productively in educational processes. Unfortunately, however, the problems involved are exceedingly complex and the body of researchers is exceedingly small. Consequently, the educational sciences are still primitive; their predictive power is low.

Some educational scientists maintain that the search for intervention guidelines arising from research is premature; that we simply do not have the necessary evidence from which to extrapolate practice. While sharing this position in general, others believe that insight into selected bodies of knowledge about human behavior is useful for educators; that it serves to "raise the level of practical intelligence" employed in making educational decisions. Still others claim that rather precise connections can be made between certain accumulations of knowledge and educational intervention, and they cite the field of learning as providing relevant examples.

Since learning is at the heart of the educational process, it is not at all surprising that research on this topic exceeds by far research on any other aspect of education. Courses in educational psychology, which presume to draw upon some of this research, are common to virtually all teacher education programs. But severe problems have limited the usefulness of such courses. The classic studies in learning are on animals rather than on humans and must be interpreted with considerable caution. Studies on human learning are difficult to design and control. The findings too often are not definitive; frequently, they are contradictory. Even though there are no one-to-one relationships between the products of research and the specifics of educational practice, even experienced practitioners look hopefully for them and are disappointed, even disillusioned, when they are not forthcoming.

Professor M. Daniel Smith maintains that it is now possible to draw from the behavioral sciences a body of knowledge that is highly suggestive for teaching. I agree. In the pages that follow, he summarizes and organizes this knowledge for the purpose of demonstrating its usefulness to those who would assist others to learn. His position on the functions of teachers and teaching is clear. Teachers are interventionists; they should manipulate the environment so as to create optimum conditions for learning. To do this, they must be rather clear on the intended learnings, be able to anticipate what will confront learners as they move toward these outcomes, and be able to recognize both appropriate and inappropriate learning behavior when they see it.

Toward the concluding pages of this volume, Professor Smith summarizes his position with precision:

In order to change the behavior of students individually and in groups, one sets up environmental situations that make desired responses highly probable, reinforces the responses when they occur, and generally attempts to create a positive emotional response both to the teacher and (through the teacher) to the subject matter. This involves presenting students with relevant problem-solving situations in a warm, accepting context, maintaining a positive relationship with students while extinguishing (largely through non-reinforcement, partly through mild punishing contingencies) behavior that interferes with productive activities, and presenting a situation where the student can set his goals, receive feedback concerning his responses, and compare his progress with his past performance in order to see if he is attaining what he set out to do.

Not everyone will agree with this position. There are those who will see it as too manipulative. They want teachers to be more passive members of educational environments in which students play virtually autonomous roles in selecting the ends and means of learning. At the other extreme, some educators view optimum learning environments as dominated by programmed stimuli, controlled by computers in such a way that students proceed through them at individual rates of speed. The teacher monitors the whole, intervening when problems occur and providing a modicum of tutoring. Whether one views the teacher in either of these roles or in the role conceived by Smith, the knowledge about human behavior which the latter sets forth would appear to be exceedingly useful.

Concluding his summary, Professor Smith makes the following observation: "All of this is straightforward enough, but is nearly impossible to achieve under many school situations." Much recent educational reform has been directed at the school "situation," in recognition of the fact that the very structure of schooling has inhibited creative, professional behavior on the part of the teacher. Efforts have been directed at graded organization, with its norm-based standards; the self-contained classroom and the burdens it imposes on the elementary-school teacher; the textbook and the limits it places on individualizing instruction; and the traditional school building with its egg-crate organization of instructional groups. But all of these reforms, important as they are, create only opportunities for effective teaching and learning; they do not assure such teaching and learning. In fact, these contextual changes frequently have fallen short of the improved schooling hoped for because teachers lacked the professional teaching skills required for taking full advantage of them.

Increasingly, we are coming to see that significant improvement in schooling will be the result of comprehensive change: in the school "situation," in instructional materials, and in teaching. Substantial progress on the first two of these is being made, although much remains to be done. Meanwhile, the knowledge base for a profession of teaching has been growing. It is to the understanding of this knowledge base and its implications for teaching that Professor Smith's book makes its timely contribution. He does this with full awareness of the complexities involved, assiduously avoiding simplification and panaceas. This is no how-to-do-it book. He searches for concepts which various theoretical positions hold in common and seeks to illustrate their possible usefulness through ample use of examples. Almost invariably, he takes a clear position regarding what he considers to be of considerable or limited usefulness and why.

This volume is recommended for pre-service teacher education classes seeking to establish a behavioral science foundation for teaching, whether under the rubric of educational psychology or methods of teaching. It would be particularly useful for seminars accompanying student teaching or internships in elementary and secondary schools. Experienced teachers will find here no rehash of their educational psychology classes (although they will discover some reinterpretation of classic studies in human behavior). Instead, they will be introduced to the fruits of research relevant to teaching and its possible implications; to a solid basis for professional self-improvement.

M. Daniel Smith considers himself to be an educator first and a psychologist second. His prime interest is in the development of education as a discipline, with particular attention to development of instructional theory. After graduating from Dartmouth College, he studied musicology and then educational psychology at the University of Michigan. He taught mathematics, science, and French in secondary schools, moving between such widely separated states as Massachusetts and Hawaii in the conduct of this teaching. Then, supported by a National Science Foundation Fellowship, he studied at Harvard, where he became especially interested in problems of teaching science in the schools. Subsequently, he focused on applications of learning theory to teaching, working for a time as a research associate in the teaching machine laboratory of B. F. Skinner. Dr. Smith received his doctorate from Harvard and then began to "write himself clear" on his ideas while teaching educational psychology at Earlham College. These ideas subsequently were polished and rewritten at the University of New Hampshire, where he is now an associate professor of education.

JOHN I. GOODLAD

Preface

This book is designed to introduce, inform, and stimulate discussion, and to encourage further reading. It takes some cognitive leaps and chances in order to make the concepts more compatible with each other and make the flow of development smoother. It limits bibliographic references to avoid discouraging the student with the recent explosion of research information. It may raise more questions than it answers, but it should launch the student of teaching on a quest for an understanding of what happens in teaching. It may also advance viewpoints that stimulate some unique thought in his teacher.

Contents

4 Conditioning and Verbal Learning 40

5 The Development of Verbal Ability 49

6 Research in Verbal Learning 59

7 Verbal Learning and Teaching 70

Introduction

Teaching involves a dual responsibility, to subject matter and to the communication of subject matter. These are not identical, although they are inextricably interwoven. To know something about learning is not to be able to teach: that takes commitment, effort, and practice, in addition to talent. There are "natural teachers" just as there are "natural athletes" and "geniuses." No profession, however, depends on heredity alone to assure its continuation and improvement, nor does it depend on mere practice without theoretical foundations.

This book attempts to synthesize theories and research relating to instruction in order to contribute to a theory of instruction. It avoids discussion of the history of theories so as to concentrate on relationships between them. In a trivial sense it presents its own "theory" of learning in an early chapter, and later develops some postulates and theories about instruction. These are intended primarily as pedagogical tools for communicating a large and complex body of concepts and processes.

While not yet a science, teaching is more than an art. Scientific understanding of its processes is increasing. It behooves future teachers to consider conflicting experimental results and gaps between theory and practice, as well as the many areas where implications of research are clear, so that they can take advantage of future advances in instruction which are implicit in contemporary research.

The emphasis on concept formation, which characterizes this book, reflects a conviction that research in this area holds great potential for the understanding of instruction. There is also a basic assumption that conditioning paradigms may be extrapolated to a vast range of human behavior; this requires one to identify the units of behavior involved, that is, the complex sets of concepts, processes, and facts that the learner uses as units and that are reinforced or extinguished as units. Through such extrapolations, analyses of "pigeon behavior," which have been so often maligned, become applicable on a sophisticated level. This has been increasingly evident in many areas of investigation, most notably in behavior therapy, the application of conditioning paradigms to counseling.

Teaching and Learning Defined

Learning is a title for a type of change in an organism. Basically it involves electrical and chemical changes in the brain, changes not amenable to observation except in special circumstances. Thus when we "teach" someone something or "tell" him about something, we assume that a change has occurred that can result in behavior different from what he would have shown otherwise.

Learning implies a storage of information or experience, and is thus based on remembering. Using or applying this information is also a learned behavior for the most part, although there are many basic hereditary mechanisms that either need not be learned or require very little learning to bring into play. While learning is based on retention and use of information, the complexities of this dual process are so manifold that we have a host of classifications for them, ranging from simple recognition or recall to higher order mental processes of an abstract or symbolic type.

All living organisms learn. Indeed, one might propose the ability to learn as a distinction between living and nonliving matter (unless it should be found that one can "teach" a sodium atom to ionize at a lower potential or illustrate some other form of learning in matter we consider "nonliving," or unless one accepts the capability to store information as equivalent to learning).

What differentiates learning from other behaviors or states of an organism? Are all organisms learning continuously? Common sense indicates that learning is a special function or process. It may be characterized as a change induced in an organism or provided by the organism, which enables it to adapt to some environmental contingency or problem. This change can be seen from two points of view. One is that the contingencies of the environment require the organism to change, or impose the necessity to which the organism adapts. Another is that the organism searches its environment and produces from within itself modifications of its behavior that enable it to act more effectively on the environment. Neither is more true or valid than the other: neither can be the only point of view. Thus, learning comes from within to meet contingencies from without; if no contingencies exist, the probability of adaptation is less, but the organism can still explore the environment physically or mentally and discover situations requiring adaptation.

The latter point of view; that is, that the organism can act upon the environment to discover discrepancies in it (as compared with past experience) or to locate contingencies which require it to adapt, implies an active rather than passive organism, a model more compatible with our human pride in our autonomy and intellectual aggressiveness. Whether it represents a basic difference in kind of learning or a superficial difference in the way one identifies or recognizes existing problems is a matter for further discussion and debate.

One implication of the "active" point of view mentioned above is that it is possible as a result of learning to change the probabilities of possible future events. For instance, a cave man who must travel from his cave to a waterhole may confront an intervening saber-toothed tiger physically, as he makes the journey, or he may confront him ahead of time, mentally. If he does the latter, there may be a higher probability of his survival. The mental anticipation may occur as a result of the intervention of an older tribal member who remembers that there are often tigers in the path: the probability of the survival of the whole tribe is greater because of the presence and intervention of this experienced person, or "teacher."

Teaching, then, implies the intervention or involvement of another organism in changing the probability that certain contingencies will be met, and therefore the probability of successful adaptation. This is not to say that the probability might not decrease rather than increase; the "teacher" in the case above may inform the student erroneously, or the student, as a result of the warning, may refuse to go after water, and thereby reduce the probability of survival of the whole tribe.

Note that this definition of teaching, coupled with the definition of learning, does not imply the use of words only, or at all. One may teach a child to cope with his environment by presenting him with simplified versions of it and allowing him to adapt to these simplified versions without verbal instruction or other guides. Indeed, the nature of play has always been at least partly an imitation in simplified form of the behavior of adults, and, therefore, a learning experience. Thus interest in the use of games in instruction is currently high.

This view of teaching is incomplete and will be extended and adapted in the course of this book. The purpose of this introduction is only to present the general purpose of the book, together with a brief discussion of the processes of learning and teaching, which are the main subjects. It might be well to discuss briefly at this time the implications of the term "instruction" as it differs from "education" or "teaching." Education is a very broad term and has come to mean administration, politics, riots, and pot, as well as teaching and learning. Learning is more restricted and basic; it is a primary concern of psychologists, who pursue an understanding of its various forms and expressions. Instruction, on the other hand, is a process in which one person intervenes in the learning of others; instruction implies manipulation of the environment and, to some degree, control of the behavior of others. It is necessary to recognize these facts and to consider the responsibilities they invoke. This is the proper concern of educators. We can no longer assume that knowledge of a subject implies the ability to teach it, nor can we dismiss poor teaching or good teaching as basically insignificant in their effects on our culture. Teaching maintains our culture, and strengths and weaknesses evident in the culture can be traced to instructional processes used many years before. We must understand the present process better, and it is to that end that this book has been written.

The Plan of This Book

The following chapters present some fundamental principles of learning and teaching. The reader will find them at once complicated and trivial, abstract and concrete, vague and detailed. He may experience some confusion and perhaps some insecurity. Some students find an objective approach to behavior very threatening: it makes them feel less human, less complex, less confident of their own uniqueness than they were before. However, understanding behavior should not in any significant sense make human beings less unique or less valuable. Rather, it should make them more appreciative of the tremendous variety in human nature.

There is another view of this subject which the student should be aware of. This is the view that the human being is sacrosanct and not a fit topic for study. Any investigation of human behavior can be labeled "mechanical" or "inhuman" or "inhumane" and therefore be suspect. This view was met hundreds of years ago by medical men, with the result that today most people do not object to having doctors understand our inner works because we assume they use that knowledge for our good. A similar attitude in respect to the study of behavior should be fostered.

Another point of view one meets in respect to this subject is that it is somehow less human or less desirable to analyze objectives and plan steps in advance: real human beings go ahead on intuition and take whatever occurs. While it is obvious that one cannot spend all of his time planning and none of it executing the plans, it is also true that in an age of relatively effective media and instructional methods we need to sit down more often and plan what kinds of outcomes we wish to have evident in the final product, that is, in the student after he has been taught. Thus this book will emphasize the need for considering and specifying the objectives of teaching, and for extending these goals beyond the conventional achievement test format into behaviors related to learning to learn, transfer of learning, and understanding and appreciation of the subject studied.

The first chapter is on conditioning. While human behavior is not identical in nature or complexity to that of lower organisms, many psychologists, anthropologists, and sociologists today treat animal behaviors as simple models for human behavior because this increases their insight into something which is hard to understand, hard partly because one has to use his own human behavior in trying to understand. There-fore, the reader is urged to accept some oversimplification in the interest of later being able to use the language thus developed in analyzing more complex situations.

The reader should not be overmotivated to get something "practical" out of the early parts of the book because one cannot build tools for analysis that quickly. There will nevertheless be attempts in each chapter to apply to teaching the concepts and processes discussed. The reader is urged to create additional examples himself for later recon-sideration.

Basic Learning Paradigms 1

There are many theories, systems, and sets of principles related to learning. This chapter presents some relatively basic ones, and then discusses relationships between them and other models of learning behavior.

1–1 Classical Conditioning

A hungry dog will salivate (an *unconditioned response*) if food powder (an *unconditioned stimulus*) is inserted into its mouth. If a bell (a *neutral stimulus*) is sounded when the food powder is inserted, and if this pairing is repeated a number of times, it will be found that the bell can elicit salivation (a *conditioned response*) by itself. Generally, then, if a neutral stimulus (the bell) is presented several times just before an unconditioned stimulus (the food powder), eventually the neutral stimulus alone will elicit the response (salivation, previously the unconditioned response, now the conditioned response). This process is called *classical conditioning*: it was first explored extensively in research by Ivan Pavlov, around 1926.

EXTINCTION

If *after* conditioning, the bell is sounded many times without presenting food powder, the dog ceases to salivate to the bell alone. If given a rest and brought back to the experiment, however, the dog will salivate to the bell again, but not as much as before. If this is repeated enough times, salivation in response to the bell will cease altogether. The process of withholding the unconditioned stimulus is called "extinction." The recovery of the response after a rest, is called "spontaneous recovery." To summarize, if the conditioned stimulus is presented many times without the unconditioned stimulus, the conditioned response decreases and eventually extinguishes. To prevent extinction, that is, to maintain the conditioning, one can present the unconditioned stimulus (food powder) along with the conditioned stimulus; this need not be done every time, but only intermittently. Since this prevents a weakening of the conditioned response, the unconditioned stimulus when used thus is called a *reinforcer*.

SECONDARY CONDITIONING

If a flash of light were paired many times with the bell mentioned above, that flash would *also* come to elicit the salivation, by itself. This is *secondary conditioning*. The bell, once a neutral stimulus but now a conditioned stimulus, has been used to "condition" the response to the light, just as the food powder was used to "condition" it to the bell. When used to maintain the response to the light, the *bell* is called a *secondary reinforcer*. The bell is to the light as the food powder was to the bell. A stimulus has been "conditioned" to a response when it comes to elicit that response by itself.

GENERALIZATION

Suppose the bell has become a conditioned stimulus for salivation, and suppose another bell of higher pitch is sounded. Salivation will occur to the new bell also, but in a lesser amount. This is called *stimulus generalization*, in that the response occurs though the stimulus is changed. (It can also be called *discrimination*, in that the response given to the different stimulus is not exactly the same response.)

CLASSICAL RESPONSES

Classical conditioning involves responses that are involuntary, especially emotional ones such as fear. These involuntary responses are elicited naturally by a variety of stimuli; that is, many stimuli existing in the ordinary environment elicit them, such as loud noises (fear), threatening motions (protective reflexes), and pleasurable physical contacts (relaxation or pleasurable anticipation). Any neutral stimulus accompanying or immediately preceding such a stimulus may come to elicit the reflex or emotion on its own. In this way one learns to "fear" such stimuli as a lightening flash that precedes thunder, a metal surface that has shocked one, or a situation in which one may have suffered embarrassment. One also learns to be "hopeful" or to "feel pleasure" in the presence of stimuli associated with food or other pleasurable stimuli. Such responses are not always obvious to an observer, so there is a tendency to overlook them when analyzing "learning," particularly in scholastic endeavors where "understanding" and "knowledge" are primary concerns. Classical responses *do accompany* these other responses, however, and are an important component of any learning situation. They involve what we generally term the "emotions," or the "affective domain" of learning, and include liking and disliking, fearing, hoping, and other more complex manifestations of feeling such as our general attitudes about certain things. These states, although hard to describe or observe, are important in that they *direct* learning; learners consciously or subconsciously incorporate them into any learning situation and are inclined to learn or repress the responses involved according to whether the emotional connotations are positive and promising, or negative and anxiety producing. These relationships will be discussed in greater detail in a later chapter.

1–2 Operant Conditioning

For many human and animal responses there is no easily identifiable stimulus or pattern of stimuli that "controls" or "elicits" responses in the way that food powder elicits salivation in a hungry animal. You lift your arm, turn your head, speak several words, smile, walk. The circumstances that evoke these responses are not easy to identify, in comparison with such relationships as food powder followed by salivation. These responses are *voluntary*, that is, they are controlled by the person himself, whereas classical reflexes such as fear are *involuntary*. Such voluntary responses are called *operant* responses, since they are used to "operate" on the environment. But what does it mean to say they are "voluntary"? It means that one can "will" them to come about, or "control" them. Does this mean, then, that they cannot be controlled or brought about by a third party, as in the case of salivation or fear which can be brought about by administering food powder or a loud noise? This question has caused a great deal of debate over the years. One answer is that human beings have a choice in what they do, and can will themselves to do or not do whatever they wish: thus a third party could *not* bring about a response that he wished to by arranging prior conditions in the right way. Another answer is that choice is a very complex matter and may be a term which merely indicates that we don't understand the nature of the conditions that bring about a certain response: this view maintains that if one can arrange conditions correctly, one *can* get another person to respond as he wishes. Of course, such an arrangement may be impractical or impossible, but conceivably if one could bring it about he could get the response he wanted.

This last point of view is called a "deterministic" one: it maintains that our behavior is determined by our environment. Whether it is entirely true or not, there are many situations and phenomena of human behavior which can be explained by *assuming* it is true, and so for the time being it will be assumed that one can conceivably identify the conditions which bring about operant responses and thereby control them.

CONTROLLING BEHAVIOR

What does it mean to assume that there are controlling stimuli for operant responses? It means one assumes that if he could identify such patterns or situations, he could reproduce them and thus evoke these responses in another person. There is much evidence that if one identifies through careful observation the circumstances that control various desired behaviors, and then reproduces these circumstances closely, the probability that these behaviors will occur is significantly high. It is not one hundred percent, but in many cases it is much better than chance, and in special cases the probability is very high. Another way to say this is that human beings are determinate systems, within limits. Classical conditioning demonstrates this, and one can assume that operant responses are governed by some similar kinds of relationships.

Why would one wish to control behavior? If one is to teach, that is, to bring about learning with a higher degree of probability than is possible without teaching or without schools, then one must be able to bring certain stimuli into control of certain responses. In classical conditioning this is done by presenting the neutral stimulus just before the unconditioned stimulus a number of times: when the unconditioned stimulus is removed, the neutral stimulus is found to have become a conditioned stimulus, in that it elicits the response by itself. Operant conditioning, on the other hand, involves responses that operate on the environment and are under the voluntary control of the learner. Thus operant responses are controlled through more complex mediating processes in the brain. The stimulus patterns which evoke these responses are more complex and harder to reproduce; sometimes they cannot be identified and reproduced at all. For example, the response of turning one's head may be controlled by a noise from the side, or by the command "turn your head to the side," or by a desire to avoid looking at someone he does not wish to talk to (because of some previous learning that makes that person undesirable or threatening or boring), or for a number of other reasons. Thus, it is not easy to evoke this response in the same sense that a classical response can be elicited; emotional responses to various stimuli are easier to condition than are operant responses.

CONDITIONING OPERANT RESPONSES

In order to learn how to deal with operant responses, that is, how to make them more or less probable under given conditions, it is helpful to turn to the simpler behavior of animals. Then, after learning how to deal with similar behaviors at that level, one can apply the knowledge to more complex human behavior. This has been done, and the results are becoming increasingly useful both in school learning and in counseling and therapy. The techniques developed this way are a bit complicated at first reading, but are basic enough to be worth the effort to understand.

Suppose one wishes to bring some simple operant response under the control of a given stimulus. If he cannot identify or control the pattern of stimuli which evoke the response (assumedly because it is too complex or varied) he can instead bring the response under the control of some simpler stimulus. This will allow him to evoke the response in a convenient, predictable fashion. How is this done? First one chooses a particular environment in which to operate; this will be relatively constant throughout the process. Then one arranges to present the learner with a certain stimulus immediately after the learner gives the desired response. If the correct kind of stimulus is given, then the desired response is observed to become more frequent in that particular environment. One concludes, then, that the stimulus, presented following the response, has somehow increased the frequency of that response. Such a following stimulus is called a "reinforcer," since it reinforces the response or makes it stronger or more probable. Another way to say this is that it increases the *probability* that the response will occur in that situation again.

Having increased the probability of the response in this way, one has begun to control it. However, one ultimately wishes to be able to produce the response by giving some simple stimulus and having the response follow that stimulus. This takes a little more arranging. What one does is make a guess as to when the learner is likely to give the response, present the stimulus which is to evoke the response, and then if the response is given, present the following stimulus. If the response is not given when one presents the preceding stimulus, then one does *not* present the following stimulus. By doing this a number of times, the probability that the response will be given after the preceding stimulus is increased, while the probability that it will be given at other times decreases: thus one achieves "conditioning."

There are special terms describing the stimuli used in the process: the "following" stimulus is called a *reinforcing stimulus* or a *reinforcer*, while the controlling stimulus is called the *discriminative stimulus* or just the *stimulus*. Thus, one increases the frequency or probability of a response by presenting a reinforcing stimulus immediately after that response. Later one presents the discriminative stimulus and reinforces the response *only* when it follows the discriminative stimulus, not otherwise. For example, suppose one wishes to teach a dog to bark in response to the command "speak." One first reinforces barking by giving the dog food every time he barks.

Then, when the dog barks fairly dependably in response to the general situation, that is, when he sees you before him in a given room with something in your hand, you can begin to teach him to bark only when you say "speak." This is done by saying "speak" and then rewarding him if he barks: if he barks without that command, or if you say speak and he doesn't bark, you don't reinforce (reward) him. To be most successful, the reinforcement must come immediately after he barks. It may be that he has learned to bark whenever he sees you, and thus it may take some time before he learns to bark only on command.

In summary, to condition an operant response to a discriminative stimulus, that is, to bring an operant response under control of a particular stimulus, one first increases the frequency of the response in the general experimental situation by reinforcing it when it occurs. Then one introduces special contingencies whereby the response is reinforced only when it is given following the discriminative stimulus, that is, the stimulus that is to control it. When it is given without that stimulus, it is extinguished; that is, it is not reinforced.

The relationship between the response, the reinforcing stimulus, and the discriminative stimulus which has been described above is sometimes referred to as the "three-term contingency," and is symbolized as follows:

$$S^d \longrightarrow R \longrightarrow (rf)$$

It is the operant "paradigm" for learning and implies that to bring about learning one must arrange the environment so that these three events occur in succession.

ANOTHER EXAMPLE OF OPERANT CONDITIONING

In classical conditioning, if one presents the conditioned stimulus several times without the accompaniment of the unconditioned stimulus, the response decreases in probability or strength: this is called *extinction*. To prevent extinction, one presents the unconditioned stimulus with the conditioned one intermittently: in this sense, the unconditioned stimulus is called a *reinforcer*. In operant conditioning, the reinforcer is the stimulus that *follows* the response. In both cases one can bring about extinction by withholding the reinforcer. Thus if one conditions a dog to bark at the command "speak" by reinforcing the barking according to the three-term contingency, and then subsequently stops reinforcing the barking even though it continues to occur when one says "speak," the dog will eventually stop responding to that command. This is extinction of an operant response. Spontaneous recovery is also observed. If one extinguishes an operant response that had been conditioned previously, and then gives the learner a rest, one will find that the response has "recovered"; that is, on trying the command or discriminative stimulus later on, one finds that the response will again be given. However, if one extinguishes, rests, and extinguishes again, one will ultimately eliminate the response for all practical purposes. Note, however, that to extinguish a response one must evoke it—this is not forgetting, but unlearning.

ANOTHER EXAMPLE OF OPERANT CONDITIONING

Suppose a pigeon is placed in an experimental cage in which there is a mechanism for delivering food. Just above the food tray there is a key which the pigeon can peck. This key operates a circuit which is connected to a food dispenser. If the pigeon pecks at the key, food is delivered to the dispenser. If the pigeon is hungry, he learns quickly to peck at the key, and does so with accuracy and rapidity. This is explained by saying that the pecking is reinforced by food.

OPERANT RESPONSES COMPARED WITH CLASSICAL RESPONSES

Operant responses are those which the learner uses voluntarily to operate on the environment, while classical responses are reflexes which occur involuntarily in response to particular stimuli. The controlling stimuli for operant responses are often more complex and harder to identify than those which control classical responses, although fear and love and other sophisticated emotions are made up largely of classical responses whose controlling stimuli are also hard to identify. In both, the conditioning process involves the substitution of a specific controlling stimulus for the stimulus or stimuli which control the response initially: in classical conditioning the initial controlling stimulus is called the "unconditioned stimulus," while in operant conditioning it is not referred to since it is not identifiable.

There is also *secondary* conditioning of operant responses, as there is of classical ones. If one has brought an operant response under the control of a certain stimulus (the S^d), then one can pair some other stimulus with the S^d and condition the response to that one also; this implies, of course, reinforcing the response when it is given to this second controlling stimulus.

1–3 Stimulus Substitution

While the two types of conditioning, classical and operant, are different in many respects, one need not assume that the cognitive processes involved are entirely different. In each case a new stimulus is brought into control of the response: in the classical case the initial controlling stimulus is easy to identify, while in the operant case it may not be. However, in the case of operant conditioning, a reinforcing stimulus is used to help establish the relationship that brings about the stimulus control. If one has brought an operant response under control of one stimulus, one can substitute another for it by pairing the two for a time: this is similar to the pairing process used in classical conditioning (pairing implies giving the new stimulus at the same time or just before the old).

Thus in each case there is a process of substitution of one stimulus for another. For example, if one wishes to condition a person to fear a light, he will present the light just before he administers some other stimulus that leads to fear—perhaps a loud noise or a physical blow. After some pairings, the light will elicit fear in the learner. If one wishes to condition a pigeon to cock his head in response to a light, and if he already does so when he hears the click of the mechanism which brings him his food, then one pairs the light with the click of the mechanism a number of times, and reinforces the response with the presentation of food in the food tray: after a while, one can present the light by itself and the pigeon will cock his head. In a more complex case, if one wishes to have a student say "cyclotron" when he sees an example of that rather complex tool for high energy research, it will not be very efficient to wait for him to say something that resembles the word "cyclotron" and then reinforce it. Instead, one shows the student the cyclotron (the neutral stimulus) and tells him: "That is a cyclotron." This kind of assertion is a conditioned stimulus for an *imitative* response on the part of the student, a response learned through some years of trial and error. So the student imitates by responding "cyclotron," and the neutral stimulus (the cyclotron) is paired with the conditioned stimulus (the statement which has been imitated or echoed). Such naming behavior is so highly learned at this point that it often takes students only one trial to learn the name of something, but it is based on a long history of learning how to learn. It is stimulus substitution at a high level of sophistication.

ARE REINFORCERS NECESSARY?

It is generally recognized that the outcome of a response has some effect on the probability that the response will be given again. There are obviously evolutionary advantages resulting from having a cognitive or mental system which reacts this way. However, some theorists feel that the *mental* relationships which make operant conditioning possible are *not* dependent on reinforcement. They regard conditioning as a matter entirely of pairing of stimuli, or of what they call "contiguity," which refers to the relationships where the new stimulus comes just before or at the same time as the old. They feel that this association is the true learning and that the effect of reinforcement on the response is a matter of *performance*, as distinct from the learning which goes on in the mind. Thus they recognize that someone may know something without demonstrating that he knows it. However, other theorists who reject this point of view hypothesize additional relationships to explain this, without separating learning from performance in this way. Neither position will be argued in this book, although both points of view will be given where appropriate.

1–4 Secondary Reinforcing Stimuli

Given that reinforcing stimuli affect performance, without arguing their effect on cognitive learning, they are still important, since the outcomes of teaching have to do with performance based on learning. One significant aspect of the role of reinforcing stimuli is the phenomenon of secondary reinforcement; it is another example of stimulus substitution, since reinforcers are stimuli, although they follow rather than precede the operant response involved.

Reinforcing stimuli are those which increase the frequency or probability of the responses they follow. Autistic children, who cannot relate to others, are reinforced with candy whenever they give the least response to any behavior of their teacher or of other children, and by this means such responses are "built up," that is, increased in frequency. However, it is not always convenient to reinforce a dog with food or an autistic child with candy when one observes a response which one wishes to strengthen: congratulatory words or smiles are easier to manipulate and administer. Thus it is convenient to substitute *secondary* reinforcers like smiles and nods and other signals, for the primary ones such as food and candy. One does this by pairing these signals with the primary reinforcers; they derive their strength as reinforcers from this association. Since such things as smiles and encouraging words have been paired over a number of years with other reinforcers, such as food, particularly early in life when the learner was a baby, they have taken on a relatively permanent reinforcing capability. Other secondary reinforcers paired more recently or less frequently with primary ones may be useful only for a while by themselves: their reinforcing properties extinguish unless maintained by further pairing.

To review, secondary reinforcers are those which have been paired with primary ones such as food, and which have taken on reinforcing properties themselves. This means that they will, when used by themselves, increase the frequency of responses which they follow. The reader has probably noticed a close parallel between the formation of secondary reinforcers by pairing and the classical conditioning paradigm. Some theorists have asserted that a reinforcing stimulus is a classical stimulus which elicits emotions of hope and pleasure: in this sense, a secondary reinforcer is simply a conditioned stimulus which elicits such emotional responses.

PUNISHMENT AND CONDITIONING

The theorists mentioned above assert that we learn responses which are followed by stimuli implying something pleasurable, or perhaps a release from something unpleasant. They also postulate that we learn to suppress responses which are followed by stimuli implying something unpleasant or threatening.

One should discriminate between *suppressing* the response and *forgetting* it. Forgetting is a complex phenomenon involving interference from other stimuli and responses; a response which is suppressed (due to fear) may reemerge without much loss of strength after the fear has been extinguished (i.e., after the organism finds that the response is no longer followed by the fear-producing stimulus), thus showing it has not been "forgotten." The "fear" is a *classical* response; the unconditioned stimulus is the punishment, the conditioned stimulus includes the punisher *and* the whole learning situation. For instance, if you shock a rat for giving an operant response which has previously been conditioned through reinforcement, he will suppress the response and show other signs of fear in the learning situation. If you then cease to shock him, the fear response (classical) will extinguish and the previously conditioned (operant) response will be found to be present as before.

SECONDARY REINFORCERS AND LEARNING TO LEARN

If a learner has been reinforced for learning in a variety of situations; that is, if the outcomes of learning, both particular and general, have been positive over a number of different situations and/or over a period of time, then many of the results of learning, such as accumulation of information, recognizing changes in one's response patterns, and the like, will have been associated with these positive outcomes, that is, with the reinforcers used (approval, reward, etc.). As a result, they will take on reinforcing properties themselves; they will become secondary reinforcers for learning. Thus learning can become reinforcing in itself, and one can be reinforced for learning *by* learning. Furthermore, the processes one uses in learning have also been reinforced and learned, and thus when one learns, one also learns how to learn; that is, one learns a particular *way* or *strategy* of learning. This strategy may be acquired through imitation or through explicit instruction by a teacher, but it is part of what one learns when one learns. This, then, is what is meant by "learning to learn."

1–5 The Nature of the Stimulus

In this first chapter, classical and operant conditioning have been described as fundamental paradigms for an understanding of learning. Stimulus substitution has been presented as a process common to them. Reinforcement as a means of arranging operant conditioning has been discussed, and the role of secondary reinforcers has been presented. The reader now has a theoretical basis for analyzing learning and for bringing it about in simple forms. At this point it is appropriate to discuss one aspect of the arrangement of learning in respect to these paradigms before we go on to some of their more complex applications. This has to do with the nature of the stimulus which comes to control the response.

In arranging for conditioning, we present a given stimulus ahead of the response: in classical conditioning one is quite sure the response will occur, while in operant conditioning one works probabilistically and reinforces the response when it occurs. While one has a certain amount of control over these contingencies, one *cannot* easily control the focus or attention of the learner and the amount and nature of the stimuli he perceives in the process of learning.

Any learning situation involves a variety of stimuli at any given time. Not all are relevant to the learning; that is, not all will be present in another situation where the response is to be given again. For example, in trying to get a learner to respond to a particular shape on a card, one may find that the learner perceives the shape, or he may only perceive the card, or he may be looking at a number of other things in the stimulus field. Even though one gets the response one wants, one cannot be sure that the part of the stimulus situation which he wants to have in control is actually in control; that is, that the learner is attending to the correct aspects of the stimulus.

Another way to view this is to say that a given stimulus which is to control a response is made up of many parts, and the learner may observe or focus on only one part or several parts at a time—not the whole stimulus. Thus if the learner is observing one part of the stimulus field, and if that becomes conditioned to the response, the next time the stimulus is presented the learner may be observing another part of the stimulus. Thus, even though the response might have been completely conditioned in that one trial; that is, be one hundred percent probable when the learner observes that same part of the stimulus, still if the stimulus is presented again, the learner may fail to give the response because he is not observing or focusing on that same part of the stimulus.

Let us put this another way. Assume that in classical conditioning if the neutral stimulus is paired with the unconditioned stimulus just once, complete conditioning results—no further trials are necessary. Then if the neutral stimulus is presented again without the unconditioned stimulus, it will elicit the response (that is, it is no longer neutral). Now this seldom happens in practice, but one may explain the fact that it doesn't happen without changing his assumption about the conditioning occurring completely in one trial. All one has to do is assume that the learner was looking at one part of the stimulus one time, and at another part the second time. To make sure the learner is conditioned to all parts of the stimulus, one will have to pair it with the unconditioned stimulus several times, maybe many times. Of course this assumes that the learner samples the stimulus parts randomly— that having sampled one part he is no more or less likely to sample that part again.

This explanation can be used for operant conditioning also, except in place of the unconditioned stimulus we have the general stimulus situation or some previously conditioned discriminative stimulus. The idea is that one can assume that learning takes place in one trial, on an all-or-nothing basis, and still see some need for "practice makes perfect." This has some interesting implications for teaching, since, if learning is a matter of sampling the stimulus until one happens to connect all parts of it to the response, then the teacher will arrange to repeat the learning situation many times so that the law of averages can have a chance to work. Some traditional approaches to teaching follow this pattern, and sometimes they are quite successful. An alternative outcome would be the arrangement of the environment so that it is more probable that the important parts of the stimulus will be observed by the learner early in the learning process: this relates to simplifaction of the environment, as well as the relationship of one learning trial to another in terms of what is changed and what remains the same.

The element of stimulus sampling is important in any conditioning or learning, and the laboratory experiments which bring about both classical and operant conditioning in a dependable fashion for quantitative study are designed so that the learner will observe most if not all of the neutral stimulus before giving the response and so that a sufficient number of repetitions will take place to assure dependable conditioning. In *all* teaching it is necessary to keep in mind that no matter how completely one arranges the environment for learning, the learner himself must attend to the relevant properties of the situation if effective learning is to take place.

1–6 Interval Reinforcement

If one reinforces a response every time it is given, then it takes a certain number of trials without reinforcement before initial extinction sets in. If one reinforces the response every time at first, then every second time, then every third, and so forth, one can build up the tolerance of the learner for intermittent reinforcement. There are two general ways of reinforcing intermittently. One is called "interval reinforcement," wherein the experimenter reinforces the first response given after a certain period of time since the last reinforcement; the other is called "ratio" reinforcement, wherein one reinforces the response every third time or every fifth time or such. Now both of these can be regular (after n seconds or every mth response), or they can be variable (after n seconds *on the average* or every mth response *on the average*). One can bring lower organisms to respond to very high ratios, such as one out of twenty or fifty. Interestingly enough, response rate *increases* under a ratio schedule. An advantage of *variable* schedules is that one does not observe a decrease in responding after reinforcement, as one does when the reinforcer is given regularly and the animal can anticipate the fact that his next response will not be rewarded if given too soon (interval) or unless given several times (ratio).

The power of such variable reinforcement schedules in maintaining responses is sometimes astonishing. Consider for instance how many times one goes to the mailbox, as compared with the number of times there is mail: often the ratio of reinforcement here is fairly high. Generally speaking, if one equates the strength of a response to resistance to extinction and frequency of responding, one makes responses stronger if one shifts them to a variable reinforcement schedule. As examples one can point to repeated trials to light an empty cigarette lighter which is known to be undependable, or the intense attention accorded a teacher who has previously reinforced behavior intermittently through the use of random questioning on items that students could answer.

Bibliography

BUGELSKI, B. R. *The Psychology of Learning Applied to Teaching.* Indianapolis: Bobbs-Merrill Co., 1964.

DEESE, J. E., and HULSE, S. H. *The Psychology of Learning*, 3rd ed. New York: McGraw-Hill Book Co., 1967.

HOLLAND, J. G., and SKINNER, B. F. *The Analysis of Behavior.* New York: McGraw-Hill Book Co., 1961.

2 More Complex Conditioning Phenomena

2–1 Discrimination Learning

Suppose one wishes to teach a learner to discriminate between two stimuli that are similar, that is, to respond to one and not to the other, or to respond one way to one and another way to the other. How does one go about this on the basis of conditioning paradigms? One might tell the learner what he wants, and the learner might be able to do it. On the other hand, experience indicates that just telling someone what is desired does not always produce the kind of behavior one wants—practice of some kind is needed. In operant and classical conditioning, processes have been developed that are suggestive for such teaching; some of these will be described here.

Suppose that a white light has been brought into control of an operant response by the three-term contingency, or into control of a classical response by pairing it with an unconditioned stimulus. Then suppose a blue light is presented as the stimulus instead of the white one. Will the operant or classical response be given? The answer is "yes and no." Yes, the response will be given to the different stimulus; no, the response will not be exactly the same or given with the same probability or the same frequency. The fact that the response is given even though the stimulus changes slightly is referred to as *stimulus generalization*. The fact that the response differs in some way or is less strong or less probable is referred to as *discrimination*. Thus the learner both generalizes (gives the response although the stimulus changes) and discriminates (shows in his response that he recognizes the difference, although he is not necessarily conscious of it).

Consider a slightly more complex case. Suppose that in place of the white light given originally, blue and red lights were given alternately. And then suppose that the response was to be reinforced when given to the blue light and not reinforced when given to the red light. Initially, the learner would give the response to both blue and red, with somewhat less probability than to the original white light, but about the same for blue and red. However, under the new contingencies of reinforcement, the response will gain strength under the blue light and lose it under the red (extinction). In this case, we can say that we have taught a discrimination between red and blue. This is not to say that the learner was unable to discriminate between them—he had to have this physical and neurological "ability" to begin with—but it does say that we have brought about a difference in the response pattern to the two where initially they evoked or elicited the same response. Now, while this is an example of discrimination learning, one should keep in mind that it was brought about through use of an initial situation made possible through generalization, that is, generalization from the white light to the blue and red ones.

Discrimination learning is a relatively simple phenomenon as described above. However, it becomes less simple when one considers the stimulus sampling concepts presented earlier. If a learner samples aspects of the stimulus situation in a somewhat random fashion in learning, as that theoretical stand assumes, then we may expect many trials to be required for some learners to discriminate, since not all of them will sample on the first try the particular aspect of the situation that makes a difference. Another implication one can draw from this is that, as in simple conditioning, one might make discrimination learning more probable by simplifying the stimulus situation in one or more ways.

One may arrange the environment so that the learner is more likely to perceive the relevant properties by making the important stimuli more vivid, or by making them meaningful in that they constitute things the learner has come to associate with learning in previous experiences. One may also arrange for the learner to have a sufficient number of trials, and perhaps reinforce him just for engaging in trials, in order to insure that he will continue to engage in the activity until he chances on the correct solution or happens to notice the important aspects of the pattern. One problem with the latter approach is that it assumes that the learner functions on one trial as if he were beginning all over again to sample the pattern, where actual learner-behavior often indicates that learners stick to an incorrect hypothesis in spite of negative feedback. This rigidity interferes with effective learning, of course, and is probably a function of some other previous learning and might itself have to be changed.

2–2 Learning by Successive Approximations (Shaping)

One way to bring about discrimination learning in human learners is to use words to help them identify the relevant or important properties in the stimulus field or pattern. However, one does not always have a clear concept of what these properties are, and therefore meets situations where he wants to bring about changes in behavior without knowing exactly what contingencies govern these behaviors. One approach to handling the latter problem is called *shaping*. In this approach to teaching one takes advantage of some existing observable response in the learner's repertoire and alters it to resemble the response one desires. This is done through differential reinforcement. For example, if a pigeon is to peck at a spot, then any pecking behavior is reinforced initially. As it increases in frequency, only those pecks which are generally directed toward the spot are reinforced. Later, when these are highly frequent, only those which are very close to the spot are reinforced. Finally, the response of pecking at the spot itself is reinforced and others extinguished.

A teacher might shape the penmanship of a student by reinforcing all writing at first, thus making it more frequent, then by reinforcing only that writing which is slightly better than the student's own norm, and by gradually becoming stricter in the contingencies of reinforcement until only his very best writing is adequate, and that far better than his best early attempts.

Related to this process of shaping is one called *fading*, wherein one gradually removes support from a stimulus pattern. For instance, suppose a child confuses *b*'s with *d*'s. One might teach him to respond correctly by coloring all *b*'s red and all *d*'s blue. Then, after he learns to respond correctly this way, one might fade the colors, that is, make them less and less bright with each succeeding trial until finally all the letters are the same hue, or are just black. This fading of the helping cue, color, results in the ultimate control of the response by the uncued stimulus. The process of altering the stimulus pattern this way can be applied to classical conditioning as well: one can weaken the conditioned stimulus for a fear response, for example, until it no longer elicits the response, and then very gradually can change it back toward the original strength while maintaining other elements of the situation in a way that makes the fear response unlikely. Eventually the learner can come to tolerate the full stimulus that originally produced fear. Whether this constitutes learning not to fear it or unlearning the fear response is a moot question.

Another use of successive approximations involves manipulation of the environment rather than the response. A pigeon can be taught to peck at a small key first by reinforcing him for pecking at a large bar, then by gradually reducing the size of the bar until he is pecking at a very small object which one would call a "key." Thus the response itself has been fairly constant, but the target has been changed (the response, of course, becomes more accurate during the process). In conditioning the discrimination between blue and red lights, as discussed previously, one might condition the pigeon to peck at the white light first. Then it could be changed to blue in very gradual steps (using generalization). Then a very dim red light could be presented alternately alongside, not strong enough to bring the response. By gradually increasing the brightness of the competing light, one could arrive at a situation where the pigeon pecks only at the blue and ignores the red. Such techniques are used to bring about learning with very few errors.

In the last example there was a process whereby a learner comes to "not respond" to a stimulus that he might be expected to respond to by generalization: it is brought about by introducing the stimulus at a strength or level so low that it does not evoke or elicit the response it might evoke if given at full strength. This process is used in *deconditioning* certain responses in therapy situations, and is often called *desensitization*. For example, if a person has come to fear a certain stimulus, say a snake, then one might attempt to desensitize him by arranging for snakes to be presented at a great distance, or by having him just think of snakes, under conditions which otherwise tend to make him relaxed and unafraid. After one succeeds in getting him to tolerate the stimulus (not react with fear) under these conditions, one can gradually increase the level of the stimulus (by bringing it closer, or making it larger, or talking about it more directly) without evoking the response. Many therapeutic processes of this type have been reported, varying from curing children of a fear of animals to eliminating fear of sexual play or sexual organs in a timid bride. Anxiety over tests is one type of fear that can be reduced through such a technique.

2–3 Avoidance Learning

One particularly important and basic form of conditioning or learning which is a combination of operant and classical paradigms is called *avoidance conditioning* or *avoidance learning*. Suppose a dog is put in a harness and his paw is placed on a grid which can be charged. A buzzer is sounded for several seconds, after which the grid is electrified, shocking the dog. The dog, on being shocked, lifts his paw, cringes, and exhibits other unconditioned responses to the shock. One of these unconditioned responses is effective in escaping the shock, that is, the lifting of the paw. This lifting response is an operant one, and is *negatively reinforced* in that the shock *terminates* when it is elicited. When shock is administered many times, the shock itself becomes a conditioned stimulus for lifting the paw, and the lifting is reinforced negatively by the termination of the shock. Now suppose there is a signal that regularly precedes the shock by a few seconds. This signal will come to elicit fear in anticipation of the shock; that is, it will elicit some of the responses to the shock before the shock occurs. This is classical conditioning, where the previously neutral stimulus (the signal) comes to elicit the response by being paired with or preceding the unconditioned stimulus (the shock itself). Now suppose that when the signal is given and fear aroused (classical conditioning), the dog lifts his paw before the shock occurs. Previously, the paw-lifting resulted in a termination of the shock; now, through association, the paw-lifting will be followed by a termination (or at least a decrease) of the fear.

Thus the response of paw-lifting is reinforced by a decrease in or termination of an aversive internal stimulus, fear. Reinforcement due to *termination* of an *aversive* stimulus is called *negative reinforcement*. What is the result? We have taught the dog to lift his paw to a signal, an operant conditioning process, using a negative reinforcer; that is, using the *termination* of aversive stimuli as the reinforcer. This process is described as *avoidance learning*.

Consider what one might expect once the dog has been conditioned to lift his paw to the signal. Remember that the signal also elicits fear of shock. Suppose the dog is given the signal a large number of times, and each time he lifts his paw in time to avoid the shock. What will happen to the classical fear response elicited by the signal? One might expect it to decrease, since it is not reinforced (that is, since the shock does not occur). This is *classical extinction.* Then if the fear decreases, the negative reinforcement the dog gets for the operant response of lifting his paw decreases, and one might expect operant extinction to set in; that is, one might expect the dog to eventually cease to lift his paw at the signal. If he does this, however, he will receive a shock; an observer might say he "forgot" to lift his paw and thus got shocked again. This is observed to happen occasionally in such situations. To explain, the buzzer is a conditioned stimulus (CS) for fear; if it isn't reinforced by the unconditioned stimulus (US), the shock, then the response (pawlifting) will extinguish, and the dog will leave his paw on the grid and will be shocked again.

2–4 The Significance of Avoidance Learning

Avoidance learning is a basic and culturally significant phenomenon. Many, if not most of the things we learn to do or decide to do having learned them, are manifestations of the avoidance paradigm; that is, we behave more in order to avoid punishment or aversive outcomes than we do to achieve positive reinforcement. One may observe that the two are similar in direction; that is, that the avoidance of aversive contingencies or outcomes is not unlike the achievement of positive or desirable outcomes in that one is improving one's lot in both cases. However, in the case of avoidance learning there is an accompanying anxiety or generalized fear of the negative outcome, which can be facilitating to the performance but is more often debilitating. Not only that, it can be debilitating physically as well, if the avoidance contingencies are frequent and regular. Furthermore, such contingencies foster defense mechanisms of a type to be discussed in a later chapter and can over long periods of time result in abnormalities of behavior which are destructive to the individual. Studies by social psychologists indicate that punitive atmospheres in schools have demonstrably negative effects on cognitive learning, partly because concern over punishment takes up the student's thoughts, which otherwise might be directed toward more constructive matters. There is much current interest in learning for the sake of learning, of utilizing natural curiosity and the desire to achieve and explore as motivators for learning. Avoidance contingencies obviously interfere with such approaches and are incompatible with them; so if a teacher invokes conventional avoidance contingencies in the classroom, the likelihood of the student becoming interested in learning for its own sake is diminished.

One may look at our society from this point of view: is it not based on avoidance contingencies to a great extent? What would happen if a new society were constructed where behavior was controlled through positive reinforcement and extinction rather than punishment and avoidance? Such communities have been discussed and described, and some have been tried, but there have not been notable successes. This may be because the human being is not made to operate in such a scheme— he needs punishment to make him run. On the other hand, it may be that avoidance contingencies are the easiest to administer, and as a result they have been used for so many hundreds or thousands of years that we have learned to operate under such schemes and no others. It may be that such a society could be made to work, if given enough support and sufficient time for working out the difficulties and if schools were designed to teach appropriate concepts and behaviors. Such a society may be our only hope of survival: punishment and aggression certainly threaten to turn our creativeness and our engineering and technical abilities against ourselves.

2–5 Sign Learning

Suppose one extends the meaning of the word *stimulus* to include sets of stimuli, that is, situations or events. Suppose one also assumes that if two stimuli occur in succession, then the first comes to elicit some anticipation of the second. Then one can look at cases such as avoidance learning as learning guided by *signs* or *signals*, that is, stimuli that anticipate positive or aversive outcomes. These signs are thus S^d's for operant responses that either avoid the aversive or achieve the positive outcomes. Much of learning is responding to various signals according to their previously established "meanings" in terms of anticipated outcomes. Each stimulus or situation evokes some anticipation of events to come, and the learner responds either to avoid them or make them more likely to occur. This *goal-directed* learning, however, is dependent on past experience and also on the interpretation of the current situation, that is, the concept one forms of the current situation. The success of this goal-directed behavior depends on perceiving such concepts and on having learned behaviors that cope with the contingencies or conflicts that arise. This can be regarded as problem solving; the styles and patterns that an individual exhibits in problem-solving processes become part of his personality. Concept formation, problem solving, and personality will be discussed in later chapters.

2–6 Sequences of Stimuli and Chains of Responses

If sequences of stimuli occur regularly, then each stimulus elicits anticipation of the others to come. As these are experienced a number of times (in a sense "practiced"), they come to function as units in controlling certain behaviors or sequences of behaviors. The ability of the brain to encode sequences of events this way, into what have been called *engrams*, is one of the unanalyzed mysteries of human thought. For example, how can one learn a list of things to get at the grocery store, code them under "things to buy," and then later remember the list? Granted that we find ourselves fallible in this area at times, it is still a question how one can encode such sequences at all. Perhaps a more vivid example would be a golf swing or the motions of an artist making a sketch: these are complex sequences of responses which are somehow encoded in the mind and which come out in sequence on command.

If stimuli occur in sequence, then each one comes to evoke some anticipation or expectation of the next. Since responses are also stimuli, that is, stimuli emitted by the learner, a response will also be anticipated by a signal that regularly precedes it, including the discriminative or conditioned stimulus which controls it. In the same way, the response itself, as a stimulus, can create an anticipation of some other response or stimulus which follows, say the reinforcing stimulus, or some other response that is part of a sequence making up some skill. What this implies is that chains of responses, or of stimuli and responses, are formed, each anticipating the one following it. Furthermore, if such a chain has some positive outcome (is reinforced at the end), then the last stimulus before the reinforcement takes on some reinforcing properties itself, and reinforces responses preceding it, and so on. Thus each response in the chain, as a stimulus, is both a reinforcer for the one preceding it and an S^d evoking the one following it.

Animals and humans behave according to such behavioral chains. Rats are taught to run mazes, series of right and left turns that lead them to food. It is found that the responses closest to the food are the strongest, or hardest to extinguish, while those toward the beginning of the maze are weakest. Humans operate in sequences of behaviors, many of which (like grasping an object) are thought of as units because they are so well learned and require so little attention. When a chain is so well formed, the signal for its beginning will evoke anticipations not only of the subsequent responses but also of the final responses, including the objective or reinforcer or outcome. In this way the mind seems to short-cut long strings of future behaviors and work ahead in order to lead the learner in profitable directions.

One key to the formation of chains of responses, which occur efficiently and reliably, is the phenomenon of changing latency of response. If one reinforces a response only when given to a certain stimulus, not only does that stimulus come to evoke or control the response, but the *time* between stimulus and response gradually decreases. This time is called the *latency* of the response, and is occasionally used as a measure of the degree or strength of the learning. There are many situations where shortening the latency of the response is important. Often one wants to "practice" a response to the point where the latency is at a minimum and also where one need not "think" about the response. In this sense it becomes more like a reflex. The capability to do so seems to attest to the evolutionary utility of such a phenomenon and to imply that a tendency to decrease the latency may be inherent. (This view, like others, is debated by some, and there is some contrary evidence.)

2–7 Probabilistic Aspects of Conditioning

A response, whether classical or operant, can be controlled by a stimulus, as has been described. This stimulus may be made up of many dimensions other than the most obvious one. For example, a learning situation has many attributes—the room, the desk, the paper, the books, the experimenter or teacher, to mention a few. If *all* these elements are considered, the likelihood that they will all be exactly repeated at another time is rather low. There are hypotheses, backed by some evidence, that the probability of a response being repeated in such a situation is dependent on the percentage of the parts of the experimental situation present as compared with the original situation. This implies that if a response is given to one situation (that is, one complex stimulus), then another situation *exactly* like it will be *certain* to evoke the response. A situation which is *nearly* the same will be *likely* to evoke it (that is, through simple generalization) but not certain to. This means that we learn responses in *one trial*, and what has been learned will certainly be repeated *if* the situation is *enough like* the original. This also means that memory is perfect where identical situations occur; nonremembering is due to differences in the later stimulus situation.

This probabilistic view of learning calls for some additional discussion. Suppose one assumes that a given stimulus situation evokes a given response. Now suppose that it is followed by two other stimulus situations, one of which is ninety percent similar to the first (having ninety percent of the stimuli in the first) and the other is eighty percent similar. Then one might expect the probability that the response will be given to the ninety percent situation will be greater than the probability that it will be given in the eighty percent situation. One might go on and say that if the situation were one hundred percent similar, the response would be a sure thing. On the other hand, one hundred percent is impossible because, owing to the passage of time, the *learner* has changed in many ways, including the accumulation of additional experiences, and thus one can *never* have a situation where things are one hundred percent similar to a previous one.

One role of a reinforcer in operant conditioning, in the early stages at least, is to add a consistent or similar element to the situation. The learner associates the response with the stimulus partly through the addition of a reinforcer, then the reinforcer acts to increase the similarity to the previous situation. Thus the probability that the response will be given is increased.

A certain amount of stimulus generalization, then, is involved in all learning, since two stimuli are never exactly the same. The probability of a response to a given stimulus may also differ from learner to learner, due to both inherent characteristics and previous learning. One may also *learn* to generalize or to discriminate, since these are responses of a complex type themselves.

There are many situations where animals and humans are called upon to respond to one stimulus and not to respond to another similar to it, that is, to discriminate. Some sociologists point out that as our culture becomes more affluent and as more people can buy what they want, we gradually become more discriminating in our choice of and opinions of things: small differences come to make a greater difference. Another point of view, related to personality, is that people are of two general types, sharpeners and levelers: *levelers* are those who tend to see the similarities between things, people, and events, while *sharpeners* tend to see differences among them. This involves what are called *learning sets* and also *attitudes*.

The learner does not or cannot attend to all properties of the environment, and he actively (although perhaps unconsciously) selects limited sets of the properties or stimuli to focus on. Thus one may presume that the learner samples the environment by attending to one of the many possible stimulus patterns and responding to it as he has previously been conditioned to respond. Assumedly, this either "pays off" (is reinforced or leads to a partial solution of his problem or avoids disaster), or it does not pay off. If it doesn't, then the learner may sample another pattern and respond to *it*. When he has found (partly by chance) the correct pattern, he has learned the response completely. This in turn implies that a learner may learn completely on the first trial, or on the third, or on the tenth, but that he does not learn partially or incrementally.

Why then does learning *appear* to be incremental or cumulative in some studies? One explanation is that while each student in a group may learn completely on one trial or another, most of them learn on one of a certain group of trials, and thus statistically learning seems to begin gradually, increase in rate, and then slow down as one approaches one hundred percent. Thus if one teaches as if learning were cumulative, he accomodates to a large percentage of the students, even though they are learning in an all-or-nothing way. When the teacher decides that enough time has been spent on a subject, he misses those students who have not yet chanced to come upon the right combination.

Some students seem to have probability more on their side than others; that is, they regularly seem to learn more quickly. This has not been explained probabilistically as yet, although it may be eventually. The stimulus sampling model has interesting implications regarding the control of learning, as well as regarding problem solving. On the other hand, it is not entirely clear what it implies regarding such processes as shaping and fading. It does imply an approach to teaching that involves putting the situation before the student and depending on him to operate on it, as compared with simplifying it and ordering it for him, but this would seem to be a too superficial interpretation to hold up for long.

Bibliography

DEESE, J. E., and HULSE, S. H. *The Psychology of Learning*, 3rd ed. New York: McGraw-Hill Book Co., 1967.

HOLLAND, J. G., and SKINNER, B. F. *The Analysis of Behavior*. New York: McGraw-Hill Book Co., 1961.

BUGELSKI, B. R. *The Psychology of Learning Applied to Teaching*. Indianapolis: Bobbs-Merrill Co., 1964.

3 Teaching as Conditioning

One view of teaching regards it as arranging the environment in order to bring about certain responses or response patterns which are less probable otherwise. This is not a restrictive view: it applies to processes which bring students to be more creative in solving problems just as it applies to teaching a student to answer "four" to the statement "Two times two equals _____." Conditioning can be applied to sophisticated behavior by expanding one's concept of what a behavioral unit is. Thus it is expected that the reader will accommodate to the level of behavior being discussed in his application of conditioning paradigms, and not expect the same types of stimulus and response units involved in pigeons pecking bars to apply to human beings in the midst of treatment for some of their "hang-ups." While the levels and complexities are different, the processes or contingencies are similar in many cases.

3–1 Conditioning Study Behavior

Studying is a complex pattern of responses controlled by discriminative stimuli just as simpler responses are. If one wants to build up studying behavior, one can invoke the three-term contingency. This implies reinforcement of the behavior, and also bringing it under the control of some appropriate stimulus. The most appropriate controlling stimulus is some special environment for studying, say a library carrel. There are a number of reinforcers which may be invoked, including food, money, passing tests, understanding, and exposure to interesting study materials. If the studying behavior is somewhat difficult or boring at first, one may use a very simple negative reinforcer, that is, termination of the studying itself. This is done by limiting the time of the studying drastically, say to three or four minutes at first, and at the first hint of boredom or tension in studying, having the student do one more sentence or paragraph or problem well and then *leave* the study space completely. By this means the behavior of studying carefully and well will be reinforced, and will increase in strength and probability. Practically, this means that the student will find subsequent study under those conditions easier, and his study time will increase.

A similar approach has been used in prescribing instruction for students in a learning clinic. Students were given diagnostic learning experiences, and programmed texts were prescribed for them (see a later chapter for information on programmed instruction). They were asked to set aside a special space for studying and to limit their daily study of the programmed text to a short period, often fifteen minutes initially. This prevented the reaction that seems to build up gradually and unnoticed when programmed instruction is used over long periods of time at one sitting. (Incidentally, this cumulative reaction seems to be similar to what one theorist postulated as "reactive inhibition," that is, inhibition built up by the act of responding itself, regardless of the response or the reinforcement which follows it.) Limited sessions each day produced improvements which were reflected in better work in school in many cases.

3–2 Conditioning and Classroom Behavior

Another application of operant conditioning of human behavior in the classroom has to do with the response of attending to the teacher and to events in the classroom in general. Consider student X who is in class daily, who has no background which has conditioned him to be interested in the particular subject, but who is normally responsive to suggestions of adults and has not been conditioned by various contingencies to be particularly aggressive or difficult. Let us now assume that there is a response complex which we generally refer to as "attending," in which, through some previously learned sets of behaviors, this student is able to filter out irrelevant stimuli and thus increase his perception of the relevant ones. The three-term contingency implies that this attending response will come under control of those situations in which it is reinforced: it will diminish in strength or probability in those situations in which it is extinguished, that is, in those situations where it is not reinforced. How can one reinforce the response of attending? By making it "pay off;" that is, by following it with some stimulus which is consistent in nature and, better still, satisfies some need of the student. One such stimulus would be the directing of attention to the student in a positive way by the teacher. How can this be done? One way is by seizing on some chance relationship between the subject and the individual and mentioning it. Another is by asking the student a question about what is going on, one that is within the ability of the student, if he is paying attention. Inability to answer would be punishing, an effect which the student might strive to avoid, either by studying more or by "turning off" (rejecting course and teacher). Questioning of each student cannot be regular or intense in a large class; on the other hand, the principle of intermittent reinforcement implies that attending behavior will be less subject to extinction if the student is put on a ratio or interval schedule, preferably a variable one. There is also *implicit* reinforcement, that derived from seeing another student reinforced; this phenomenon is a little tricky to handle. Some research implies that in certain situations implicit reinforcement works negatively—that is, a student observing another being reinforced on a certain task will do less well on that task than if he sees another student punished (mildly, verbally). Other research indicates that generally if one student is reinforced for giving the correct answer, other students will also learn that answer. The response of a student to the behavior of another depends on whether the other is seen as someone to imitate, and whether the reinforcement or reward is seen as relevant or important.

Related to this, and to be discussed in a later chapter, is the phenomenon of social facilitation. Learning is found to proceed more effectively when the student is isolated, whereas performance of a learned set of responses is better under group conditions, when the student performs before his peers or adults. Generally, however, attending behavior of individuals in a group is maintained by providing opportunities for it to be reinforced on an intermittent schedule. This implies communicating with the class partly through questions and answers, and reinforcing answers, questions, and comments initiated by the student. This in turn implies a view of teaching behavior that is interactive rather than dominant. Another approach is through division of the class into smaller groups, where interaction is possible for more students at a time. Here, however, it is best to train student group leaders, who then bring out responses of various members of their groups.

Avoidance learning is often evident in tutorial and classroom situations. The many behaviors exhibited by students preparing to study or to take a test, such as getting their materials ready, getting something to eat or a glass of water, asking questions about various matters not entirely related to the task (all rather irritating to the adult or teacher), are examples of behavior reinforced by the postponement of the aversive situation anticipated by the student. More generally, studying to avoid the aversive outcomes, both immediate and long range, of not doing well is all too prevalent. Talking to students about such matters will not be very effective, since the contingencies which reinforce avoidance behavior remain. In some cases the threatening nature of the situation can be so severe to a student that he is unable to control or suppress avoidance responses that *interfere* with learning. Such behavior has been called *defending* as differentiated from *coping* behavior. Such students are trying desperately to *avoid* learning, so attempts to help them learn end often in failure.

3–3 Managing Student Behavior

Teachers often face problems such as those just described, as well as the more moderate but ever-present problem of interfering desires and the aversive nature of some learning situations. One key concept which is useful in dealing with these problems and maintaining motivation is the concept of partial reinforcement and scheduling of reinforcement. It is important to note that the amount of reinforcement is not the most crucial factor in improving performance; very small reinforcers, relatively weak, can be used effectively if they are scheduled properly. They can be used following weak responses which the teacher desires to strengthen. They are available in the form of stimuli or experiences that the student has learned to find desirable—they are "what works." Praise, approval, feeling of accomplishment on an individual task, a chance to be alone, a chance to run and play—any or all of these can be effective as reinforcers at the appropriate times. However, the teacher must face the fact that it is easier to react negatively to an undesirable behavior than it is to patiently build more positive behaviors to take its place through a long-range program of selective reinforcement. It is more difficult to be alert for initial manifestations of a behavior one wishes to shape, and then to reinforce these immediately and discriminatingly, than it is to hold up a finished performance as an example and act disappointed when students fail to imitate it exactly. Punishing-behaviors on the part of the teacher are reinforced by momentary compliance or spurts of energy, but they are not effective over longer periods of time in changing the behavior of students without carefully scheduled programs of reinforcement. However, long-range programs require more concentration on the students' behaviors by the teacher, and thus are more difficult and less convenient to apply. As a result, aversive approaches involving punishment are reinforced by the conditions of teaching.

Teachers who employ conditioning paradigms, on the other hand, have been observed to become more positive about their teaching and more patient with students. This results partly from the decreased use of punishment which such processes imply, partly from increased confidence in their own ability to cope effectively with situations that arise. Such strategies require the teacher to develop an ability to observe his own behavior rationally, and this is done best through situations where the teacher can receive feedback concerning his behavior. Without such situations, teachers often develop behaviors that interfere with learning. Some teachers, for example, wait longer for the answers of good students than they do for the answers of poor students, although they do not realize it; this makes it more likely that the poor student will fail to answer correctly, and to a degree punishes participation by the poor student. This in turn results in better achievement by those students whom the teachers see as "good," whether due to their performance in class, their reputation as students, or their IQ and aptitude as given on their records. Other teachers make discipline problems for themselves by recognizing small misbehaviors in the classroom and commenting on them or reacting to them in other ways, thus reinforcing them and increasing their frequency. Still other teachers discourage student participation in class in general, by cutting off student responses through their tone of voice or lack of receptivity and patience. A teacher who excuses a class when it is noisy at the end of the period reinforces noisiness.

It is often difficult to convince a teacher that he or she should deprive a student of attention and personal interaction if he misbehaves, yet the same teacher often finds it very easy to punish misbehavior and thereby reinforces it. One reason for this may be that the teacher is reinforced by "letting go" and giving punishment, while withholding attention from the student creates tension in the teacher, which is aversive, and thus such extinguishing behavior is punished.

The reinforcement and extinction of behavior as described above does not always involve verbalization; much of it is nonverbal in nature, and thus often overlooked by teachers. On the other hand, one way of bringing about changes in behavior is to build up *mediating* verbal behaviors in a student which lead him to change. Ideally, one would want to condition certain verbal responses concerning the implications of a given behavior so that they would be thought of by the student *before* he made the "wrong" response, for example, before he misbehaved. This would be in order to teach him to think of the consequences of his actions before he acted. Thus the teacher needs to reproduce or simulate the contingencies which lead to the misbehavior, and to condition the student to think the appropriate things under those conditions. For instance, the teacher will teach the student to think, "If I do this, then such and such will occur, and I don't want that" or some such chain of responses when the controlling stimuli occur. Over a period of time this will result in "looking before leaping." However, such control of the environment is not always available to the teacher. As a substitute, one may condition the verbal behavior following the wrong response, thus associating it with the response and eventually bringing the student to anticipate the response and give the verbal behavior first. For example, a student in an elementary school may be asked to write, "If I _____ then I will have to stay after school" or "If I _____ then _____ will not like me." This kind of learning task is repeated either at intervals or each time the child misbehaves, possibly with increasingly complete response behavior on the part of the child (that is, he fills in more and more of the contingencies himself), until the thoughts are well learned and probable in the event of some likelihood of misbehaving. This differs from traditional punishments like, "I will not throw spitballs in school," in that the outcomes of the behavior are learned, not just the fact that the behavior is forbidden. Another difference is that the verbal training is given without the punitive and disapproving attitudes of the teacher, which conventional punishment usually involves, thus avoiding negative side effects in classically conditioned attitudinal responses. Another important factor is, of course, the truth of the statement of outcomes: if the student is taught that a certain behavior will result in loss of a privilege or in detention, and if that behavior does *not* result in such an outcome, then the exercise will only teach the student about hypocrisy. It should also be pointed out that more abstract consequences of misbehavior may be effective and cause the teacher less inconvenience, such as, "If I _____ then Miss _____ will be displeased" or "We don't _____ because it makes it more difficult for others to enjoy class." These contingencies are also more convenient to carry out. The conditioning of verbal mediators described here is a general and powerful tool in controlling behavior, and is not incompatible with counseling and therapeutic approaches. Some of the interactions with these fields will be discussed in later chapters.

3–4 The Scheduling of Reinforcement and Classroom Behavior

A response reinforced every time can be extinguished quickly; a person put on a *variable* schedule of reinforcement is more likely to persist in his responding. If one wants attending behavior and studying behavior to be maintained then ultimately some intermittent schedule of reinforcement should be put into use. One form of reinforcement for such behavior is the providing of some outcome or "pay-off" for the behavior. Quizzes and tests are such an outcome; so also is the use of what one has studied in class discussions. If these are put on an intermittent schedule, that is, if the teacher plans to have one of a number of kinds of pay-off for study behavior, regularly at first, then intermittently, one may expect study behavior to be maintained at a fairly high rate.

In utilizing the principles of intermittent reinforcement, experimental data are suggestive. A variable ratio schedule (every *n* times on the average) ordinarily results in a high steady response rate; thus one may reinforce studying behavior through giving a quiz on it every third assignment on the average but not regularly every third assignment. One should also consider the classical responses conditioned by such a strategy; some students might develop high anxiety in such a situation, where a fixed ratio would give them less concern. On the other hand, a fixed ratio would result in a decline in behavior after reinforcement. This decline is much more evident after a fixed *interval* reinforcer— say, a quiz every five days, or every Friday, which leads to the familiar "cramming" just before the quiz and the "lay-off" from studying afterward. Another example might be reinforcement of class response every ten minutes on the average by complimenting the class or by telling a joke. This would probably give a fairly constant rate of attending behavior, where doing this on a fixed interval of ten minutes would probably give a high degree of attentiveness just before the compliment or the joke, with a falling off immediately afterwards. On the other hand, one

might give such reinforcement after a certain number of student responses instead: then the students might respond very frequently in order
to get more jokes—if the teacher had a sufficient store of them for this.

3–5 Punishment and Its Effects

Punishment results in classical conditioning. If a teacher punishes a
student, then the teacher comes to evoke responses associated with the
event, such as anxiety and guilt. This is one of the purposes of punishment; it is also one of its drawbacks. If a teacher is associated with
pleasant situations, for example, positive group feeling and a sense of
accomplishment, then the teacher comes to evoke responses associated
with the pleasant situation. This emotional response to the teacher can
also have cognitive overtones, as in the case of a teacher who successfully handled a disturbance that occurred while a film was being shown;
he evicted the disturbing students. Later he was rated by his class as
"more expert at showing films."

Generally, punishment is a two-edged sword which should be used
with discrimination. The objective is to bring the student to avoid responding the same way again, but if no substitute responses are available, or if the student feels that he has been treated unfairly, or if he
sees it as a contest between himself and the teacher, then the process can
backfire. Furthermore, a teacher who punishes frequently and has few
other positive aspects either in personality or teaching behavior will
come to elicit responses in the student which are generally aversive and
which therefore interfere with their learning in the classroom. Students
learn partly through a sense of identity with the teacher, a desire to imitate; if this feeling is absent, there is less learning. On the other hand,
the teacher who does not punish when punishment is called for or
expected is in equally bad straits. Students look for guidance and protection, for security: the teacher is a source of security. If a student
cannot learn in class because the teacher does not keep the environment
free from interfering stimuli, then the student loses respect for the
teacher and finds learning not worth the effort. One theorist has suggested that punishment is only effective when the student does not know
that the response is wrong or punishable; once he has learned this, if
he makes the response again, one can assume that punishment will not
help. Generally this is a very significant observation. If punishment
makes the response increase then it is by definition a reinforcer. If the
response stays at the same level, punishment is not doing any good.
However, it might require several punishments to convince some students or groups that the response is (pragmatically speaking) wrong.
On the other hand, if one uses punishment with groups who have long
since learned that the response is punishable and in that sense wrong,
one may find that the punishment is ineffective and perhaps acting as a
reinforcer—the person or group may find the behavior of the teacher

entertaining. It is also possible, and probably more prevalent than we suspect, that the sequence of behaviors of doing something wrong in class and being punished is a powerful negative reinforcer for the deviant behavior. The students involved may find the cognitive behaviors which they are called upon to produce too difficult and may become anxious over their inability to function adequately in the situation. They avoid this anxiety through deviant behavior. In this sense, such deviant behavior is a defense mechanism; this topic will be discussed in a later chapter. The teacher should be careful not to abet this process by behaving toward the student in such a way as to allow him even more of an escape. Often, simply proceeding with the business of the class and ignoring the deviant behavior will suffice to extinguish it, since it is then unsuccessful in distracting the class and in avoiding the cognitive requirements of the situation.

Discussions such as the one above obviously do not cover situations where the pressures of the environment outside the school and the relationship of subject matter to the students' future produce more serious and difficult behavioral problems. The basic relationships are the same, but the degrees are different. Most of the processes discussed in this chapter assume a normal situation where the students see the school as at least partially relevant to their future, and do not experience great distracting influences in their environment outside school walls and hours. However, a number of reports from teachers in more difficult school situations attest to the fact that if one presents subject matter in a way and on a level that does not punish students by being too demanding or unreal or foreign, one may achieve surprising success even in more difficult environments using some of the processes outlined in this and the next chapter.

3–6 Dealing With Anxieties Through Conditioning

Anxiety is generalized fear, a classical response. If a child has been conditioned to fear something because it has been associated with a fear-producing stimulus, he can often be cured of his fear of that thing by its being presented many times *without* the fear-producing stimulus. Initially it may be necessary for the presentation to be of very low intensity, either by having shown the feared object at some distance or by use of some other protective measures, before it is gradually brought closer or the protection is removed. This process, discussed previously, is called *desensitization*. It is accomplished by presenting a weak form of the conditioned stimulus (thus making extinction quicker, or making the conditioned response less probable, or both), and then gradually increasing its strength. In a classic experiment of this kind many years ago, a small boy was conditioned to fear a rabbit by sounding a gong behind him when the rabbit was presented to him. After he had been taught to fear it thus, the rabbit was presented at a distance without the gong, and gradually moved closer: this desensitization process was reported to be successful.

A current approach to therapy for maladjusted persons occasionally makes use of a similar process. For instance, a patient who fears a certain kind of situation, say a party, may be partially hypnotized (while in therapy) to make him relax and then be asked to signal in some simple way when a thought occurs that is threatening to him. The therapist then suggests a number of different situations that might occur, initially far removed from the one that causes the concern but working gradually closer to it. If the patient signals that the therapist's descriptions are causing him concern, the therapist backs off and talks about something else. Gradually, through introducing ideas closer and closer to those which are feared, the patient is brought to tolerate the thought of the fear-producing situation without a negative reaction. Then he is gradually prepared to enter the actual situation through desensitization to increasingly realistic simulations. Such treatment also includes the conditioning of responses that enable the patient to cope with the situation better, assuming that he may have some behavioral *deficits* in addition to interfering responses.

A similar type of classical fear-response is observable in testing situations. The aversive outcomes of tests, plus the rigid and authoritarian atmosphere in which they are sometimes administered, results in their being seen as aversive and as signs of aversive outcomes. The anxiety is a covert response, not always clearly evident to others or to the student himself. This results in defense mechanisms that repress or avoid recognition of the anxiety itself as well as the causes of it. Repeated testing experiences will not necessarily reduce this anxiety, unless they are accompanied by measures that make the test situation more attractive and less threatening, measures that increase the probability of success of the student (and thus decrease the probability of failure), and therapeutic processes whereby the student expresses his anxiety and confronts it without being made to feel guilty about doing so. In spite of this, however, desensitization involving relaxation-training can be effective.

An alternative or complementary approach to dealing with test anxiety is to increase the sophistication of the evaluation process so that the tests themselves are only one of many components of the evaluation, others being classroom contributions, writing of papers, independent study and reports, contributions to group projects, and the like. Also, since one of the primary contributing factors in anxiety in the classroom is often the teacher, steps can be taken to reduce anxiety through teacher behavior that accords the child more security and is less threatening.

Desensitization can be used to alter a variety of classical responses, from fear of the dark (by dimming lights in the bedroom gradually over a long period of time) to reactions of untrained horses to carrying weight (gradually putting on increasingly heavy weights). One form of this process, which is more under the voluntary control of the teacher and involves old-fashioned will-power, is that demonstrated when a teacher suppresses her conditioned response to snakes in order not to show fear to her class. Here, she may eventually learn to tolerate the snakes if she carries this out frequently.

In another approach to eliminating a response, the stimulus is given so frequently that the response gradually disappears in a way that seems attributable to satiation. This process was involved in a rather amusing case in which a patient in a psychotic ward who hoarded towels was cured by presenting her with several towels a day. After the total number of towels in her room reached about six hundred, she began to become satiated, and ultimately ceased hoarding towels altogether.

The converse of satiation is of course the effect of a novel stimulus. An old textbook with a new cover, or the same old lesson presented by a different teacher, can stimulate an increased interest. A visitor to class can discuss the same topics the teacher has been discussing but may be accorded much greater attention than the regular teacher.

Distraction is a factor in conditioning and learning. Responses learned under distracting conditions tend to show decreased resistance to extinction; evidently distractions "weaken" the relationship. On the other hand, the occurrence of distracting stimuli during extinction can increase resistance to the extinction process. Thus it seems that distractions interfere with whatever process is going on; it also implies that extinction may be thought of as a process of learning *not* to do something.

3–7 Learning Not To

One of the most difficult things to learn or to teach is not to do something one has learned to do. How does one get rid of a response that one does not want? This is a basic question involved in therapy and in coaching athletics as well as in teaching cognitive abilities. Desensitization has been given as one way of getting rid of a fear response or other classical response. Extinction is of course another way—bringing the response to be given without reinforcement, either classical or operant. This is also called "negative practice." A more frequent approach to getting rid of responses is punishing them. This leads to avoidance learning. Unless the teacher reinforces the fear involved by intermittent punishment, the fear will extinguish and the former response may show up again. Another technique is to strengthen a response that is incompatible with the one to be eliminated.

BASELINES FOR CONDITIONING

In applying either classical or operant conditioning to either building desirable behaviors or reducing undesirable ones, one needs to observe carefully the frequency of the behavior involved before he begins.

Human memory is fallible, and human observation is inconsistent; as a result it is wise to record data concerning the frequency of a behavior over a period of days before trying to alter it. Then, whether one punishes the behavior or reinforces it or induces stimulus satiation or desensitization, one can observe progress by referring to the cumulative data. For example, a high school girl recorded the frequency of her own sarcastic verbal behavior at four per hour over five days. She then introduced self treatment by giving herself a painful shock after each sarcasm. Her rate decreased to one half sarcasm per hour over the ensuing ten days.

A response, once eliminated, will reappear unless the treatment is given intermittently to prevent this. Schedules for the maintenance of such learning have not been explored thoroughly and as a result are not well understood.

3–8 Conditioning Group Behaviors

Groups can often be conditioned as individuals are. In one interesting study a group of children was brought to an unusually high degree of attention-giving during lessons by reinforcing such behavior with what were called "more probable behaviors." This meant that the behavior of quietly attending to some lesson was reinforced by behavior initiated by the command "run and scream"; the students would do so, and it was observed that the attending behavior which preceded this show of energy increased in probability and frequency.

On the other hand, such behavior as that used above can mislead the students in their expectations, and expectations are important in the interpretation of teacher behavior. Groups are conditioned to expect certain things of a teacher, and when these expectations are not realized, the group members react in much the same way a dog does to shock; that is, they show a number of maladaptive behaviors, aggression being one of them. Once a strict, authoritarian teacher has conditioned a group to his approach (and groups are more malleable toward the beginning of a school year), he is less likely to frustrate a class and initiate aggressive responses on their part than a teacher who has been more permissive and led the students to expect more consideration. This is not an argument in favor of authoritarian approaches across the board, but rather an observation on teaching strategies and perhaps on the simplicity which makes authoritarian measures attractive.

3–9 Conditioning and Cognitive Processes

There is an extension of the concept of reinforcement which borders on the area of communication theory and which is referred to ordinarily as "feedback" or "knowledge of results." If a student is asked to perform a task, and does so, then he is more likely to perform it correctly another time if he is given information concerning the acceptability or "correctness" of his response. Other things being equal, students learn better if they are given information concerning the correctness of their responses. A corollary of this is that optimal learning requires that most responses be correct, since errors will result either in feedback being punishing (which in turn will interfere with learning if too frequent) or in learning the wrong response. Generally these considerations imply that a student should respond actively in order to learn most efficiently.

Suppose a student is told that two and two are four. If he is asked later to give the sum of two and two, assuming he interprets the command "give the sum" correctly, he may give it or he may not. If he does give it correctly, it is a moot question whether giving it increased his learning. One may argue that he knew it, and that giving it did not contribute materially to learning since it was already learned. On the other hand, one may say that even though he gave the answer correctly, the response probably had become "weaker" during the interval since it was first acquired, and that its being repeated and reconfirmed in the answer made the response stronger and more useful. If he does *not* give the correct answer, there is yet some doubt as to whether he "knows" it or not: there may be some intervening reason which leads him to withhold the answer—perhaps he has been chewing a big wad of gum and can't speak without revealing it. Generally, however, failure to answer indicates some problem of interference or lack of original understanding.

What if the student responds incorrectly? One may correct him and tell him to respond another way; if he can follow such directions, well and good—one may get the correct response. On the other hand, even if one gets the correct response this way, does it imply that the student has "mastered" this or that he "understands" two and two? He may simply be imitating what the teacher has asked him to say and not actually understand the question.

Some information on the question of active response has come from research in programmed instruction. Here it has been shown that active response in the form of writing the answer as compared with simply "thinking" it does not pay off when the subject matter is very simple but does pay off when the subject matter is complex or difficult. Experiments in problem solving indicate that students may solve a problem more quickly if they engage in overt verbal behavior concerning their hypotheses and solution processes than if they keep them to themselves (this does not imply that the verbalizations have to be correct). There has been some research in the requirement of active response at intervals during a motion picture film about science. Here too the students who made active responses performed better on a test of understanding of the principles of the film.

3-10 Achieving Control by Relevant Stimulus Properties

A stimulus is made up of many parts: which one or set of these controls the response? One may alter the stimulus presentation in ways which are designed to make it more probable that the student will observe certain elements of the stimulus. One may on the other hand change observing and scanning and eye fixation behaviors of the student, translations of stimuli into internal representations, and other mental accompaniments of learning. These last behaviors are classified as "mathemagenic" behaviors, and while they are not directly observable, there is increasing evidence that they can be modified and shaped through special learning contingencies. One such contingency, for instance, is the inclusion of questions following paragraphs or groups of paragraphs in a text. If these questions are encountered regularly, the kinds of observing and translating behaviors they require are differentially reinforced, and the student gradually comes to use them more frequently. This process obviously involves a greater risk of error and a greater tolerance for errors on the part of the student than in more carefully programmed instruction where responses are required more frequently and feedback is more clear. It may be that such risks are necessary if one is to achieve the kind of stimulus control that the responses should have, rather than a simpler and less effective substitute which is an artifact of the teaching situation.

It is not hard to get a correct response; students are great imitators and can readily pick up cues or hints. What *is* difficult is to arrange for the response to be controlled by the correct stimulus. Take for example the previous problem, teaching that three times two equals six. If one has the problem, "three times two equals _____," then the response is "six." It is easy to get this response. You can ask the student, "What rhymes with mix but begins with *s*?" or just tell him to say "six." However, these do not assure you that the student will say "six" the next time he is asked "three times two equals _____." If he does, it still does not imply necessarily that the student will respond correctly when given the statement $3 \times 2 =$ _____. There is also a possibility that the student will respond "six" when given the statement "three *plus* two equals _____," since generalization operates regardless of the intent of the teacher. Teaching then becomes a matter of searching for basic, appropriate, and powerful stimulus situations to control responses, ones that will provide a frame of reference wherein most other relevant situations can be subsumed. One way of approaching this in the example given is to provide students experience with concrete objects that can be arranged in sets of two and then "added" in some predetermined fashion to get the total; this *enactive* mode of learning in a sense underlies and in another sense subsumes the more formal knowledge. This quest for ways of subsuming concepts and processes into more powerful approaches to a problem will be discussed further in later chapters. It is one of the more fascinating and potentially productive avenues of investigation in teaching-research.

3–11 Initial Versus Final Stages

One can use shaping in teaching a variety of responses. If, for instance, one wishes to teach a class to be quiet, one may reinforce them for being quiet just before being excused by holding them over if they are not. This increases the probability of their being quiet at that time, and of being quiet in general also. One may make one's standards for this increasingly strict over a period of time, so that a class which is terribly unruly at first may by degrees be brought to be very quiet. There are techniques which accomplish this all at once, but they require a type of control that is more difficult to maintain. For example, if a student has bad handwriting, one may reinforce certain gross aspects which are under the student's control, say making capitals at the beginning of a sentence or making his *a*'s legible, and gradually through successive stages make the criteria more rigorous, always rewarding the student at each stage for successful completion (this also implies that any other approach would not work, since he could not be successful at all without an initial relaxation of the standards). One may also shape the behavior of a good student in a similar manner, by requiring successively increasing standards for him to achieve the *A* that he is accustomed to. Teaching in general may be looked upon as a process of shaping, of gradually expecting more and more of the student; this also relates to the general view of teaching proposed in a later chapter on concept formation, where it is pointed out that to teach means to simplify the environment, which in turn means to make the environment in some sense unreal or untrue to life. A crucial element in the process is the gradual altering of the learning contingencies so that ultimately the student operates in a close approximation to the criterion situation, or as one might put it, to real life.

TEACHING BEHAVIOR CHAINS

In a chain of behaviors which lead to a goal, those which are closest to the goal are learned first and strongest. A rat running a maze learns the final turns leading to the food box most quickly. This fact has interesting implications for teaching. One is that it may be more efficient to teach the final behaviors in a sequence first, and work backwards to the beginning. For instance, in one application of this principle a teacher ties a child's shoe until she reaches the final pull on the laces, which she asks the child to do. When he has mastered this, she goes through the whole performance and lets him complete the last *two* steps, and so forth until she has worked her way back toward the beginning. Research on such an approach to teaching has not been replicated sufficiently to present it as a hard-and-fast principle, but it is a technique worth considering in simple serial learning, particularly that involving motor responses.

3–12 Relating Conditioning to More Complex Behaviors

As pointed out in the previous chapter, much learning can be analyzed without identifying the reinforcing stimuli, by assuming that they consist of secondary reinforcements associated with the conditions of learning or the subject matter itself: thus we need not look for the reinforcing stimulus for learning a poem in English class, since most students will learn it, assumedly because they are reinforced through many channels for learning (anticipation of approval, of grades and thus approval, plus implicit reinforcement from the poem itself, and from studying and reading generally). If, on the other hand, learning does not take place, one may find it helpful to analyze the situation from a reinforcement point of view, to identify what is missing. If one does so, it must be remembered that the functional stimuli in most practical situations will be complex patterns of simpler stimuli and also sequences of stimuli. The controlling stimulus for studying mathematics, for instance, may be a situation made up of a conducive environment for studying, anticipation of a pleasant nonpunitive class situation for discussing problems met in studying, anticipation of reasonable success in a quiz on the material, anticipation of some success in understanding the material, and lack of interfering stimuli resulting from anxieties in other aspects of life—social problems, competition from other subjects, competition from demands of other activities, and the like. Cognitively speaking, the stimulus for a correct response to a mathematical problem may be a sequence of stimuli related to the symbolic presentation; if all the elements are present but are out of sequence, this may interfere with understanding; for instance, a student may respond correctly to the problem $3x - 2 = 4$, but may be unable to cope with $4 = -2 + 3x$. Interesting and unexpected outcomes are emerging from experiments with the effect of sequencing; for instance, it was found in one experiment that while students remembered information given in correctly patterned sentences better than that given in incorrectly patterned sentences, they learned more from one of two forms of "scrambling" the sentence than from the other, and the better form was the one that was more thoroughly scrambled. The conclusion was that the interfering effect of scrambling the sentence was partly balanced by the greater attention given to unscrambling the meaning in the more difficult of the two.

A FINAL NOTE ON APPLYING CONDITIONING

Many problems in classrooms come about because teachers reinforce, inadvertently, behaviors they do not want and extinguish behaviors they *do* want. It is very often possible to improve a classroom situation by following two basic rules: (a) reinforce desirable behaviors by attending to students who show them, and (b) extinguish undesirable behaviors by ignoring them. If (b) does not work, mild punishment may be effective as long as (a) is used also. Thus one should *notice* the student who is working productively, not ignore him, and one should *ignore* the student who is procrastinating or disturbing, not notice him.

Bibliography

BANDURA, ALBERT. *Principles of Behavior Modification.* New York: Holt, Rinehart, & Winston, Inc., 1969.

ULRICH, R., STACHNIK, T., and MABRY, J. *The Control of Human Behavior.* Glenview, Ill.: Scott, Foresman and Co., 1966.

WOLPE, JOSEPH, and LAZARUS, ARNOLD. *Behavior Therapy Techniques.* Oxford: Pergamon Press, 1966.

4 Conditioning and Verbal Learning

4–1 Verbal Stimuli and Responses

The conditioned stimuli of classical and operant conditioning are substitutes for the stimuli they replace. They signify that some event is imminent, either an unconditioned stimulus (food powder, shock) or a reinforcing stimulus contingent upon an operant response. Thus one may think of them as signs or signals. As signs, they may be classified in terms of their relationship to what they stand for or predict. Some stimuli are *concrete* in that they originate with three-dimensional objects in the environment, although transmitted via light or sound waves as well as touch and smell. Others are *iconic*, in that they are facsimiles of the concrete object, such as drawings or photographs. Finally, there are *symbolic* stimuli which stand for concrete objects, and for many other things including concepts and processes; these symbolic stimuli have no physical or spatial correspondence with the things or ideas they refer to. A horse is a concrete stimulus; the picture of a horse is an iconic one; and the word *horse* is symbolic.

Most stimuli are transmitted by light or sound waves, although some impinge on the receiver through sensory nerves (a blow, a shock). In a similar sense, most responses are produced through physical acts (also responses); that is, one may draw a picture and thus produce an iconic stimulus, or one may type a word and produce a symbolic one, but in both cases the response is made through a chain of physical responses. Typing is an example; the typing process must be highly overlearned before it becomes completely the tool of the writer, and even then if one concentrates on the thought involved, one's accuracy is liable to decrease.

Responses can be of various types also. Purely motor responses, or physical responses, are a basic type, and have been called *enactive* by some investigators. Enactive responses can be iconic or symbolic in intent, as with sign language and semaphore, respectively. Oral responses (speaking) are mainly symbolic, while textual responses (writing) are either iconic or symbolic.

There are various transformations within the symbolic mode that a learner is called upon to make in learning to respond. He may be called upon to echo the verbal behavior of another, as when he is told to "repeat after me." He may be asked to transcribe what another says, as when told to "write this down." These are not trivial behaviors for the young child. Echoic behavior, for instance, has no correspondence with its model other than the final result; for example, hearing the word *elephant* gives no inherent cue as to how one goes about *saying* "elephant." Saying it must be part of the listener's repertoire of already learned responses if he is to repeat it correctly, and it is quite different from recognizing the word and acting upon it in some other way. In addition to echoic and transcriptive transformations, there are those in which the learner sees a word or picture and copies it (this includes the iconic mode as well as the symbolic), and in which the learner reads a word and translates it into sound.

Responses are stimuli. If *A* emits a stimulus, we say that he has "responded." Responses also *produce* stimuli: one hears or sees himself responding through stimuli produced by his own responses. Reinforcing stimuli can be primary (food, water, warmth) or secondary (sight of food, water, fire, or things associated with them). Secondary reinforcers in operant conditioning are also conditioned stimuli for classical responses; for example, presentation of food to a hungry animal as a reinforcer for some operant response also stimulates both salivation and feelings of pleasure or hope associated with food; these are classical responses. Consider an operant response reinforced by the presentation of food to an animal by the trainer, in a particular dish each time. The trainer and the dish become associated with the food and thus become conditioned stimuli for salivation in anticipation of the food. Now suppose that the trainer makes certain motions which indicate that he is going to get food. These motions will also become conditioned stimuli for salivation; as a result they will reinforce operant behavior (responses) which precedes them; that is, these motions indicating that the trainer is about to get food become secondary reinforcers. Now suppose that the dog barks and immediately (by chance or by design) the trainer initiates those motions which indicate that he is about to get food; then the barking will be reinforced. In a sense one might say that the dog has learned to "speak" to his trainer, in that his bark has been reinforced by the behavior of the trainer in appearing to go for food, not by the food itself. One may also say that this is just part of a chain of responses leading to the attainment of food, and that is true, but still the bark that "brought" the behavior of the trainer is not directly associated with the primary reinforcer and is to this degree "verbal" in nature.

4–2 Defining Verbal Behavior

This discussion of the dog and the trainer has laid the groundwork for a definition of social behavior and subsequently of verbal behavior.

Social behavior will be defined here as behavior reinforced by the behavior of others. If one offers a bit of food to another person, his behavior is reinforced by the resulting expression of gratitude of the other; this expression of gratitude is also social behavior, having been reinforced in the past by the approval of parents or by further helping behavior. Similarly, if in baseball a pitcher offers a pitch to a batter he is reinforced by the batter hitting it (in batting practice) or missing it (in a game).

Verbal behavior can be defined as social behavior that stands for something else and has a low degree of correspondence with the thing it stands for. For instance, a signal that resembles the act of eating is reinforced by the behavior of another person who brings food as a result; this would be an iconic verbal stimulus. The words "I'm hungry" have a similar function but less correspondence with the actual eating. Thus they constitute a *symbolic* verbal stimulus (or response, depending on your frame of reference). Even more to the point is the expression, "Would you please bring me some food." The degree of abstractness, or lack of correspondence to the referent, is related to the degree of "verbalness." Ancient writing systems had different degrees of correspondence to their referents, and their power was generally an inverse function of that degree—that is, the lower the degree of correspondence of the stimulus to its referent, the greater the power of the verbal system.

4-3 Reinforcing Verbal Behavior

While verbal behavior, as an aspect of social behavior, is reinforced through the resulting behavior of others, the resulting behavior need not be limited to what is specifically appropriate to the stimulus. For example, if a child says, "May I have the salt," he may be reinforced by passing him the salt, but on the other hand it is possible to reinforce him with the approving phrase, "You said that very well, Johnny." Such generalized reinforcers as approval are sometimes called *transsituational* in that they do not depend on the particular situation for their reinforcing properties: they are general because they have been associated with a number of different reinforcing situations. This use of generalized reinforcers is one of the important tools of teaching language, whether in the home or in the classroom. A child can be reinforced for imitative behavior in the presence of a stimulus which is to control a certain response; for example, a parent says, "That is a cow, Ann," to which Ann replies "cow" while looking at the cow. She will be reinforced by the parent for saying "cow" and by sight of the actual animal will also gain some control over the response (*if* she was focusing on it or "perceiving" it). She will not have formed the *concept* of cow from this one exemplar, but it is a beginning. Generalization will assist in identifying other cows, as will the instructions of her teacher or her friends, and corrections by both.

The use of generalized reinforcers is often *too* convenient. For example, if one asks for the salt in French when one is in France, one gets the salt: if one asks for it in French in a French class, one gets a good grade. The first reinforcer is *intrinsic*, the second *extrinsic*. The nature of the reinforcement is too often divorced from actual relationships which build language originally. Students feel the difference, and this results in lower motivation. If one can't take the student to France, then, he might at least simulate France in the classroom.

4–4 Conditioning, Verbal Behavior, and Humanism

Conditioning analyses can be applied to verbal behavior without denying that the human organism has a hereditary propensity or aptitude for learning. The ability to make such transformations, the more basic ability to utilize responses and stimuli which "stand" for something else, and the ability to be reinforced by stimuli far removed from primary reinforcing stimuli are basically human qualities, although elements of them are observed in lower organisms. Again, the ability to use signals which have no correspondence with the objects or phenomena they refer to and to use them as titles for whole groups or sets of phenomena is more characteristic of the human species than of others, although others show forms of it. Thus the uniquely human ability to learn verbal behavior is shown in the degree of abstractness and indirectness in representation and implication that can be utilized by the organism in stimuli and responses. At present, we can analyze only broad classes or types of such behavior.

Even a single word is a chain of responses (letters), and learning *any* chain calls upon the hereditary capacity to encode such chains and then reproduce them when needed. This hereditary capacity is not enough by itself: learning is required in order to realize this potential. Ethnologists have observed that there are certain environmental "releasing mechanisms" for hereditary behaviors, situations that bring out the latent ability of the learner, ability acquired through heredity and not previously tapped. Behaviors brought out in this way, however, are quickly conditioned to other stimuli in addition to the particular "releasing mechanism," and thus very soon acquire the status of "learned" behaviors. Furthermore, learned responses may be added to the hereditary ones to carry them out or express them. For example, a small chick must learn to walk, although he has the innate mechanisms for it, and certain stimuli bring out the attempts to walk; only *after* he walks can he get around in such a way that the pecking mechanism can be released by some object on the ground. When it is released—by an object of a given size and appearance—he can learn to discriminate further between various types of objects having the proper shape and size, so that he does not peck at specks instead of food, and so that he can discriminate between kinds of foods.

In a previous discussion it was observed that a listener must have the word "elephant" in his verbal repertoire in order to understand what is being referred to by the person who utters the word. This exemplifies an important aspect of verbal behavior, namely, that both speaker and listener must have a common repertoire consisting of a large set of responses of the same form. More than this, these responses must be under the control of the same stimuli. If one man says "elephant" and the other visualizes an apple tree, the communication will be somewhat inefficient! Thus a large part of learning a language consists of specification of the correspondence between the verbal repertoire (learned by the child, largely through imitative behavior) and its controlling stimuli. This ranges from a very specific control (saying "please" on command) to control by different stimuli and selecting from a number of responses (saying either "house" or "domicile" or "abode" to different examples of this general concept). Furthermore, a single stimulus may strengthen and control many responses; for instance, the stimulus which evokes *house* may also evoke *window* or *chimney* or *home* or *love*.

4–5 Verbal Discrimination Learning

Suppose a child is reinforced for eating apples; for purposes of illustration, consider the stimulus to be the sight of the apple, the response, biting it, and the reinforcement, tasting it. If the child sees a wax apple and bites it, he will not be reinforced by the taste. In the future he may "discriminate." Consider again two similar stimuli of a textual nature, "2.5" and 2·5". The response "10" is reinforced in the presence of one, not the other (which is which depends on whether you are in the United States or Great Britain). Discrimination learning is of course a basic element of verbal learning. Its converse, *generalization*, is a process wherein students generalize their responses to similar, though not identical, stimuli, giving the same response to one stimulus as to another resembling it, whether this behavior happens to be desirable or not. Learning to read and learning to listen both require a large amount of discrimination learning, perhaps even more than they require generalization. This probably results in a learning set on the part of most students which is discrimination-oriented; that is, they have been corrected so many times for generalizing incorrectly that generalization per se is largely extinguished. This fact has been lamented in recent years by those who would foster creativity in the classroom, and many ways have been sought by which this over-learning of discrimination tendencies can be combated. One might also hypothesize that the learning of the *concept* of discrimination learning might contribute to discrimination between races and between other types of groups. It may be that as new and better teaching comes into use one may arrive at some balance, so that a generation may be produced which is not "discrimination-bound," as it were, and which can be creative in its social (as well as its academic) behavior.

4–6 Abstraction

A child is shown a red ball and prompted to say "red"; if he is then shown a blue ball, he is likely to say "red" again, since it is the ball that controls the response as well as the color. However, if he is shown a red ball, then a red triangle, and then a red house, each time being prompted to say "red," or if he knows what a ball, a triangle, and a house are, and thus can have the color emphasized as a component, he may begin to say "red" to any object of that color. "Red" is an abstraction (or rather, "redness" is); it is the name of a property or set of properties that always occurs as part of a larger set, never by itself. Abstractions are similar to concepts, which will be discussed in Chapter Eight. The basic process involved seems to be opposite to that involved in discrimination, but actually it is not, since it requires discrimination between things that are red and things that are not, and between redness and other qualities of a given stimulus. On the other hand, it does encourage the recognition that more than one stimulus can control a given response, which is to some degree antidiscriminatory.

4–7 Translation

The response "commutative principle" to the stimulus "$A + B = B + A$" can be considered a case of translation from symbols to words, just as the response "3" to the stimulus "three" can be considered a closer translation from words to symbols. A skilled bilinguist cannot necessarily translate from one language to another at will: he may not have been reinforced for forming intraverbal bridges between them. A skilled mathematician or physicist may not be able to translate his symbolic processes into word explanations, partly for the same reason. An experienced teacher may have been conditioned to provide such translative behavior, but this translation may suffer from incompleteness or inaccuracy because the concept involved has no word equivalents. A practicing mathematician may never *need* to translate $D + B = B + D$ into "commutative property under addition," although he must know whether it is considered to be operating over a given system. Translative responses, therefore, should not be taken to represent the ultimate objectives of learning, although some translation is necessary for the carrying on of the learning process.

If an American translates French into English, his available repertoire is greater than if he translates from English to French. The same is true of translation from symbols to words, as compared to words to symbols, in mathematics. One's reading or listening vocabulary may differ in extent from one's writing or speaking vocabulary; this fact may be exploited in certain instances as a source of reinforcement;

that is, one may try to recall a word and succeed, and then reinforce himself by saying or writing it.

TRANSCRIPTION

Closely involved with translation is the problem of *transcription*, which means the writing down of what one hears or sees. When a student is asked to construct a response, he must recall the response and also write it down; it is not obvious whether these two are distinct behaviors, but it would seem so. Thus to evaluate learning one should provide instances where recall or recognition can be demonstrated by means other than by writing down, or else one should make sure that the transcriptive behavior is part of the student's repertoire. This same relationship is involved at higher levels in the problem of expressing one's thoughts on an essay examination, where the writing itself is a large part of the task.

4–8 Verbal Chains

Some verbal behaviors arise when one person desires another to act in a certain way, as noted previously, while others involve response to verbal behavior, that is, verbal behavior reinforced by other verbal behavior. The latter can be termed *intraverbal*. Suppose event B evokes event C; that is, suppose C is reinforced when it follows B. Also suppose that B is evoked by A for the same response. This results in chains of behaviors in which a given event is both response (to a preceding event) and stimulus (for a following event). In verbal behavior such chains are very common, for example, "Four score and _____" will evoke a predictable response in most readers.

All behavior and thus all learning is sequential in nature; thus all behavior involves chains. Indeed, the identification of such elements of behavior as "stimulus" and "response" represents an artificial separation of the ongoing environment into discrete components, when, in fact, stimulation never ceases either from without or within and responding is continuous in a variety of forms. Attempts are made to cope with this reality by accounting for multiple causes for a response; that is, by seeing responses as given to combinations of stimuli and by accounting for complex sequences of behavior through the concept of chains.

One aspect of a verbal chain of behavior has received little experimental attention but seems basic to learning: if one learns a chain in which each response is also a stimulus, this chain may be given overtly as recognizable responses or may be "run off inside one's head," that is, practiced covertly. Either way, it seems that if one practices such a chain a number of times, each stimulus-response gains a measure of control over other stimulus-responses in the chain as well as over the one immediately following. This seems to result in the possibility of short-cutting, or jumping from an early stimulus in the chain to a later one; this short-cutting can come overtly (perhaps going through the other elements mentally but not saying them). It is not clear whether it can also happen covertly, or whether it is really a matter of going through all elements of the chain but at high speed. Either way, this enables a learner to handle long chains of responses quickly and covertly and to express and use the results of these chains (that is, the connection between the first and last stimuli) as elements of other chains, as units. Thus, once learned thoroughly through practice, the entire chain can function as a unit, in that very little time is required to go from the first to the last "link."

This reduction of learning to a unit to use in other learning is a powerful tool. It enables the learner to cope with ever-increasing complexity and variety without becoming overtaxed with the burden of going through all the elementary steps of all the processes that together form the larger concept or process or skill with which he is dealing. Some research into memory has indicated that one can keep in mind approximately seven units of information at a time. These units can be keys to a complex and extensive fund of information, but they must function as units if other such units are to be retained (for some current task) as well. For example, one can remember a number like 38420679508348965 if through previous experience the triads 384, 206, and so on function as units, that is, have some previous meaning which enables one to remember them as units or have a history of repetition so that they become units for the learner.

4–9 Conditioning Imitative Behavior

No unconditioned stimulus elicits the spoken sound *ball*, nor is it likely that a child will spontaneously emit a spoken sound close enough to the sound *ball* to be shaped into the correct one. Thus verbal responses are not learned through a direct conditioning paradigm. On the other hand, there is a general response, *imitation*, which is learned and then used to acquire verbal responses. Human beings and some animals seem to have a hereditary predisposition to learn to imitate, and our culture has many contingencies which reinforce this behavior in various forms. (The more complex pattern of behavior called *identification* is based partly on imitation and is discussed in a later chapter.) Experiments have been performed that demonstrate environmental contingencies that lead to imitative behavior; the experiments indicate that there is an *imitative response* and that it is acquired in a manner that can be described by basic learning processes. The author's limited observations of young children indicate that imitative behavior is learned very slowly, over a long period of time.

Consider then a child who is asked to respond "boat" when told, "Say *boat*." The correct response is called an imitative one, but there is nothing in the sound of the word *boat* that can be imitated by the muscles controlling the formation of the word. This must be a trial-and-error affair. Imitation of the physical movements of another person is also a complex behavior, but somewhat more basic; few of us carry it to anything near its potential development as demonstrated by the fascinating performance of a mime! Saying "boat," then, is imitation only in the sense that the response sounds like the stimulus: it must actually be learned through a slow process of trial and error in forming the words. The child must also learn to discriminate between correct and incorrect sounds so that he may monitor his own sound production, in order to come close to the correct intonation.

Another example of simple behaviors which are actually complex is that of writing the word *boat* when one hears it. Again there is no correspondence between the stimulus and the response. The sound of *boat* actually becomes a discriminative stimulus for a chain of muscular responses which produce a symbolic (verbal) stimulus on paper, one which we have learned to translate back into the sound of *boat*. Any grade-school teacher knows that this does not happen automatically; it must be shaped carefully. Thus, if "boat" is the answer to a question, some students may be able to perform the necessary mental processes to get the answer, but may *not* be able to translate the answer into speech or writing. As a result, others will assume that they are ignorant or stupid.

A simple example of the converse of this comes from the field of speech correction. In some cases defective speech can be improved not by concentrating on the speech production of the student, but rather by teaching the student to discriminate between certain similar sounds. Once the student has been taught to discriminate, he can hear his own errors and will learn to correct them. Another example comes from research in teaching writing: one assumes that writing difficulties are motor in origin, that is, that students need to learn to make their pencils go in the right way by training the muscles. In some cases, however, it has been shown that if they can be taught to discriminate correctly between different letters, they are then able to write the letters correctly where they couldn't before. The muscular ability was not lacking, rather the cognitive discrimination necessary to direct the muscles. Again, it has been shown that some of the difficulty in learning to write comes from requiring letters that are too small; when allowed to write on a chalkboard with large letters, children who otherwise could not write were able to produce very legible versions of the letters. These examples are given to emphasize the necessity for careful analysis of the behaviors involved in any learning process, and are not to be taken as an expert's recommendations for teaching in these specialized fields.

Bibliography

SKINNER, B. F. *Verbal Behavior*. New York: Appleton-Century-Crofts, 1957.

The Development of Verbal Ability 5

5-1 Developing Verbal Behavior

There is much disagreement as to the correct theoretical model for describing how verbal utterances are learned early in life. A simple reinforcement model would have children building response chains through trial and error, in imitation of adults, over a period of years, with differential reinforcement of such chains by their parents; this involves a long-term, large-scale shaping process involving the parents, other adults, peers, and the environment. Imitative behavior is certainly an important element of the learning, since children imitate the sayings of their parents and other adults and children, from single words on up to complex sentences. Imitation itself is a learned behavior and has been conditioned in laboratory experiments with children. There is some question as to whether language development proceeds from the very simple (words, phrases) to the complex (sentences), or whether children learn phrases and sentences (through imitation) and through them identify the parts (the words and ultimately the letters). This reflects the whole–part controversy which has gone on in one form or another since the days of Gestalt psychology and before. It may well be that the complexity of the unit which the child learns initially, or early in life, is partly a function of the kind of unit which is most frequent in his environment; it is also possible that learning proceeds both ways—toward the more complex through a process of synthesis, and toward the elements of the learned units through a process of diagnosis or analysis which comes about through comparing different examples of the same kinds of phrases or sentences. For example, a child may learn to say, "Pass the butter" and may go on from this to build other sentences such as, "Please pass the butter" or "Pass the butter and the salt and the milk" or "Please pass me the butter quickly"; on the other hand, through experience with other exemplars of a similar utterance, such as, "Pass the milk" and "Pass the bread" and "Give me the book" and the like, he is forming concepts of the function of parts of speech (implicitly), and the meaning and use of specific words (pass, give, and the like). This does not imply that he necessarily learns each of these independently through imitation; he may well generate a "Pass the _____" sentence himself through use of other elements of his vocabulary. (This implies that he has also formed the concept of substitution.) At the same time, he can learn the meaning of new words through hearing them used in a familiar sentence pattern and observing the context (the situation) in relation to it. One example of grammatical behavior induced through such experiences is found in research where children are asked to complete such statements as:

This is a rak. Now here is another one: there are now two of them. We can say, "Now there are two _____."

The fact that they respond correctly, that is, with the plural of rak, "raks," indicates that this response is controlled by a fairly complex stimulus pattern, which consists of the type of situation and the sentence pattern.

5–2 Stages of Early Verbal Behavior

One can analyze verbal behavior from the point of view of the learning of the child to do various things in which verbal stimuli or responses take part. Fairly early he may respond to verbal stimuli without being able to reproduce them himself: if someone says, "Pat the doggie," he may do so without being able to say "pat" or "doggie." Later he will be able to say "doggie" when he sees one. Children practice these behaviors ad infinitum; learning is very slow at this level, and repetition seems to add to the strength of the *type* of response as well as the individual response itself. Later, perhaps around the age of three, the child begins to express verbal responses which he is using as mediators; for instance, he may say "Go out" and then go out. Research in concept formation shows that somewhat later the child will use words to help solve simple problems even though he does not express the words.

It is important to remember that verbal responses, like others, require contingencies that lead to the response's being given and then reinforced. Since a host of behaviors which we take for granted are learned through long and complex but often somewhat random series of experiences in early life, the relative paucity of effective learning contingencies in the environment of the culturally deprived is currently a matter of great concern. Such conditions leading to later difficulty in learning are not entirely the result of poverty, however; children of high economic status can also be so deprived. Deprivations are often at the root of cases of children who are "underachievers," who "have the ability" but "can't learn." The origins of such behavioral deficits are not always recognized at present and are often attributed incorrectly to physical or neurological disabilities going by such titles as "dislexia." The important point to be gained from the type of analysis introduced here is that one can very often identify the hierarchy or pattern of behaviors which make up a given ability or understanding and on the basis of this hierarchy can diagnose learning difficulties in terms of gaps in the student's background of learning, that is, in terms of behaviors which he does not possess (has not learned) or which he has learned and which interfere with his understanding or ability. Then one can arrange for the learning of such behaviors or the extinction of others, or both, and remedy the situation.

The work of Montessori in the early 1900's and, recently, that of O.K. Moore and others shows what can be learned by very young children when the necessary contingencies are carefully supplied and arranged. Montessori taught three- and four-year-olds to read as a matter of course; Moore's students publish their own newspaper by the age of six to demonstrate that they understand what they are reading. The definition of verbal learning as an aspect of social behavior, that is, behavior reinforced through the intervention or mediation of behavior of other persons, emphasizes that verbal learning benefits from a highly structured environment marked by the personal involvement of adults as well as peers. Such an environment need not be aversive or discouraging to creative thought.

5-3 A Psycholinguistic Approach to Verbal Behavior

Another approach to analysis of verbal behavior, one not entirely different in its observations but somewhat different in intent, concentrates on the structure of verbal behavior, without primary concern for the ways in which it is learned. This approach hypothesizes that there are certain basic structures in a language from which, by the proper use of general rules, one can generate all the acceptable utterances in the language. (The concept of acceptable utterances might be taken to imply some differential reinforcement of verbal behavior by the community.) Some proponents of this *psycholinguistic* approach feel that there may also be structures which are basic to *all* languages. They point to experiments which suggest that very young children of diverse cultures show common inherent propensities for verbal structures, some of these at odds with the structures characteristic of the culture into which the child is born. This implies that the child ultimately learns the structures of its own culture and abandons the basic ones which conflict. This is not hard to accept: one might hypothesize that through evolution man has developed neurological capabilities and predispositions adapted more to one type of utterance than to another, and it would be presumptuous to assume that one particular language makes use of all these hereditary capabilities perfectly or completely.

One aspect of this psycholinguistic point of view regarding learning of utterances emphasizes that children learn sentences and parts of sentences as units, rather than learning individual words. The psycholinguists regard pieces of discourse as patterns or frames which the learner files away in a kind of dictionary or storage area: as more and more of these are learned, common properties among them lead to a formation of rules governing their use. This process is largely inductive and probably not consciously recognized by the learner. (A similar inductive development of rules will be discussed in relation to concept formation.) These rules can then be used to manufacture or generate other pieces of discourse, substituting different words to suit different occasions. There is some disagreement as to this rule-forming and rule-using process; for example, some feel that separate rules are learned for forming active declarative sentences as compared with passive declarative, while others feel that the active declarative sentence rule is formed first, after which transformation rules are learned to change from active to passive voice. In general, this area of thought is characterized by an interest in forming models that describe the processes by which grammar is formulated into practice and in the development of language in general.

The model of learning proposed by the psycholinguists is based on the formation of basic sentences called "kernel sentences," which contain the main part of the information to be communicated, in concentrated form. Sentences that are heard by the learner are reduced by him, for storage, to appropriate kernel sentences, plus "footnotes" related to syntactic structure. If called upon to reproduce the sentence, the learner provides the basic pattern, plus some corrections to it as filed in these footnotes. This analytic approach eventuates in a complex scheme for analyzing sentences into rules (transformations) by which one can generate all the correct utterances in a language. A simple example of the generation of "The boy hit the ball" is given below.

Rules	*Application to Specific Case*	
1. Sentence implies noun phrase, plus verb phrase $(S \rightarrow NP + VP)$.	S $NP \qquad VP$	
2. Noun phrase implies article plus noun $(NP \rightarrow T + N)$.	$T \qquad N$ (The) (boy)	
3. Verb phrase implies verb plus noun phrase $(VP \rightarrow V + NP)$.	$V \qquad NP$ (hit)	
4. Noun phrase implies article plus noun $(NP \rightarrow T + N)$.	$T \qquad N$ (the) (ball)	

One can substitute other words in the appropriate categories; for example, "A bird" for "The boy," "swam" for "hit," and "a truck" for "the ball"! The resulting sentence, "A bird swam a truck," would be grammatically correct and would be reinforced by an audience of linguists under appropriate conditions, that is, where the grammatical correctness and not the meaning was most important. However, the fact that children do not generate "A bird swam a truck" habitually, implies that such utterances are extinguished through lack of desired response in others, because they have no meaningful referent situation.

5–4 Environmentally Produced Verbal Tendencies

In the language of certain Eskimo tribes, there are about thirty different words for snow; in some cultures in warmer environments the same name is used for ice and snow both, as well as for cold. The language of a culture is to a degree shaped by its environment. Since people use language as a mediator for thought, or as a vehicle for thinking, the kind of thinking that is characteristic of a culture is modified by its language. The meanings of some passages in French novels are only approximated in the English translation; one must read it "in the original." We have very little understanding as yet of the implications of these different thought patterns and attitudes that result from language differences. A similar situation exists in relation to differences in social class. The middle-class teacher of poverty-stricken students faces a culture and language different from her own. Norman Mailer has commented on this in a recent work ("The Steps of the Pentagon," *Harper's*, March 1968) :

These blacks moved through the New Left with a physical indifference to the bodies about them as if ten Blacks could handle any hundred of these flaccid Whites, and they signaled to each other across the aisles, and talked in quick idioms and out, an English not comprehensible to any ear which knew nothing of the separate meanings of the same word at separate pitch (Maoists not for nothing these Blacks!) their hair carefully brushed out in every direction like African gorillas or huge radar stations on some lonely isle, they seemed to communicate with one another in ten dozen modes, with fingers like deaf and dumb, with feet, with their stance, by the flick of their long wrists, with the radar of their hair, the smoke of their will, the glide of their passage, by a laugh, a nod, a disembodied gesture, through mediums, seeming to speak through silent mediums among them who never gave hint to a sign.

5–5 Stimulus Modes

In the initial definition of verbal behavior, certain stimulus modes were mentioned, namely concrete, iconic, and symbolic. These become important considerations in teaching. For example, very young children are unable to use pictures of squares and crosses and the like as cues to tell them under which box some food has been hidden. However, if they are first presented with the same problem using three-dimensional representations of the figures, they are able to solve it and then go on to solving it with two-dimensional figures. One explanation of this, derived from communication theory, is that the three-dimensional stimulus has more information. If so, to explain the fact that they can go on to use two-dimensional figures successfully, one must postulate that learning involves a reduction in amount of information given, at least in this case. This might imply that concrete stimuli are required generally in the early stages of learning, then iconic, then symbolic. The Swiss psychologist Piaget has, over years of research in cognitive behavior of young children, found many situations which demonstrate that children process information in different ways at different ages, and that their thinking becomes less dependent on the presence of concrete stimuli as they mature. By giving children of different ages a set problem and observing their solution processes and asking them questions about their behavior, he has concluded that they proceed through stages of cognitive behavior described as *preoperational* (forming concepts from experiences and concrete stimuli), *concrete operational* (solving problems involving concrete stimuli with the stimuli present), and *formal operational* (solving problems in the absence of the concrete stimuli, or thinking ahead of one's physical activity and anticipating the solution).

Piaget's work has been primarily descriptive; his interest is in the maturation of cognitive processes and the growth in the ability of children to cope with their environment. His conclusions have been interpreted by other theorists to imply that there is a necessary sequence of stages of learning in any subject which may not be bound to the maturational levels proposed by Piaget; that is, it may be necessary for a student, regardless of his age, to have gone through the preoperational and concrete operational stages of dealing with a subject before he can function effectively in the formal operational. This to some degree parallels the three classes of stimuli: concrete, iconic, and symbolic. For example, consider the concept of energy as taught in physics and chemistry. One current view is that energy should be regarded as a hypothetical construct which is used to describe the relationships between physical changes, such as the number of revolutions of an electric motor shaft, the amount of electricity used, the change in temperature of motor and surroundings, and the distance traveled by the vehicle which this motor propels. To "understand" this concept at the abstract level it may be necessary first to have enactive experience with some of the phenomena on which it is based (as obtained in the laboratory and in working with such vehicles), then iconic experience in relation to illustrations used to represent these phenomena and their interactions. Whether one can understand if one skips one or more stages is a question that cannot be answered categorically at this point; it depends on one's definition of "understanding," among other things.

5–6 Symbolic Thought

One of the marks of human thought which separates it from that of lower organisms is its ability to deal with things that are "not there," in other words, to deal with past and future events and to manipulate images and memories in order to predict and control the future. Verbal behavior and verbal thinking are part of this process, and words are one of the tools used in such thought. It is a mark of maturity to be able to go beyond the immediate stimulus field and to anticipate future possibilities on the basis of present and past experience. Some have said that the young child is "stimulus bound," and to a greater extent so are lower organisms.

The age of adolescence is characterized by a noticeable increase in ability to deal with symbolic stimuli and formal operational thought, to break free of the immediate stimulus field and think beyond it, to manipulate ideas partly for the sake of doing so. This ability, of course, is built up over many years but seems to reach a "take-off" point about this time. This does not necessarily mean that understanding of a concept or process can come about without some background of experience with concrete manifestations or exemplars of it, or without iconic representations to codify the relevant dimensions in a way that has some correspondence with the original. It implies rather that around the age of adolescence the learner begins to become aware of the possibilities in symbolic thought in areas where he has adequate background experiences to support such thought and may tend to extend this type of thinking into areas where this experience is less complete. This often results in a tendency to intellectualize matters and to assume one understands them because one can manipulate the verbal titles and rules and definitions which relate to them. There is often a marked contrast between the confidence that learners have in their understanding of ideas and their ability to apply what they know to problems of various types. There are also contrasts in the abilities of adolescents to deal symbolically with different subject matters, for some of which they have the requisite background but not for others. Thus the frustration and agony one observes in some otherwise good students when it comes to dealing with mathematics, where the background for the symbolic thought requires experience with numerical and arithmetic "phenomena" (that is, relationships and problems) which they may have overlooked or taken lightly before as well as experience in generating numerical and arithmetic examples of the concepts in order to see firsthand how they work. Problems here often relate to inexperience with a "discovery" approach to learning as well, where the necessary experience of getting a wrong answer and having to try a number of possible solutions may be threatening to good students who are used to getting right answers and who are threatened if they produce errors.

5–7 Inductive and Deductive Thinking

Inductive thinking is a process of describing sets of stimuli or complex arrangements of them, particularly physical phenomena, in terms of past experience, that is, in terms of some general rule or hypothesis. It involves discriminating between elements of the phenomena and also between the present phenomenon and past phenomena (experience). It also involves generalizing from current to past experience, through rules or descriptions in which the words one uses have been formed themselves through past experience. The processes involved are close to those of concept formation. A more abstract kind of inductive thinking is that involved in forming descriptions or rules or hypotheses from experiences or phenomena which are described in words. Since these word descriptions are themselves distillations of the actual experience described, the important dimensions of those experiences have been emphasized already, and thus it is often easier to induce new rules or generalizations at this level than to do so from observation of the physical phenomena or examples themselves. Induction is not solely based on generalization, then, but it emphasizes that aspect of learning; the direction of thought involved has also been described as "divergent" and "thematic," and persons who think this way more than others have been described as "levelers," as contrasted with "sharpeners," who see differences rather than similarities among situations primarily. This process or direction of thought is also related to what has been called "creativity."

Deductive thinking involves the use of general rules to arrive at specific outcomes or examples of them, that is, by taking a general description and then generating specifics. When only one statement or theorem or rule is involved, this generating of examples is also related to "creativity." However, when more than one rule is involved simultaneously, the task is to create examples or additional statements which are implied by combinations of the original ones. Sometimes one can generate examples which satisfy the various rules or theorems, and then by induction go on to create a new rule or theorem: this new theorem may be either narrower or broader than any of those from which it was created. This is all based on past experience, and the conclusion will be tested against past experience and new experience. It is not impossible, however, to arrive at a formulation of experience which is new to the creator and to others as well, and which can be used to codify experience in a more effective way.

Generally speaking, deduction is a convergent process, reducing a number of conditions to some statement or example which satisfies them all; in this sense it is related to "convergent" thinking and associated with high "intelligence" rather than creativity. However, as indicated above, the outcomes of deductive thinking can on occasion be highly creative; thus, the outcomes are a function of the situation and of the thinker, who can impose his personality on the process.

Consider the formation of a theorem about triangles. If one measures two or five or seventy-five triangles, he may conclude inductively that their angles add up to 180°, particularly if he has some experience with variation in measurement and a grasp of the elements of statistics. Now consider the theorem, "All triangles have angles that add up to 180°." One must make a judgment as to the probability of previous theorems (used to prove this one) being true; the added generality of the deductive proof rests on this. To form the theorem inductively one identifies common properties among his measurements; to form the theorem deductively, one identifies common properties of the basic concepts used (parallel axiom, alternate interior angles in one proof.) To apply the theorem to a particular triangle, one identifies the subset specified by the theorem itself and then compares it to the particular situation (the triangle). There is a subjective aspect involved in these processes which is pedagogically important; that is, if one has not had the concrete experiences that make up the "inductive" conclusion, he may have less "faith" in the verbal rule (the theorem), even though the latter is based on previous theorems which he accepts. In such a case, the student might say the statement is not "meaningful" because he has no referent for it. On the other hand, if he has been conditioned to find the deductive conclusion satisfying, he may not need the type of "understanding" that requires such referents. Thus one can see that the effectiveness of the two approaches may be affected by their different requirements in terms of previous conditioning. To compare them pedagogically, one must consider the previously conditioned behaviors needed, the immediate behavioral requirements, and the long-range requirements of the discipline involved. It may be, for instance, that the students need to be acquainted with the deductive approach, but that to use it the students must have learned the other concepts required. In following this deductive approach, they may eventually have to be given enough experience of an inductively oriented nature to form the concepts on which deduction depends. This suggests that there is a "best" sequence in learning, perhaps even a necessary sequence, which involves the nature of the learning experience. It suggests that students must first acquire concepts inductively, through experience with actual examples, before they can deal with the same concepts deductively or abstractly. This relates to the sequence mentioned previously, involving enactive, iconic, and symbolic modes; that sequence may be invariate, or it may apply generally to a certain class of learning behaviors.

5–8 Frequency and Repetition

To use a sentence or a phrase one must treat it as a unit, a unit that can be emitted correctly without paying primary attention to producing it. This requires that the function be relatively autonomous, which in turn requires that the latency of the various responses which make it up be short, and that their probability be high; that is, they must be given quickly and easily and be highly reliable. It was observed in the first chapter that repetition of a set of contingencies results in the learner's "seeing" different aspects of the stimulus, thus extending the control of the response by the stimuli involved and making the response more probable. At the same time, the repetition decreases latency and makes the chain of behaviors more reliable as well as quicker and more convenient to treat as a unit. If one repeats the response under the correct conditions many times, he will have "overlearned" it, thereby contributing to the retention of the response, since an overlearned response is retained or remembered longer or more completely.

The use of repetition in learning has been theoretically unpopular for some years. The concept of "drill" has been anathema to many educators. Yet it has been an important part of teaching practice all along. Its unpopularity has been due to the use of "drill" in an unimaginative and unproductive way; its ineffectiveness often results from structuring that allows irrelevant stimulus properties to control the response and thus fails to invoke the correct or desirable elements of the stimulus situation for controlling it. This will be discussed further in the following chapter.

Bibliography

CHOMSKY, NOAM. *Topics in the Theory of Generative Grammar*. The Hague: Mouton, 1966.

CHOMSKY, NOAM. *Aspects of the Theory of Syntax*. Cambridge, Mass.: MIT Press, 1965.

DeCECCO, J. P., ed. *The Psychology of Language, Thought, and Instruction*. New York: Holt, Rinehart, and Winston, 1967.

Research in Verbal Learning 6

6–1 Serial Learning

There is a very active field of research in verbal learning which is basic and not primarily oriented toward applications to teaching, but which is still *suggestive* for both teaching and learning. In one type of research, a student sits in front of a memory drum, a device that reveals to him one of a list of syllables every few seconds, hiding the rest. The first syllable may consist of the three letters *NOX*, for example, and the second may be *RIV*. The student is asked to anticipate (to say) RIV when he sees NOX, and when he sees RIV he is asked to anticipate the *next* syllable. Syllables like these are called *nonsense syllables*, although they have meaning due to their similarity to parts of words, both in appearance and sound. Some are easier to learn to anticipate than others, partly due to their greater "meaningfulness." One can rate them for meaningfulness by asking a number of people to describe the associations that are called up by each one: some will have more associations on the average than others, and are thereby termed more "meaningful." As will be described below, this meaningfulness is related to the difficulty in learning a list of such syllables. What does this "learning" consist of?

Suppose a student is shown the syllable NOX and asked to anticipate the next in the list, RIV. The list is given below:

NOX RIV BAP FOL SUG MES KOR RAL SOK LEV

He cannot see RIV when asked to anticipate it. When RIV is finally shown, after a few seconds, he is asked to anticipate the next syllable. Then, after going through the list, he is asked to try it again. This goes on until he reaches some arbitrary criterion, say twice through the list without an error, or five times, or more.

Each time he responds (anticipates) the experimenter writes down a + (if he is right) or a 0 (if he is wrong). The table below shows part of the results from such an experiment with one student, each row representing one time through the list, and each column giving the record of errors for one of the syllables in the list. On Trial 2 of this experiment, for example, the student anticipated only the first syllable correctly, while on Trial 5 he was wrong on positions 2, 4, 5, 6, 7, and 8 (that is, on RIV, FOL, SUG, MES, KOR, RAL; conversely, this means he correctly anticipated NOX, BAP, SOK, and LEV.) Incidentally, the order of the list is kept constant, and the response is correct only if it names the *next* item on the list—it will not be correct if the subject anticipates number 7 instead of number 6 when he is shown number 5.

Trial	Position in the List (assuming a list of ten)									
	1	2	3	4	5	6	7	8	9	10
1	0	0	0	0	0	0	0	0	0	0
2	+	0	0	0	0	0	0	0	0	0
3	+	+	0	0	0	0	0	0	0	0
4	+	+	0	0	0	0	0	0	0	+
5	+	0	+	0	0	0	0	0	+	+
.	.	.	.	.	.	.	.	.	.	.
.	.	.	.	.	.	.	.	.	.	.
.	.	.	.	.	.	.	.	.	.	.

6–2 The Serial Position Curve

Averages based on data from many students over many experiments done by different people in different places show that correct anticipations occur early in the learning period for syllables toward the front of the list, a little later for those near the end, and much later for those in the middle. If we had put down the data for more trials, plusses would have appeared in the middle eventually. Their late appearance seems to reflect some kind of interference, perhaps from syllables at the beginning, perhaps from those at the end, perhaps from both, and perhaps from other factors as well. The syllables in the list are chosen to be of equal "meaningfulness" so that this factor does not affect the shape of the curve, which is plotted using data like that in the table above. The serial position curve is shown in Figure 6.1.

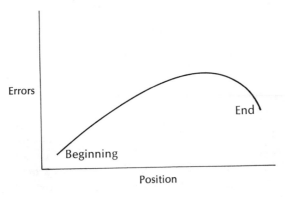

FIGURE 6.1

The fact that the peak of the curve is just past the middle has caused some difficulty for theorists, and debates over the implications of this curve are still going on. Some evidence indicates that the response is controlled by a number of aspects of the stimulus situation, among them the preceding stimuli, the following stimuli, and position in the list.

Lists made up of meaningful words, or of syllables that resemble familiar words or parts of words in sound or appearance, are easier to learn than lists that are less meaningful. This is somewhat surprising since more meaningful syllables and words have more associations; one might think that these would interfere with the correct anticipations, since they would call up other associations to compete with the correct ones. There is some evidence that this does happen but that the positive effects of familiarity outweigh in importance the interference from the other likely responses. This may be due to the greater availability of the response for recall, that is, the ease with which the learner can bring the response (the next syllable) out of storage in his memory and give it. One might guess that recalling is partly a matter of bringing likely responses out of memory storage and then somehow inspecting them to see whether or not they are really correct. If this is true, then the familiar or meaningful responses would be easier to "find" in one's memory; they are used more often and thus one has had to find them more often.

Another interesting aspect of this kind of learning has to do with the similarity between the syllables in the list. The more similar in appearance, sound, or meaning, the harder it is to learn the syllables *in order*, that is, to anticipate correctly when the order of the items is unchanged. On the other hand, such similarity between items aids the learning when *free* recall is the criterion, that is, when one is asked to give as many of the items as possible without worrying about the order in which they appear.

The fact that meaningfulness or familiarity aids in the learning of the list; that is, that a list with similar syllables can be recalled more easily if order is not relevant, can be partly explained by assuming that the syllables are stored in some way when originally viewed, and then recall involves a search for their storage location (this approach is suggested by the operations of modern computers). Such a search would be easier if the syllables were related to some group of words whose location or address was well known from previous experience. Also, if a group of syllables is similar, it might mean that they are stored in the same general location, and thus finding one of them aids in finding the others. Thus a list with similar syllables is easier to recall, but this facilitation interferes with getting them in order. In brief, similarity *interferes* with *serial anticipation*.

A related phenomenon has been found in the teaching of reading. Emotionally loaded words, such as *hate, wish, kiss* (as compared with neutral words such as *come, keep, busy*) were learned more quickly when presented on flash cards to a group of children. It may be that the former verbalizations are stored in more immediately accessible areas.

6-3 Speed of Learning and Retention

There is another phenomenon of interest related to retention, wherein retention is measured by the number of trials needed to relearn a list after some time has elapsed. Suppose two groups of students, X and Y, learn the same list to the same criterion, and suppose Group X learns it more slowly, on the average, than Group Y. Now suppose the two are asked to relearn the list a week later. Which group will relearn more quickly? The answer seems to be that they will each relearn it with the same speed; the amount of difficulty in learning does not determine retention, as long as both groups learn it *to the same criterion*. We may also expect, then, that if two lists are of unequal difficulty and are learned to the same degree, retention will be the same for the two.

6-4 Applications of Serial Learning

Since all learning is in a sense serial, in that it occurs in time, we may expect some situations analogous to serial learning to become apparent in more practical learning situations. When presented with a series and asked to recall in order, one may expect that responses at the beginning and end will be fresher than those in the middle. One also expects meaningfulness in general to contribute to ease of learning, but not necessarily to retention, except where ease of learning enables one to learn something more thoroughly in a given trial. One would also expect similarity between items to be a confusing factor where order is important, but to facilitate learning where it is not.

The recall of prose passages of certain special types evidences some of the characteristics of serial learning mentioned above. In one experiment, the passages were constructed to show different levels of meaningfulness; a low level, for example, might have been the following:

> We bought in tent for delta fay one sight . . . ,

while a higher level might have been:

> Grass does nothing for but to buy the pond in the dell. . . .

The highest level of meaningfulness is exemplified by:

> We were watching the sun come up over the placid ocean. . . .

It was found that while the second level was quite a bit easier to recall than the first, the *third* level was little, if any, easier to recall than the second. This would imply that overall meaningfulness is not the only important factor in retention: here the second level seems to be near optimal in its resemblance to ordinary prose, even though the over-all meaning is not equal to that of the last level.

6–5 The Curve of Forgetting

An early learning theorist by the name of Ebbinghaus initiated the use of nonsense syllable lists to study learning. He used himself as a subject most often and explored many facets of the topic now being discussed. One outcome of his research which has always attracted interest is simple and striking and yet, as will be seen, somewhat misleading. After learning a list to a certain criterion, say, X times through without an error, Ebbinghaus would go for some time (hours, days) without practicing the list and then would relearn it and record the number of trials required. He varied systematically the amount of time between original learning and relearning and found that the longer the time, the greater the number of trials he needed to relearn the list. This was attributed to forgetting, which was generally envisioned as a sort of brain leakage or growing fuzziness of the mental trace of the previous experience. Ebbinghaus found that the most forgetting occurred soon after the learning, and that one forgets at a slower rate as one becomes older. A representative curve is given in Figure 6.2.

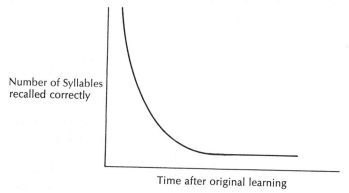

Time after original learning

FIGURE 6.2

This does not tell how forgetting comes about, but it is an empirically derived picture of a phenomenon relevant to learning and deserves serious consideration. It implies that whatever we learn we forget soon after we learn it. (Of course, review or practice are not taken into account here.) There is another interesting fact about the curves that Ebbinghaus discovered by using himself as a subject, however, one which leads one to continue to explore the phenomenon of forgetting.

When in recent years investigators replicated Ebbinghaus' experiments using college students as subjects, students who had not previously learned lists of nonsense syllables, they found that their retention of the lists was far better than Ebbinghaus' data showed: furthermore, they found that the more experience the students had had with such lists, the poorer was their retention. It began to be apparent that learning lists of nonsense syllables interfered with learning other lists of similar content. This was evidence of proactive interference or inhibition, that is, interference from previously learned material.

This effect has confirmation in some of the phenomena to be discussed below, as well as in the old student complaint:

> Why study at all?
> The more you study the more you know,
> The more you know the more you forget,
> The more you forget the less you know,
> So why study at all?

6-6 Paired-Associate Learning

While serial learning has many aspects that resemble conventional learning, there is another kind of learning involved in research that goes a step further in sophistication. Suppose one presents the stimulus BAV and then presents it again with the stimulus ROS following it; for example:

> First presentation: BAV
> Second presentation: BAV–ROS

The second presentation implies that ROS is associated with BAV. Now the next presentation will not have either or both, but rather will have a new stimulus syllable; let us say it is MUX, followed by MUX–SIM. Thus the learner is given the first of a pair, and asked to anticipate the second. The order in which the pairs are given is varied each time the learner goes through the list of pairs. This experimental paradigm is called *paired-associate learning*.

As in serial learning, previous learning affects the learning of paired-associate lists in much the same way but with some variations. One difference is illustrated by the following experiment:

A paired-associate list is formed where all (the first words) are related to each other (interitem similarity) and all (the second words) are related to each other also.

> elephant—green
> lion—red
> tiger—blue
> rhinoceros—yellow
> Maine—window

California—door
Texas—ceiling
Michigan—floor

The student would be given "elephant" and be required to say "green" to be correct. There were sixteen pairs, four groups of four, two of which are shown above.

Many college students asked to learn this list were unable to reach criterion (several times through without an error) in a large number of trials.

How can one explain their failure to learn? Most of the errors were responses from the second list, but they were attached to the wrong first word. They learned it, and they didn't. The implications are that there is a very strong pull between words in the same category; this may be what is responsible for the difficulties found in serial learning with interitem similarity. Here it is so strong that it cannot be overcome. It will be well to remember this when we discuss concept formation.

Suppose students are asked to learn two paired-associate lists, one after the other, as below:

List X	List Y
A–B	A–C
fos–rel	fos–siv
gav–gox	gav–mub

Note the relationship between first words of pairs; this is symbolized by calling this an "A–B, A–C paradigm." If we had instead the following list to learn after X:

List Z

fos–ril

we would call it an "A–B, A–B' " paradigm, due to the relationship between second syllables.

6–7 Inhibition Paradigms

Consider the effect of learning A–B on learning A–B'; since the first syllables are the same and the second ones similar, we might expect the learning of A–B' to be easier than if A–B had not been learned. This ordinarily is the case and is called *proactive facilitation* or *positive transfer*. How does one demonstrate this experimentally? One has two groups of students, one of which learns A–B and then later learns A–B'; the other learns A–B also, then later does not learn anything. Both are finally asked to relearn A–B, as in the following diagram:

	Day One	*Day Two*	*Day Four*
Group 1:	Learn A–B	Learn A–B'	Relearn A–B
Group 2:	Learn A–B	. . .	Relearn A–B

Group 1 would relearn A–B more quickly than Group 2, where the groups were equal originally. This effect of learning A–B' on learning A–B again is called *facilitation*; since it has worked "backward" in a sense on the learning of A–B, it can be called "retroactive" facilitation. Suppose instead of learning A–B', the first group learned another list, A–C, as in the original given above:

Group 1:　Learn A–B　　Learn A–C　　Relearn A–B
Group 2:　Learn A–B　　　. . .　　　Relearn A–B

Here the first group would relearn A–B more slowly than the second, indicating that the learning of A–C interfered with their learning of A–B. This would be retroactive inhibition. Now suppose that we have a different experimental setup, where one group learns A–B initially but the other does not; then both groups learn A–C:

Group 1:　　Learn A–B　　Learn A–C
Group 2:　　　. . .　　　Learn A–C

Now if Group 2 learns A–C more quickly than Group 1, we will hypothesize that the learning of A–B interfered with the learning of A–C. This would represent the effect of *past* learning on learning something in the present; the previous experiments represented this in a sense also, but not as clearly. Here we have what is called *proactive inhibition*, or *negative transfer*; that is, the learning of A–B interferes with the learning of A–C. If it had facilitated the learning of A–C, then we would have had proactive facilitation, or *positive* transfer, or what is ordinarily spoken of as *transfer*.

There has been a great deal of research involving these inhibition paradigms; some of it has had implications for classroom teaching and learning, while some of it has seemed to show applications of basic conditioning phenomena. For example, in the second retroactive paradigm above, the time between learning A–C and relearning A–B can be varied. If one changes the relearning of A–B from very soon after to some time after the learning of A–C, one finds that the inhibition caused by A–C *decreases*. This seems surprising until one notes that in the learning of A–C there are a lot of intrusions of responses from A–B. This might imply that the A–B responses are being extinguished during the learning of A–C. If this is so, then one might expect them to recover, and the fact that increasing the time between A–C and A–B improves performance implies that some kind of recovery process is indeed working.

6–8 Distribution of Practice

Suppose two groups learn the same list, and instead of learning it to a given criterion, both learn far beyond the point where they can go through without error (this is called *overlearning*). Both devote the same number of trials to the learning, and this number is made large to overcome slight differences in initial learning speed. The groups differ, however, in that one learns in blocks of trials separated by time, while the other learns through massed trials with no rest; for instance, if the total is eighty trials, one group learns in blocks of twenty while the other does all eighty at once. If the two groups are compared in terms of relearning the list later, there will be little if any difference between them. However, if the inhibiting effect of this learning on the learning of *another* list is examined, a *great* difference is found. The massed learning group has a much harder time learning a new list, while the distributed learning group has relatively little difficulty in learning a new list. The massed practice results in greater inhibition with other learning; the distributed practice results in little interference with later material. This effect seems powerful enough to affect educational practice significantly.

6–9 Mediation

Another area related to proactive and retroactive effects is that involving *mediation*. Consider two lists of paired associates; the first is made up of such pairs as these:

soldier—pipe
dog—leaf
hatter—pot

and the second is made up of pairs such as these:

arm—then
organ—tan
just—hold

Would there be any difference in speed of learning the two lists? Soldier is related to "sailor," and that in turn to "hornpipe," and thus to "pipe." "Dog" goes through "tree" to "leaf," and "hatter" through "tea party" to "pot." While not every learner would think of these relationships, generally speaking the first list would probably be learned more quickly because of the possible "mediators" involved. Such mediators have been reported by subjects learning paired associate lists made up of nonsense syllables as well as lists made up of words. The use of past associations to build such verbal "bridges" and thus to make the task more "meaningful" demonstrates one source of the general effect we have called *proactive facilitation* or *positive transfer*, although this is of a somewhat more random variety than is usually implied when one uses the term *transfer*.

Research in mediation has reproduced such facilitating effects under laboratory conditions by teaching students relationships which are new to them and then by using these relationships as mediators for other learning. For example, learners may be asked to master an A–B list, such as fav–boj, and then a B–C list, such as boj–muz. After this they are given an A–C list, for example, fav–muz. They learn it more quickly than a control group which has not learned the others, or which has learned only one of the others; thus mediation has been demonstrated experimentally.

Other experimental paradigms of this sort are as follows:

$$1: \quad \text{B–A, C–B, then A–C}$$
$$2: \quad \text{A–B, C–B, then A–C}$$
$$3: \quad \text{B–A, B–C, then A–C}$$

In 1, B is the mediator, but a backward association is involved; this yields weaker effects. In 2 is found an example of what is called *stimulus equivalence*, in that A and C acquire a relationship or association (again, as evidenced by the quicker learning of A–C as compared with a control group); this relationship is acquired through the learned relationship with B as a response. This seems to imply that if two quite different stimuli are associated with the same response, they can come to be seen as similar or related.

Suppose that the first part of the third paradigm above is used, that is, B–A, B–C, but without the A–C. Then suppose an additional list, A–D, is learned also. Would C–D be facilitated due to the response equivalence brought about by the first two lists? Early attempts to demonstrate this were not successful; some later ones were more so. The effect seems to be present, but weak.

6–10 Learning Sets in Verbal Behavior

It was previously observed that children learn the "naming game," that is, they learn that the response "horse" to the statement, "That is a horse," is reinforced, and that the thing pointed at or the unique feature of the environment at that time is the thing called a horse. This "naming game," which is played so continuously in certain periods of life, is an example of what is often called "learning to learn," or alternately, the "formation of learning sets." That is, children learn how to learn names; they learn various stimulus complexes which indicate that a thing has a particular name, and they also learn to recognize the conditions under which it behooves them to learn, conditions which suggest that they will have to use what they know in some situation. This implies that one teaches learning sets by setting up conditions under which learning of a given kind pays off; this pay-off may be in the form of a test, or it may be in the form of making the learning a key for some positive reward, or it may become the condition for teacher approval. Suppose one wants to teach problem solving: one brings together a class of problems, exposes the students to them in an ordered sequence, giving feedback after each one. The student learns to give general responses such as "asking oneself what the problem is" or "looking for a common property" or just "attaching the name to the object," and those enable him not only to learn the particular response at hand but also to learn more efficiently other responses of this kind when the situation demands it. If the teacher provides cues to make the student more likely to attend to these relevant attributes of the problem or the solution, without telling him *how* to solve it, he makes a significant contribution. This procedure will be discussed in more detail in a later chapter on problem solving.

As information proliferates and job requirements change in our culture, learning how to learn becomes more important, while learning to cope with particular problems or to do particular tasks becomes less so. Yet one can only learn how to learn by using some particular learning task as a vehicle. This implies changes in the process of education which will be discussed in several parts of this book. Generally, they take the form of problem-centered and process-centered curricula, and student-centered individualized instruction.

Bibliography

COFER, C. N. and MUSGRAVE, B. N., eds. *Conference on Verbal Learning and Verbal Behavior.* New York: McGraw-Hill, 1961.

UNDERWOOD, B. J. and SCHULTZ, R. W. *Meaningfulness and Verbal Learning.* Chicago: Lippincott, 1960.

7 Verbal Learning and Teaching

7–1 Discrimination, Induction, and Deduction

In teaching a student to appreciate a sonnet, one may condition him first to discriminate between the sonnet form and other forms of poetry, although one might instead teach him the salient features of a sonnet to such a high degree that he would automatically recognize anything which was *not* a sonnet. This implies a combination of inductive learning (learning a discrimination by being reinforced for identifying something which is a sonnet and not reinforced for identifying something which is not) and deductive learning (being given rules for recognizing a sonnet and applying these rules). The student will be conditioned further to discriminate between good and poor uses of simile, metaphor, and such devices. Ultimately, again through a combination of inductive and deductive approaches, he will be brought to recognize "good" and "bad" examples, and the various shades of excellence, as well as the particular preferences of his professors, of his peers, and of poets and literary people in general.

Other aspects of verbal learning are suggestive of strategies and decisions on a larger scale. For instance, the effect of distributed practice on interference has implications for curriculum organization and scheduling which should be explored. It suggests that one might remember different subjects in his curriculum better if they were distributed among each other in terms of classes and study time. Thus, reducing numbers of courses taken simultaneously and studying fewer subjects "in depth" might not be the best approach for long-range understanding and retention. As another example, the relationship between retention and difficulty of learning (speed of learning) implies that material which is harder to learn will be retained as well as material which is easy to learn, and that the frequently heard postulate that "meaningful" material will be retained longer is not of itself necessarily true. What is probably true is that more meaningful material is learned more quickly and in a given amount of time is learned to a higher degree. Thus it is retained more completely because it has been learned better, or overlearned, not because it is meaningful per se. There is some evidence, actually, that less meaningful material is retained better when learned to the same degree as more meaningful material. If one considers interference as the prime source of "forgetting," then this makes sense, because less meaningful material is by definition and experiment material that is less frequently used and less frequently met; as a result, there is less chance that similar but confusing material will be encountered subsequently, thus less chance of "interference," thus better retention.

Another aspect of verbal behavior which is important to consider in practical learning situations is that of mediation. Where mediators are available from previous experience, or where mediators are provided by a teacher, learning is quicker. In a sense, the subject is more "meaningful" to the student; for a given time spent, learning will be more thorough and retention will be better. It is also a short step from "mediators," as discussed previously, to the use of concepts in categorizing and ordering learning and then to hierarchies of concepts. This will be discussed in another chapter.

7-2 Teaching Paired Associates

In paired-associate learning, the greater the similarity of the stimuli to each other, or of the responses, the greater the difficulty one encounters in connecting the response to the stimulus. The difficulty is due to interference from "clustering" of terms that are similar in sound, appearance, or, particularly, in meaning. Since generalization is involved, this implies some need to teach discriminations between the terms. Thus if steps are taken to teach a student to discriminate between stimuli involved in such learning, the learning will be facilitated. Thus the better one knows the various responses in respect to each other, the less "similar" they are in that one has more cues by which to differentiate between them. These cues may take the form of mediators in the learning, since the associations taught to make the terms more meaningful may also be used as mediators between the stimulus and response terms. Thus "mediation" opposes the effect of similarity between stimuli or between responses. One-trial learning experiments which indicate that stimulus-response connections are formed on an all-or-nothing basis imply that mediation is an important means of learning; that is, one either "finds" a link or one doesn't, and the link is what makes the "connection" which leads to the response to the stimulus. One can relate this to a memory-storage model, saying that the learner is searching his memory for such a mediator. In that case, it might be easier to "find" the mediator a second time, and thus there would be some decrease in the latency of the response with practice.

These considerations suggest an approach to the learning and teaching of paired-associate-like materials, and paired-associate paradigms are often met in learning tasks. One can help the student by differentiating between stimuli and between responses. A program of learning which emphasizes such discriminations would facilitate the process. One can also help by emphasizing various possible links between words and sounds or whatever the pairs consist of. This might amount to something close to reinforcing creativity in some cases, since one would reward students for unique though appropriate connotations or relationships. This implies that playing with language, acquiring funds of "useless" connections and information, and seeing relationships among things that are not always considered related might pay off in learning. Such a view is somewhat different from one which will be proposed later, where the need to teach the most powerful basic concepts so that learning may build logically is advocated. The view given here is analogous to a "look-see" approach to reading, while the other may be compared with a carefully structured "phonic" approach. Probably neither in itself is sufficient for optimal learning and transfer. One needs a carefully designed structure of concepts and processes combined with a large fund of potentially useful but not immediately applicable information.

A one-trial learning model and a related information-storage-and-retrieval model imply that learning is the relating of previous knowledge to present tasks, of finding mediators between the stimulus and the response. The implication is that once one finds the "link," then learning has been accomplished. If this is so, then why repeat or review something after it is learned? How can later learning "interfere," and how does "forgetting" come about? Evidence has been given that interference *does* occur, and there seems to be little doubt that review *is* helpful. There is little evidence on which to base decisions as to amount and scheduling of this review, however. Several possible explanations of this seeming paradox offer themselves. One is that the connections between stimulus and response must be repeated in order for the latency to decrease to a point where the response is useful in other tasks. Another is that subsequent learning may involve similar mediators, and that confusion is thus possible. Review would be a matter of discrimination learning, then, to keep the proper mediators in place. There is also evidence that review is most effective when it comes after other material has intervened between it and the learning. This also implies interference from subsequent connections. There is also a continuing problem after learning of generalization among responses and stimuli in the lists. The review may consist of a continuation of the original learning, a distribution of learning sessions, if you will, to make the procedure less subject to interference as well. There is also the need to maintain the learning by continuing both to extinguish old erroneous responses and to keep the new ones strong.

7–3 Teaching Composition

There are certain aspects of teaching composition for which a shaping model is suggestive, together with discrimination learning applied to verbal behavior. The correlation between improvement in understanding of grammar and improvement in ability to write has been shown to be rather low in several studies, suggesting that conventional approaches to the teaching of English are not optimally designed to produce students who can write. One basic ability which needs to be taught is discrimination between good and poor writing, which calls for the presentation of exemplars and identification of their desirability by the student, reinforced or extinguished by the teacher. Another ability is writing clear, well-structured sentences and paragraphs. Again the student needs models to work from, then needs to respond himself and have some feedback as to his success. Much of this could be carefully structured so that the teacher does not need to "correct" every last attempt. Model situations with exemplar descriptions of them could be provided the student so that he could imitate, monitor his own progress, and revise before presenting the teacher with a final product. Early attempts at composition should be reinforced on the basis of their relationship to the student's own previous work, and not red-pencilled on the basis of grammar and spelling, when the objective is to reinforce clarity of expression and style; this requires some focusing on the crucial aspects of the student's behavior. Finally, it would seem worthwhile to shape a particular essay or description through a number of stages, so that the student can correct his mistakes and improve his work on the basis of that particular paper. It might be demanding too much of his ability to generalize to expect him to apply the feedback to a completely new paper without first working out the difficulties on the original.

7–4 Teaching Remembering

There is an empirical body of evidence and practice, not of a formal research nature but nonetheless convincing, which has important implications for the study of retention. This content is often expressed through commercial courses and workshops for the improvement of memory, and while one cannot treat these as scientifically sound engineering processes, one can assume that they are reasonably effective. One of the assumptions which underlie such approaches to improving memory is that the ability to form mental pictures is highly important in retention: if someone tells you about something, you visualize it. This seems to be a method of coding large amounts of information for storing it for future reference. However it works physiologically and neurologically, it is something worth considering for practical use.

Another assumption is that the ability to associate mental pictures with each other is important. If you visualize your living room, you see not only the couch and some chairs but the coffee table and some things on the coffee table. You may also see familiar people in the room. A further step in this process of putting images together or synthesizing them, as it were, is the formation or creation of novel situations by associating pictures which do not ordinarily go together; for instance, you can visualize yourself riding on the tail of an airplane in your nightshirt with an umbrella trailing behind, turned inside out, and a baby tiger holding on to your back. Whether such a picture is appropriate to any purpose or has any advantages in its visualization is another matter; one advantage such a picture might have is that, being unique (that is, a unique formulation of several familiar things), it may be easier to recall than a picture which is quite ordinary. This matter of standing out due to uniqueness is part of the figure-ground perceptual phenomena that Gestalt psychologists investigated in some detail, but they did not exploit this for such practical purposes. In more recent research in mediation, it has been shown that pictures sometimes function more effectively than words as mediators for a paired-associate task.

Along with these basic abilities of visualization and combination of visual images, the "memory expert" takes advantage of another basic fact of retention, namely, that it is easier to recall something familiar than something new. As we have hypothesized earlier, this may have to do with the accessibility of the material in storage, with our ability to find the image or word. Along with this, there is the ability to attach new things to old, to make associations (visual for the most part) between something new to be remembered and something old that is already remembered, that is, accessible in memory. Thus, if you want to remember something new, you associate it with something old; if you wish to remember several new things, you associate them with several old things. To make this process more efficient and enable one to practice it, the memory expert provides a list of familiar things which the learner makes even more familiar by going over it time and time again, associating pictures with the words in the list so that he can associate other pictures with them. For instance, one might pick such words as coffee, Socrates, and ferris wheel to begin with: associated with them would be a steaming cup (perhaps with a coffee can beside it), a bust of Socrates, and a ferris wheel. These would be the first three of a list that might be as long as ten words (in one such system, each of the words and pictures also refer to a number from one to ten, for use in other parts of the system). How are these lists used? Consider the partial list we have made up—coffee, Socrates, and ferris wheel. Suppose now you are sent to the store to buy bananas, bacon, and pork chops. Then you might visualize slicing bananas into your coffee and eating them with a spoon out of the cup, with the coffee running over into the saucer; also, you might visualize Socrates sitting down to a modern breakfast of bacon and eggs, with the slices of bacon being oversize and drooping over the edges of his plate, as he stares down at them quizzically; finally, you might visualize a ferris wheel full of pigs instead of people, where every once in a while one of the carriers dumps over into a giant frying pan and the pigs are turned into pork chops and sold to the people at the carnival. This seems very complex and hard to remember, but the association with the familiar list (it is not familiar to you as yet, so you can't get the benefit of it), the unique and memorable situations which you have visualized, and the efficiency of this visual coding of the happenings or situations all contribute to make it practically certain that you will remember to get bananas, bacon, and pork chops. Thus the concept of familiarity as an aid to recall can be harnessed in an artificial situation which can be very useful in everyday requirements on retention, partly because the requirements which our society places on memory are so random and arbitrary and unconnected that they benefit from some system which makes them make some kind of rational sense, no matter how wild and unique.

Does this kind of approach work for studying verbal material connected with some subject, say, history or mathematics? The answer is a qualified yes, to the extent that the particular subject is arbitrary and random (or is taught that way). One can imagine a history course where the requirements are arbitrary enough to make such a memory system pay off; one can imagine another history course where the concepts, processes, and facts are so interdependent and related that the course is its own memory system, and learning is an ever-unfolding series of related ideas. The same can be said of mathematics: despite the closely-knit nature of its theoretical structure, it can be taught so badly that some memory system of an arbitrary nature might be helpful. On the other hand, it can be taught in such a way that an ever-increasing number of complex concepts and processes are subsumed under an ever-*decreasing* number of more powerful postulates and theorems, so that the more complex the subject becomes, the simpler it is to comprehend in its entirety. No *arbitrary* memory system is needed here; again, the course *is* the system.

7–5 Providing for Proactive Inhibition

The physicist assumes that a body in motion will remain in motion unless acted upon by an outside force. It might be well to assume that a student will learn whatever is given him to learn unless acted upon by some previous interfering learning or some current interfering stimuli which distract him or get him on the wrong track. One way to prevent the interference by previously learned material is to bring it out and label it as wrong, that is, to give the student ample opportunity to verbalize and thus give responses that occur from previous experience; these can then be labeled as "incorrect" by the explicit or implicit response of the teacher (hopefully not punitive). This process is analogous to extinction; it also implies a student-centered approach to teaching, since one is probing for the responses of the student to relevant stimuli, and then responding differentially to his responses. It also implies something of a discovery approach to learning in that the student is bringing his personal past experience to bear on the topic; however, he is not formulating the questions himself, and so is not indulging in pure discovery. If one were to allow him to formulate the questions himself, though, one might get to the problem areas (cognitive) more quickly. Whatever the theoretical framework for this practice, it is very important to recognize the seriousness of the problem of dealing with interference from past learning; one would almost hope to have completely naive students rather than ones whose concepts and processes had been formed poorly. Generally speaking, it is more difficult to teach a student with previously formed, erroneous concepts and processes than to teach one who has a reasonable background in the subject but no previously learned concepts and processes which relate directly to the subject. This is not to say that correctly learned related concepts and processes would not be invaluable, only that learning often interferes as much as it helps.

7–6 Maintaining Verbal Learning

Verbal responses can be extinguished unless maintained. It is quite likely that this applies to mediating responses as a subset of verbal responses. Furthermore, when two responses are available to a given stimulus, it seems likely that the one with the shortest latency wins out, other things such as meaningfulness and relevance being equal. If one is learning a new response to an old stimulus, or "sharpening up" a response under such conditions, the new response initially has short latency and is dominant, that is, is given instead of the old response. If one evaluates the learning some time later, however, one may find that the old response has regained dominance; this would seem to relate to the greater familiarity and firmer storage of the information or equipment used. Thus one must maintain responses once they are conditioned. This involves having them given from time to time, which is in turn "review." Furthermore, it is becoming more and more obvious that teachers spend more time than needed in introducing new material and less time than needed in reviewing old. If one learns (teaches) Topic A, and then Topic B, then to maintain them both one needs to review A and B together, before going on to Topic C. When finishing C, one needs again to review A, B, and C. This review is tedious for the teacher, and more so for the text writer, but repetition is still the mother of learning, and for the reasons given above.

Maintaining responses implies increasingly complex cumulative reviews, but this can be ameliorated by combining a number of previous concepts or processes into one problem, and by building the subject so that review is implicit in the learning of new material. This again implies that the review requirements will be a function of the subject matter as well as of the teaching approach. Discrete sets of facts without common subsuming principles or concepts will require either continually expanding review efforts or dropping of required information as it accumulates. The latter case calls for attention to broad subsuming principles and for studying situations as exemplars of the principles rather than as collections of facts to be remembered. However, the concepts, processes, and principles are based on facts, and so facts themselves cannot be eliminated or dismissed lightly.

7–7 Complexities of Applications

The engineering or technology of instruction is full of complexities not entirely covered by what little theory exists at this point. For example, in one study, similar but potentially confusing passages were interpolated between the reading of a given passage and the evaluation of the students' understanding of it. In this case, the interpolated material was expected to interfere with learning. As it turned out, that group which read such passages was superior in its performance on a later criterion task. The investigator concluded that the similar-yet-different material required the student to clarify the concepts gained in the first passage, to reconsider it in some way, thus resulting in better understanding of it. In another study, two different approaches to analyzing electrical circuits were introduced one after the other. A subsequent test indicated that the groups which had only the first method, without the second one in between it and the test, did *less* well on the test, as would be predicted by the retroactive inhibition paradigm. In both cases, it seems, the expected inhibition occurred, but in the former case this inhibition was recognized and the students overcompensated for it.

7–8 The Function of Drill or Practice

As mentioned before, frequency in verbal learning has its place, as does review of past material. This implies some need for drill or practice involving concepts and processes which have been presented. Such drill or practice should involve all the contingencies which are to control the response, and should not introduce irrelevant cues which shortcut the mediating processes which are to be involved. Unfortunately, it is possible to give such drill or practice *without* reproducing the contingencies, substituting instead other contingencies which may subvert the learning. Thus drill can be either good or bad, depending on the way in which it is done.

For example, suppose the student is to learn to handle a simple linear equation, of the type $ax + b = c$, by subtracting b from both sides and then dividing both sides by a. If this has been taught in a meaningful way initially—either inductively, by having the student discover the solutions himself, aided by past experience with the type $ax = c$ and the type $x + b = c$, or deductively, by reviewing the previous types and then, through exposition, by giving them the combined solution, or through a combination of both—then the practice or drill will have the objective of repeating the process with increasingly complex variations in irrelevant, and then to some extent relevant, aspects of the problem. The initial problems in the drill might involve different letters, for example, $fx + t = m$; then the order of the terms might be varied, for example, $m - gx = a$; later the complexity of the expressions would probably be increased, for example, $x(a-t) + af = g^2n$. It should be pointed out, however, that this kind of structuring and ordering of drill can become an end in itself, a self-defeating end; it would seem that after a certain point the drill would have fulfilled its function, and that additional complexities and variations of the basic problem might be of academic interest but not contribute significantly to the ultimate goal of understanding the process well enough to deal with it in a new situation. Furthermore, since the student knows it is a drill and on a certain topic, each problem is redundant to that degree; that is, it is not the same as a situation where a number of different processes might be used to find the solution. Part of the problem of using the process is in recognizing it as applicable or not applicable, and in such a drill this kind of discrimination learning is not fostered. Furthermore, there is a temporary repetitiveness involved in such drill, which makes the correct responses highly probable, more so than when one comes upon the same problem in the context of another problem or several others. This is related to knowing what is being drilled, also to the temporary effect of repetitions.

In summary, then, the purpose of the drill is to reduce response latency and also to increase retention, since overlearning increases retention or makes the responses involved easier to recall or to find in the memory storage. It is also to bring the student to be more familiar with the material, to give him an opportunity to see more aspects of the problem, something which seems to occur when one goes over a problem a number of times. On the other hand, certain dimensions or properties of a drill situation, such as repetitiveness and redundancy, are inherently irrelevant and to some extent interfere with the application of the behavior. Thus there would seem to be a possibility that there is an optimum drill period for each learned behavior or for each application of a learned behavior. For example, one would concentrate more on decreasing the latency and increasing the accuracy of arithmetic processes for a student who was going to be calculating payrolls or cross-footing accounts than for a student who was going on to abstract algebra and graduate study in topology. At least, this is an easy and seemingly logical conclusion which is often made concerning such matters. However, there is another side to this which should be considered, and it is that we are undertaking or even presuming to decide for a student in advance and without consulting him whether he will undertake to prepare for a career as a clerk or a mathematician; some may say that the choice is necessary and that the instruments are available to aid us in making the decision, but such instruments are reliable predictors only in respect to large numbers of people, not in respect to individuals. These instruments are also of questionable validity in respect to the tasks or behaviors which the learner is presumably to undertake or in respect to which his aptitude or ability is to be measured. The matters of reliability and validity will be discussed in a later chapter.

CODA

Obviously verbal behavior is too complex and all-involving to be analyzed and reduced to theory. This chapter has only mentioned a few aspects of it which have come under investigation and which are suggestive for both practice and further research. Verbal behavior will be involved in other chapters in this book as well, obviously, and so this treatment cannot be said to end here, but only terminate temporarily.

Bibliography

JONES, CHARLES. *Learning.* New York: Harcourt, Brace, and World, 1967.

8 Concept Learning

8–1 Concept Described

As we have seen, the unit of behavior used in classical and operant conditioning is the *stimulus*. Moreover, a stimulus emitted by the learner is called a *response*, whereas one which follows the response and makes it more frequent is a *reinforcer*, and one which precedes and "controls" it is a *discriminative stimulus* (or *unconditioned stimulus* or *conditioned stimulus*, depending on the conditions and the response). Further, *stimulus substitution* is a basic form of learning. The "meaning" of a controlling stimulus has to do with its implications regarding reinforcement.

In discussing verbal learning, we again found the unit of behavior to be the stimulus, or stimulus and response, but, as we discovered, in some cases several stimuli have the same response, or several responses are controlled by the same stimulus. The meaning of a stimulus has to do with its implications regarding reinforcement by the behavior of others, since verbal behavior is regarded as a form of social behavior.

As verbal behavior builds in complexity, meaning becomes more difficult to establish. Consider a word; it does not refer to a single object or act or function, but rather to a group or class or set of these. Thus the relationship between a word and the real world it describes is not the same as the relationships between the world and an individual's momentary perception of it. The Russian psychologist Vygotsky has observed that just as there is a dialectic leap between absence of consciousness and sensation, so there is another equally important leap between sensation and thought. The qualitative distinction is the presence in thought of a generalized reflection of reality, the essence of word meaning. A young student in an economically depressed area asked, "How can we understand the words when we haven't had the experiences they stand for?" This ability of a word to function as the title for a group of past experiences, and thus to act as a mediator for applying past experience to the present, is one of the miracles of human thought.

In analyzing cognitive processes, there seem to be two basic relationships. In one, a number of stimuli come to control a common response; in the other, one stimulus controls a number of responses. The response "dog" is an example of the first, being controlled by a large number of stimuli representing different breeds, sizes, and shapes of dog. An example of the second is the stimulus "pound," which controls a number of responses, among them "weight," "cake," "place for errant dogs," "hit something with a mallet." The same word can function both ways. One should not assume from the examples given that the only responses possible are iconic or symbolic. Sitting down, as on a stool, is an enactive response associated with the idea or concept of "chair," and can be elicited by a large variety of objects with chairlike potential.

Learning can be viewed as a process of ordering and simplifying one's perception of his environment, which is infinitely complex otherwise, and coding the results of this process for future use. This coding is done through words primarily, but words themselves are only symbols or titles or representatives of the coding or of the simplifying process. Knowing the word does not take the place of having the experiences to which it refers.

One aspect of the process of ordering and simplifying, including both experiences and titles (words), as well as ways of referring to or describing them in terms of other experiences, is called *concept formation.*

8–2 Concept Defined

A concept is a relationship between a set of stimuli (the *exemplars* of the concept) and a smaller set of responses (the *titles*). This relationship may be expressed through words (the *rule* or *definition* of the concept).

Concept is a concept. One exemplar of it has the title "dog." The exemplars of the concept *dog* are many, and there are other titles, such as "canine." One can give a number of rules or definitions of it: a typical one would begin, "A four-legged animal with. . . ."

Another exemplar of the concept *concept* has the title *metaphor.* Its exemplars are sets of symbolic presentations (stimuli), each a verbal chain. They are to be found in poetry and prose. One such is the famous line, "It is the East, and Juliet is the sun." One rule or definition might be: "A metaphor is a phrase or combination of phrases which calls attention to aspects of events not ordinarily attended to in practical everyday communication, which as a response to the environment is controlled by unique properties and which is not ordinarily reinforced by others." Such a definition is sophisticated in respect to behavioral paradigms, but might not be acceptable to a professor of literature.

A concept whose exemplars consist of sequences of stimuli rather than a pattern of simultaneous stimuli can be called a *process.* An exemplar is the solution of a simple linear equation. Such a sequence is encoded in the brain in some unitary fashion and can be manipulated cognitively as a unit, yet when called from storage it results in a *chain* of behaviors. Another example of a process is the phenomenon we have called *extinction*, a sequence of events leading to the decrease in strength or probability of a response. It is a *sequence* of events, as compared with a pattern of simultaneous stimuli such as that involved in the concept *house*.

8–3 The Concept of Stimulus Expanded

Any stimulus situation, or environmental situation, in which some response or other is expected to occur, can be viewed as an indefinitely large number of individual stimuli or elements or dimensions. Were it possible to attend to all of these individually, one probably could not provide unique responses to them all, certainly not at the same time. One might also regard any response as made up of smaller responses, and relate each of these to some stimulus dimension, but even then it is doubtful if one could account for them all. A response, then, represents some reduction in the complexity of the real world, in that it is controlled primarily by some subset of the stimuli which precede it. For instance, in a busy city scene one's responses may be governed primarily by the sight of a bus stop (if one is waiting for transportation) or by the color of a small disk of light hanging over the street (if one is driving) or by the marquee on the theatre one is passing, or simply by one's own thoughts. One adapts to many familiar aspects of the environment and either suppresses the perception of them or responds rather automatically to them (the two may amount to the same thing).

Thus, one can divide any stimulus situation into a subset of stimuli which have primary control over the response and the stimuli remaining which are relatively unimportant. This control is determined in part by the contingencies of the situation in respect to the responder, as implied in the illustrations in the previous paragraph. This control is also determined by the configuration of the stimuli and their relative intensity and duration and by their similarity to configurations or patterns involved in past learning. This division into what has been called *figure* (the important aspects) and *ground* (the rest) is somewhat arbitrary; it may eventually be more useful to give a relative "weight" to each of the properties of the stimulus situation, and thus to recognize that *all* properties exert *some* control over the response, even though the amount may be negligible. This is similar to recognition of the pull of the gravity of the moon on someone on the surface of the earth: theoretically it is there, but it is generally negligible in practical problems involving weight.

As an example of this control, consider an operant response learned in a room with an electric fan humming in the window. The sound and sight of the fan will to some—probably negligible—extent control the response. In addition, the sight and sound of the fan will elicit an emotional response parallel to that (or those) experienced during the learning (classical conditioning). However, one may never notice this control. The sight and sound may have negligible effects, and also they may evoke other responses since others have been learned with the same background—thus the small effect there is cancels out in that it elicits many different responses which compete with each other.

8–4 Example of a Response Controlled Primarily by a Common Subset of Properties

Suppose a seven-year-old child is shown a set of three blocks so constructed that a toy can be hidden under any one of them, and suppose that one has several such sets varying in size, color, texture, and such. In each set, let us suppose there is one block that is different from the others; for example, in the blue set, suppose one block is a darker blue than the others. Now one picks a set, hides a toy under the odd (darker) block, and then asks the seven-year-old to find the block. The child is given several trials on each set, until he finds the toy regularly on the first try.

After doing this with several sets, the child is observed to locate the toy on the first try with each subsequent *new* set of blocks; he may never have seen the particular blocks used in this criterion (test) situation, and they may vary along a dimension which has not been used before, that is, along the dimension of texture, whereas the others have varied in size or color. Thus the "oddness" must be controlling the response. ("Oddness" here resembles an abstraction, as defined previously.)

What would happen if the boy were told initially that the toy was "under the odd block"? Would he "learn" to locate the toy more quickly? Would the nature of the learning process be different? What if children of different ages were given this problem, and their average solution times and their solution processes were compared? Would older children do better than younger, and would there be a steady decrease in learning time according to age? If there were, would it be the result of physical and neurological maturation, or the result of experience, or would it be the result of adding to their vocabulary? Would there be a difference between the solution processes of children who were verbal, that is, who could speak intelligently and fluently, and children of the same age who were not?

In research with similar problems, it has been found that older children do better generally on such·a problem, also children who have formed a more complete vocabulary; they do this even though they are not given any rule for the solution such as "the toy is under the odd block." This might be explained by saying that they are using words as mediators for thought, even though they don't express them, and even though they aren't given any words to help them.

If one were to take a number of children of the same age and give them the rule verbally before they tried the problem, one would find that the rule had varying degrees of facilitating effect. This would imply that their "understanding" of the words in the rule or directions varies in degree. This would assumedly be a function of their different previous learning experiences, although such differences are often explained by alluding to differences in "intelligence" (intelligence itself is a mixture of various general abilities, and is thus a general achievement level). Other differences due to age and vocabulary will be discussed later in this chapter.

8–5 How Concepts Are Used

When a child makes errors in the process of learning, one can explain his behavior either by calling it "trial and error" or by saying, "He is testing various hypotheses and receiving feedback." The "hypotheses" are concepts. One might explain the greater effectiveness of older children in solving a task like the one above by saying that they have a larger number of concepts or hypotheses available to be tested, and thus they are more likely to find the right one. This resembles the stimulus sampling view of conditioning. One might also assert that they are more experienced in hypothesis testing or trial-and-error learning and are as a result more persistent; this would be especially true if they had been successful in the past in such endeavors. In stimulus sampling, this would increase the probability of "drawing" the right hypothesis. They also have more experience in recognizing a successful outcome; after all, when the child finds the toy under the box, it is not necessarily reinforcing, since he may not want a toy anyway and may simply be searching because the experimenter indicates that he should search. Perhaps such a game is not part of his past experience, and he has to learn to play it or to anticipate some positive outcome for playing it. Positive outcomes might include such things as the approval of the experimenter, a feeling of achievement, or enjoyment of the particular toy due to past positive associations connected with it. These too are concepts. It is possible that such outcomes are aversive to him, due to previous conditioning of classical associations involving fear.

Thus, one may also view the odd-block problem as one where the learner uses concepts formed in the past, such as color, size, and number. If the learner has not learned to involve color in dealing with the environment, then he will not recognize as easily that one of the blocks is an odd color, since he will not attend to that property or dimension or attribute. Even though he may be able to recognize in some way that one block is darker than the others, he may not have learned to "connect" this with some other property of the situation, that is, the absence of the toy, or to use the relationship effectively. Thus the solution of this problem, or the formation of this concept of "oddness," or the use of the concept "oddness," is very much a function of other concept learning and other problem-solving experiences. If the child has not formed the concept of "oddness" previously, it may well require a very long series of experiences with different sets of blocks before he arrives at the criterion behavior, selecting the correct block the first time. It might run the experimenter out of new sets of blocks!

The ability to "form" a concept for the solution of such a problem (that is, the ability to adapt behavior or learn a new response due to contingencies of reinforcement which one meets in the environment) is a hereditary faculty of the mind, particularly the human mind, but it is also present to various degrees in lower organisms. Its evolutionary usefulness seems obvious. Such concepts are formed very slowly, through many trials. This too might be of evolutionary advantage, since if one formed a concept on the basis of a few trials, one might be forming large numbers of them which do not "pan out," which are based on chance contingencies which do not reflect the environment accurately. In a primitive environment, with its great complexity and uncertainty, there were probably very few concepts that were useful to man. Another advantage to having concept formation come about slowly is that it is more efficient to use other concepts already formed if they are effective in achieving results or gaining reinforcement or solving the problem. Thus we may avoid "from-scratch" concept formation until we have exhausted all possibilities of utilizing concepts already formed. This latter view might be altered to include the possibility that all concepts are formed on the basis of other concepts, and thus it may be a matter of using less complex concepts where possible, rather than putting together a new formulation of the old learning, which requires a certain amount of energy and a certain amount of anxiety during the learning process. This anxiety, in turn, probably stems from anticipation of negative outcomes, since when one is trying out a new "bag of tricks," one often finds that it does not work in certain situations and is thus punished for responding in that way. That is, one uses the new hypothesis in a number of situations which it does not apply to, thus learning to discriminate between appropriate and inappropriate ones. Conservative leanings are reinforced by the real world, and one must be able to tolerate aversive outcomes if one is to learn new methods.

There is another possible behavioral difference between the solution process of those who have had previous experience involving the formation of applicable vocabulary and the process of those who have not.

It relates to the concept of "insight." Children who have learned what "oddness" is, and who might therefore test this as one hypothesis, may be observed to "catch on" to the solution suddenly, due to the fact that they have finally "thought of" or "tried" the correct hypothesis where others were incorrect. They do not have to "form" this concept, since it is already relatively well established, so there is little uncertainty when they arrive at the correct one. Such an "all-at-once" solution process is often referred to as *insight*. It seems to be made possible by previous learning, learning which was originally of the slower, more inductive, concept-formative type.

8–6 Precursors of Concept Learning in Previous Chapters

In the discussions of verbal learning, an abstraction was defined as a response to a common property among different stimuli. Redness was an example, abstract in that it could not exist apart from the stimuli to which it belonged. In a sense, any response to a subset of stimuli is an abstraction, since no stimulus or set of stimuli exists apart from others which make up the particular situation; for example, a dog is always part of some background. This is another view of the "figure-ground" relationships discussed earlier in this chapter. Thus, "oddness" can be viewed as an abstraction or as a concept.

In the discussion of intraverbal behavior the interference of inter-item similarity with serial and paired-associate learning was discussed. It was found that syllables or words that either look or mean the same tend to cluster in free recall and tend to facilitate that recall, although they make serial anticipation and the connection of associate pairs more difficult. A paired-associate list was described, in which students were unable to connect response words to stimulus words, due to the fact that the response was related to others from the list, and the same for the stimuli; this was an unusually strong example of this clustering. This affinity of words or syllables that are similar in looks or meaning is also involved in concept formation and identification. A concept refers to a number of things (words or objects or subconcepts) which have something in common. Dog is a concept, so is red. Energy is a concept, also house. In order to study this crucial area in teaching and learning, and to make this study most rewarding in terms of applications to teaching, we will begin with a definition of concepts that is a bit abstract itself.

8–7 Basic Research in Concept Learning

Careful, controlled research requires simplified learning tasks and quantitative criteria. Figure 8.1 shows a number of cards used in research in concept formation. As is evident from the display, the exemplars involve three dimensions, shape and number and shadedness

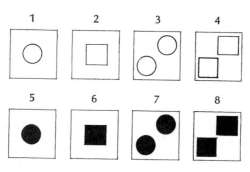

FIGURE 8.1

(shadedness might also be called color, involving black and white only). A card is presented to a student and he is asked to respond in a way which indicates whether it represents a *positive exemplar* (that is, whether it is an exemplar of the concept to be learned) or a *negative exemplar* (that is, whether it is *not.*) For example, suppose the experimenter decides in advance that the correct concept will be "black square"; this means that cards with black squares on them will be positive, others negative.

The experimenter may present exemplar Number 2 (Figure 8.1) and ask him to push one button if he feels that it is a positive exemplar and another button if negative. After he pushes one or the other, a light over the button becomes red (if he is wrong) or green (if he is right); thus he receives information or feedback concerning his response. This is similar to paired-associate learning in that each exemplar has a response, but different in that some of the exemplars have one response (positive) and the rest have another (negative). Thus the population of cards (exemplars) is classified into two sets, one the concept, the other not.

DIMENSIONS OR ATTRIBUTES OF THE CONCEPT

One concept which the experimenter could have decided to make "correct" using the cards above is the one with the title "black circle"; this title is also a rule in abbreviated form, meaning "all cards that have black circles," or "all cards in which the figure is both black and circular." This involves two of the three dimensions or attributes of the exemplars, shape and color; number is not used. Thus shape and color are said to be *relevant*, and number is said to be *irrelevant*. In this case, as in many others, the dimensions or attributes of the exemplars are concepts in their own right: "square" and "circle" are concepts, and they are part of the more general concept "shape." These are *learned* in early life, and do not depend on hereditary mechanisms for recognition. People who have been blind and then had their sight restored have had to *learn* them, and if the sight was restored too late they could not do so adequately.

Suppose one asks a student to stand on his head every time he sees a card with a blue figure on it. If he is shown a card which has a blue circle, a white background, and a yellow border, then he will so respond; to do so, however, he has to "ignore" attributes that are unimportant, such as circularity, color of background, and presence and color of the border. As another example, many dogs have collars, but collars are not relevant to the concept "dog," since they are found on many other animals as well. Another factor to be considered is the number of "levels" or variations in a given dimension or attribute. If one knows in advance, for instance, that the color of the exemplars of a concept will be either blue or red, then it is easier to deal with this dimension than if it can be *any* color.

DOMINANCE OF ATTRIBUTES

Some dimensions or attributes of a concept are more obvious than others; that is, there is a higher probability that the correct response will be given if they are present than if others are present. This means that concepts with noticeable or obvious or distinct properties will be learned more easily than concepts which do not have such properties. This seems analogous to the function of "meaningfulness" in serial and paired-associate learning. Such dominance is partly due to previous learning: one notices that which is familiar. It is also due to such attributes as size and intensity: the bigger, flashier, louder the stimulus, the more noticeable or dominant it is. This matter is also related to the "figure-ground" concept of the Gestalt psychologists, who pointed out that in any stimulus pattern, certain parts stand out from the rest. One perceives part of the pattern as the "figure" and the rest as the "ground" or "background." For the reader, the particular word or phrase he is reading is the "figure," and the rest of the words and the book and the table it is lying on are "ground." Exemplars that stand out, that are more noticeable, that are more dominant lead to quicker conceptual learning, just as more meaningful words lead to quicker learning of lists. Concepts which have many such exemplars are learned more easily.

One property of exemplars of a concept which contributes to distinctiveness or dominance or meaningfulness is the relationship between levels or varieties *within* a given dimension. For example, if one of the relevant dimensions of the concept is color, exemplars might have different shades of the same color, or they might have different colors entirely. Learning is facilitated by using the different colors as compared with using different shades of one color. This again seems to contribute to distinctiveness and/or dominance.

8–8 Types of Concepts

Given the set of cards as before in Figure 8.1 (see page 87), what would it be like to try to identify a new concept which one had not met before? It is difficult to find examples of something completely new, since newness is relative. The sequence of exemplars given below, with feedback, is given so that you can try to identify a relatively new concept. Try it.

First exemplar: Card 1   Your response (positive or negative) _____.

Feedback: Positive is correct.

Second exemplar: Card 2   Your response _____.

Feedback: Negative is correct.

Third exemplar: Card 6   Your response _____.

Feedback: Negative is correct.

All the other cards are given as exemplars, and the feedback indicates that all are negative except 8, which is positive. If there were several examples of each card, and they were presented in random order, do you think you could come to identify the positive ones correctly every time they showed up? What is the concept; that is, can you give the rule? Is there a convenient title?

This concept could be described vaguely as "opposites in all dimensions," but there are other pairs which would satisfy this, so it is not a unique description. There is no simple title for it. Yet it *is* a concept, in that it has exemplars and a rule, albeit a complicated one, and it could be given a title—we could call it "gloop" or something like that. If one were to have extensive practice identifying this concept, a "gloop" would come to have meaning and to be familiar. In this sense, then, one is *forming* a concept rather than identifying a familiar one. On the other hand, if one didn't already know what circles and squares were, what numbers were, and what shadedness was, one might never be able to learn it—in other words, it is built on other more basic concepts. They are more basic in that they were learned earlier. It might be possible, however, to teach them (that is, squares, numbers) by first teaching this concept which is new to us. It might turn out to be a very basic relationship which is relevant to many of the others and thus might contribute to learning of the major concepts. The search for such basic, powerful, inclusive concepts is becoming more important as information explodes around us. We need to look for powerful subsuming concepts to help us process more information more easily.

ANOTHER "TYPE" OF CONCEPT

Some review of concept "types" may be in order here. Given the same cards, suppose Number 1 is presented and one guesses that it is positive and finds out that he is wrong. Then suppose Card 2 is presented and one guesses that it is positive and is correct. Now Card 1 appears again (one may or may not remember he has seen it before): it is identified as negative, and the feedback indicates that this is correct. Card 6 is now presented, identified as positive by the learner, and the feedback indicates the response is correct. Card 4 is presented, identified as positive, correctly. Can you begin to identify the concept? Card 5 is identified as negative: this is correct. Card 7 is presented, identified as negative. Feedback indicates this is *wrong*. Card 8 turns out to be positive, also Card 3. What is the concept; that is, do you have a rule for it, or a title?

Most students will have more trouble with this than with a concept like "white square." Such concepts are not used as extensively in every-day existence. To some extent, one is "forming" it as he learns it. Some research indicates that once it is "formed," once it becomes as familiar as the basic "white square" type, then it is no more difficult to identify than the basic type. This new type of concept is called a *disjunction*, whereas the "white square" type of concept is called a *conjunction*. The disjunctive concept is "square or two or both."

The example of a concept given initially in this discussion of research in concept learning was "black circle"; this concept can be regarded as a combination of the two basic concepts "black" and "circle," where only those figures having *both* are positive exemplars. The rule might be stated, "All figures which are both black and circular."

Other kinds of relationships are possible. Consider all figures that are *either* black or circular or both; this is a different set of exemplars, including those from the first one (black circle), plus others. Such a concept has been termed a *disjunction*. If you have learned the set-theoretic approach to such relationships, you will realize that the conjunction is the *intersection* of the two basic sets, where the disjunction is the *union* of them.

In the study of logic, there are four basic relationships which enter into our thought processes. Conjunction and disjunction are two of them; the others are *implication* and *equivalence*. In implication, we say, "If something is true, then something else is true"; for example, "If it rains, we will put on our coats." In equivalence, we say that something is equal to something else: this has a particular connotation. "*A* and *B* are equal" means that *A* implies *B* *and also B* implies *A*. It is thus a reciprocal implication, or one-to-one correspondence.

These basic relationships can be considered to be types of concepts. The implication relationship is used extensively and is sometimes described as a principle; for example, "If there is a change in one attribute of the system, say the electric potential, then there will be a corresponding change in some other attribute, say, the heat." This is part of a statement of implication relevant to the concept of conservation of energy.

In cognitive behavior (thinking), there are also processes for using these basic relationships or types of concepts. One of these, for example, is substitution: if A is equivalent to B, then any concept or process which involves B involves A as well. For example, if two parts of a car are equivalent, then one can be put in place of the other.

ADDITIONAL COMMENTS ON TYPES OF CONCEPTS

A black circle is a conjunctive concept; exemplars must be both black and circular to be positive exemplars. A strike in baseball is a disjunctive concept: the ball must be within the strike zone, or it must have been swung at and missed by the batter, or both. "When the humidity reaches saturation, then water condenses and one gets rain or fog" is an implicative concept, or a principle; it has a before-after dimension, among others. "Two plus three equals five" is an equivalence. The sum of two and three corresponds to five, and vice versa: one can be substituted for the other. In all of these concepts or processes or principles there are exemplars, titles, and rules, although sometimes the title and the rule are very similar and other times the title is one of the exemplars.

Each of these concepts is made up of attributes which are themselves concepts: in "black square," blackness is an abstraction learned through induction at an early age, usually, and is based on ability to discriminate between colors and ability to recognize absolute value of colors without another color for a referent, although the latter may be derived from the former. Squareness is a relationship between straight lines, but it may be learned as a thing in itself rather than as a synthesis of lines and angles; that is, one does not really have to know what a straight line is or what a right angle is to learn to recognize a square and call it by name. In this sense, squareness is also an abstraction, although it can also be handled deductively by rule in terms of other more "basic" concepts. Equality of two-dimensional vectors is a concept which involves a conjunction of equal length and equal direction; length and direction are basic concepts which have to be learned first. It might be possible in a course in modern geometry to analyze length and direction into subconcepts themselves, and thus to see *them* as conjunctions or disjunctions, but they are probably *learned* as *units* in most cases. "All men are created equal" is a principle that is basic to our form of government, at least theoretically. This can be viewed as an implication, namely "X implies Y" where X is "all men" or just "men" and Y is "equal." The latter implies "equal to each other" or "the members of the set are equivalent along some dimension or dimensions"; this is equivalence, another type of concept.

In analyzing concepts in this way, the question of what is "basic" can be answered by determining which unit was learned first. This relates to the problem of units of learning. Many after-the-fact logical analyses of the real world do not reflect the actual hierarchy of conceptual learning behavior that went into them. One can define a square as a four-sided closed figure whose sides are equal and whose angles are right angles, but this does not mean that the concept "square" was synthesized originally from these subconcepts by the learner, or even that one should teach it in the "natural" order even if one could. Square as a concept was probably learned through concrete stimuli involving enactive responses, then later through iconic representations, long before some symbolic treatment of it became possible. In a similar way, many analyses of human cognitive behavior have little to do with the way the behavior actually develops; thus, to approach a subject according to its "logical" structure is not always the most logical *teaching* strategy.

8–9 Concept Identification Versus Concept Formation

Consider the original set of cards used to describe and define concept learning. If one knows what a circle is and what black is, and if one has had previous experience with conjunctive concepts, then responding correctly to the cards when "black circle" is the concept is a matter of identifying the right cards by putting the right concepts (previously learned) together. One can test hypotheses about the right "combination" by selecting a card as positive and getting feedback on one's choice. One may have "insight" into the problem eventually, implying that the most recent hypothesis was correct.

In such a situation, where the "ingredients" of the solution are well known and the particular pattern is the solution, the phenomenon of "insight" is frequently observable, in that subjects (students) will "catch on" suddenly, either after trial-and-error behavior that seems aimless or after contemplating the situation and then trying one of the exemplars. This "aha!" phenomenon has been found to follow some trial-and-error behavior, often of the covert or "thinking" type where various possibilities are manipulated mentally. This insight is often observed to occur during the learning trials *before* the student can describe in words the solution that he is using; that is, a student may begin to identify positive exemplars correctly before he can put into words the process or rule or relationship that he is using to get the correct answer. This seems to imply that insight is not necessarily consciously verbal, although verbal ability may facilitate the process even though the student does not express it overtly.

Such a learning pattern, based on previously learned concepts, is called "concept *identification*," as compared with concept *formation*; it implies that the basic "ingredients," the concepts on which it is based, have been well-learned already. Concept *formation*, then, would be a situation wherein the exemplars are not made up of attributes that have been previously learned, or wherein the relationship is of a new type.

In relation to learning *types* of concepts, it is found that conjunctive concepts are more easily learned than disjunctive ones, at least in most cases. However, when students have been exposed to a number of disjunctive concepts, so that they are accustomed to the kind of relationship involved, there is evidence that disjunctive concepts are as easy to identify as conjunctive ones. This implies that the difference in difficulty is due to a difference in previous experience with the type of relationship; it also implies that in the case of the disjunctive concept the student is ordinarily in the process of *forming* the relationship. This requires a series of experiences with it, which might be described as "trial and error" to some degree, in that they require the conditioning of a new relationship through an inductive process. Also, it implies that there are no previously formed concepts whose titles may be manipulated cognitively (in the form of rules) to help the student operate effectively with the new relationship.

The discussion above begins to seem somewhat circular in nature, due to the lack of detailed understanding of the cognitive mechanisms involved. It may be resolved for the time being by assuming that the student is testing hypotheses as he tries to cope with the problem, the hypotheses being previously formed concepts. In cases where the hypotheses do not lead to desired or anticipated outcomes, he forms new ones inductively through a trial-and-error or conditioning process, and this is a process that can be described as concept "formation" rather than "identification." It seems probable that where the basic concepts are well known, the identification aspect is most important, involving testing of hypotheses until one is found which works. On the other hand, since this testing is one additional experience in using the hypothesis and getting feedback on it, it is to some extent a learning situation in regard to that hypothesis, and thus to some degree a matter of concept *formation* as well. Thus, while we may be putting familiar things together rather than learning something new, the *process* of putting them together in a new way *is* part of the "something new" that is learned.

8–10 "Understanding" Concepts

Concept learning involves responses to exemplars (identifying them as positive or negative), responses involving the title, and responses involving a rule. If one gives the title of a concept as a response to an exemplar, it may be said that he "knows" the concept or has "learned" it. A similar estimate may be made if the student gives the rule. However, the title(s) and the rule(s) are essentially tools for the *use* of the concept, means by which past experience may be brought to bear on new exemplars or on new concepts and problems. This implies that proper criteria for "understanding" a concept would include (a) identifying new exemplars as positive or negative, (b) forming new exemplars, given the title or rule, or (c) using the concept in forming or identifying a *new concept*. For example, one may be able to give the title "triangle" to a familiar exemplar of that concept, or one may be able to give a definition of triangle, or both, but part of the test of one's understanding of the concept must be whether one can identify new exemplars, whether one can construct a new exemplar, and especially whether one can utilize the concept in a situation where triangles are involved in other things, such as in analyzing the forces involved in hanging a sign from a wall. In the latter case, the title and definition might function as covert (unexpressed) verbal mediators in the application process, but would not be evident in the final responses (solution).

Concept formation research indicates that students show understanding of concepts, in the form of identification of new positive and negative exemplars, before they are able to verbalize this understanding, that is, give a rule or definition. Thus there is an enactive mode of responding which indicates understanding just as clearly as the iconic and symbolic modes do. However, when the student does arrive at a point where he can give the rule, his behavior becomes more certain, or his understanding becomes more "complete." This is possibly because he has related the new situation to past experience through the use of words, i.e. titles of the concepts of which the past experiences are exemplars.

While one might postulate that responses in the symbolic mode imply the greatest probability of transfer, there is reason to believe that transfer can take place on the basis of responses (learning) in the enactive mode alone, that is, that students can identify new exemplars and use the concept in new learning *without* coming to the point of stating a rule or definition or giving the concept a title. Some research in guidance and discovery in learning implies that there may be advantages to restricting learning to the enactive or iconic modes in some cases, or in some phases of the learning procedure, because it leads to better transfer.

8–11 Number of Dimensions and Learning Difficulty

Research indicates that the more relevant or irrelevant dimensions there are, the more difficult a concept is to learn. This finding leads one to question the popular assumption that "realism" contributes to understanding. Since "realistic" presentations have large numbers of dimensions, many irrelevant, "realism" may in some cases *interfere* with learning. This has one important qualification, however, namely that the phenomenon of *redundancy* interacts with the number of dimensions. Redundancy will be discussed in Chapter 10.

8–12 Ways of Presenting Concepts to Students

Research in concept identification involves the presentation of exemplars, both positive and negative, for response by the student; he receives feedback after his response. Word descriptions are omitted from such research in order to create a situation more nearly resembling the identification of more complex concepts where the titles or rules are not as helpful or clear or understandable. For instance, if one were to tell a student in advance that the title of a certain concept was "simile," and then ask him to identify positive exemplars of it, he might not have success since "simile" would be a new word. If on the other hand one were to give a definition, such as "simile is a description using *like* or *as*," the student's performance would improve but might still not be adequate since he could mistakenly identify *any* phrase using *like* or *as* as a simile. Thus the formation or identification of the concept depends on the use of exemplars to varying degrees and in various ways. Basic research, then, often begins with exemplars rather than rules, in order to explore the ability of learners to use different kinds and amounts of information.

In teaching concepts in a practical context, such arrays of exemplars are often used after a rule is given or derived, but there are cases where they are used before the rule is given or even without a rule. In some cases, there is no adequate rule, since words do not describe the concept adequately; for example, word description of the concept whose title is "sunset" would inevitably fall short of the real thing. This is partly because one component of the concept "sunset" is an emotional one, involving classical responses, while other components are color and design that cannot be expressed adequately in words.

SIMULTANEOUS VERSUS SUCCESSIVE PRESENTATIONS

If exemplars are to be given, one has a choice as to the format of the presentation. This choice may well be crucial, for reasons to be discussed now. The most common way to teach a concept by example is probably to present one example, then another, then another, pointing out relevant and irrelevant dimensions and asking for some response on the part of the student that indicates that he "understands." (Often, unfortunately, the question asked is, "Do you understand," to which the student may well answer "Yes" to avoid displeasure, whether he understands or not.) Another way to present exemplars, one which makes greater demands upon the teacher in terms of organization of materials, is to present all the possible exemplars (or a subset of them) *simultaneously*, and to allow the student(s) to select from them those which they think are positive (or to select and tell whether it is positive or negative). This requires more complex learning behavior since the student selects his own exemplars and may require feedback on them. This implies the existence of some strategy on his part in order to process the information he receives.

Consider two situations. In one, the student is presented with one exemplar and then another, *by the teacher.* In the other, *he selects* possibilities one after another from a simultaneous presentation of several exemplars. Suppose that in each case the two exemplars are the same; that is, the sequence happens to be identical in both cases. Also, assume that in both cases the student receives feedback after each exemplar, and that in the first case the teacher leaves the first exemplar in view while presenting the second. What differences exist between the two situations, in terms of the student's learning behavior?

Suppose that all but one of the dimensions of the second exemplar are the same as those of the first exemplar; that is, suppose only one dimension or attribute changes, for example, the color. Suppose also that the first exemplar is positive, that it *is* an exemplar of the concept. There are two possibilities for the second exemplar, positive or negative. Suppose that it too is positive. This implies that changing the color made no difference, that is, that color is an irrelevant dimension (this is based on the assumption that we are dealing with a simple conjunctive concept).

In the case where the teacher presents the exemplars, there are several possible approaches also. The teacher may say, "This is a positive exemplar, and so is this," and then ask what that implies; or he may ask, "Is this one positive?" in each case, and then confirm or contradict the student, and then ask him what the information implies; or he may simply continue to present exemplars, with feedback, until the student begins to get them all right, in which case he may assume the learner "understands," or he may then ask the student to formulate the experiences in a general rule of operation. What the teacher asks of the student in these terms is partly a function of the developmental stage of the student, but we are assuming here that the student is capable of forming a symbolic representation (that is, a rule) at this level of complexity or with this type of concept. While these options are open to the teacher, one may reasonably ask which of them is most probable, given not only limited patience on the part of the teacher, but also the demands of other students on him for time and attention.

What of the case where the student selects the exemplars himself? He may or may not have some hypothesis which he is testing. One possible one would be "Is color relevant?" although it need not be expressed in words, either overtly or covertly, in this way; that is, he may act "intuitively" to test his hypothesis, which means that he selects the proper exemplar for testing it but cannot put into words the reasons for selecting that exemplar. At this point, some theorists might argue that he is not testing the hypothesis if he is not using words either overtly or covertly but is operating according to trial and error. On the other hand, since students who *have* adequate vocabularies and language abilities are observed to perform more adequately in such tasks even though they are not conscious of such hypotheses, such a conclusion is open to question. There have been cases where students have been impeded in their problem-solving process by being asked to verbalize the rule or by being given hints. There are other cases where verbalizing of mental processes by students has been helpful to them in solving a problem, even though the verbalizations do not indicate correct processes in all cases.

It seems from this cursory analysis that a student may engage in hypothesis-testing behavior, whether the teacher presents the exemplars one at a time, or presents them all and allows the student to select. However, if there are alternate strategies, the teacher presentation is likely to be such as to make one strategy most helpful and thereby to diminish the likelihood of using others. This is "good" if one is trying to shape a certain kind of learning strategy; it is "bad" if one encourages a student to use a strategy that is less powerful than others he could bring to bear on the problem.

There is another element of difference in the two situations, successive presentation by the teacher or selection by the student from several alternatives. This has to do with choice. In the situation where the student can select his own exemplar, he has a degree of autonomy and is to some extent "on his own." He may not make good use of this choice, but it is one element of any valid criterion situation, since ultimately he must be *put* on his own. If one can inject an element of choice and autonomy into the learning, then, without sacrificing too much in the way of shaping learning strategies and without bringing too many confusing errors into the picture, it is worthwhile.

If one compares more extensive presentations of exemplars according to the simultaneous-successive dimensions, one meets other important differences. If a student is given one exemplar at a time, one after the other, without being able to see the previous ones, the load on his memory is in certain ways greater than if all the exemplars are spread out before him and he can select one and then another, or than if the teacher leaves some past exemplars in view while presenting the next one. On the other hand, the more one puts or leaves before the student, the more complex the stimulus field becomes, and potentially the more confusing; thus the simultaneous presentation can be overdone and can make it difficult for the student to focus on one exemplar at a time or to process all the information. Thus even in the simultaneous situation, a teacher may help the student by selecting exemplars for him, at least at first, and by discussing the implications of positive and negative feedback in terms of strategies of learning, that is, discussing what the feedback means or how one can process the information in order to become able to identify other exemplars correctly. This might be called *guided discovery*.

Another important factor is the pacing of the learning. In the successive situation, the teacher controls the pace of the presentation; this may be too fast or slow for the learner. In the simultaneous presentation, where the student can select for himself, this pace is under the student's control. However, it is possible for the teacher to let the student pace the successive presentation, although such behavior is perhaps a little less probable than when the student has full control over the selection.

Bibliography

BOURNE, L. E., JR. *Human Conceptual Behavior*. Boston: Allyn and Bacon, 1966.

BRUNER, J. S., GOODNOW, J. T., and AUSTIN, G. A. *A Study of Thinking*. New York: John Wiley and Sons, Inc., 1956.

BRUNER, J. S., OLVER, R. R., and GREENFIELD, P. *Symposium on Cognitive Growth*. New York: John Wiley and Sons, Inc., 1966.

HUNT, E. D. *Concept Learning, An Information Processing Problem*. New York: John Wiley and Sons, Inc., 1962.

How Concepts Are Learned 9

9–1 Learning Strategies

Consider Figure 8.1 again (see page 87). Suppose you select Card 1 and get a red light, indicating you are wrong. What have you learned? That the concept is not just "one," or "circle," or "one circle." It might be "unshaded," or "unshaded square," or "two," or "two squares," or it might be disjunctive like "two or unshaded or both" or "square or two or both." Now suppose you select Card 2 next, and it is positive. The concept might still be "unshaded" or "unshaded square." It can't be "two" or "two squares," but it might be "two or unshaded or both," or it might be "two or square or both." So you select Card 3. This is positive: by this you know that it must have a "two" in it, although it is not *just* "two." If you have had previous experience with disjunctive concepts (as you must have, if you were to have thought the things it said you did) you probably begin to suspect what the concept is. We had you make a mistake earlier, however: it couldn't have been "two or unshaded or both," since Card 1 is unshaded: therefore it must be "two or square or both."

If the cards had more dimensions, there would be more different cards, and this would be more difficult. If one knows in advance what type of concept is being identified, one has a much easier time. For example, if one knows that the concept is conjunctive, then one can adopt a simple strategy for solving the problem. The first step is to find a positive exemplar, then to choose the next exemplar so that only *one* dimension of the concept is different on the new card. If the next exemplar is positive, then changing that one dimension has not made a difference; that dimension is irrelevant, since the concept is a conjunctive one. Then one can go on to choose another exemplar in which one dimension only changes, this time a different dimension; if the next exemplar is negative, then one may conclude that the dimension which changed *is* relevant, that is, it makes a difference.

One could have gambled a bit, and instead of changing only one dimension changed two of them. Had that been the case, and the next exemplar were positive, then one might conclude that neither of the two dimensions were relevant. On the other hand, if the next exemplar were negative, it would not be possible to tell which of the two made a difference, or whether both of them had to change in order to change the feedback.

The strategies mentioned above, called "conservative focusing" and "focus gambling," respectively, are based on the assumption that the concept is conjunctive. Strategies involved in identifying the type of concept (conjunctive, disjunctive, equivalent, or implicative) and in identifying the particular concept within those are assumedly more complicated. They have not been analyzed or investigated as extensively or in ways that are immediately applicable to problems of instruction. However, such strategies are implicit in any learning behavior, and thus in so-called trial-and-error learning as well as in the more overt and verbal strategies evident in hypothesis testing. It is important to realize this and to analyze the strategies inherent in any learning task, as well as to analyze the kind of strategy which a particular teaching approach shapes or encourages. It has been pointed out very often that too many teachers teach "to the test," in that they achieve criterion behaviors regardless of means. But in this age of proliferation of facts and concepts and of increasing complexity in our approach to dealing with our environment, it is becoming more and more important to concentrate on the processes by which students learn, so that they may be able to cope with the concepts and processes of tomorrow without being inhibited too greatly by the less powerful concepts and processes of today.

9–2 Mediation in Concept Identification; Reversal Shifts

The concept formation research described so far has been useful in identifying and clarifying basic concepts of learning and teaching which are useful in analyzing more complex situations. Much of the research in concept formation is, however, of a less quantifiable and analyzable kind, but is also more sophisticated and closer to learning as we experience it daily. One experiment* which seems to fall in between the basic and applied levels is the following, which involves a developmental aspect in respect to the mediation of previously learned concepts (verbal mediation). It uses the two cards shown in the diagram in Figure 9.1. The experiment involved three phases and used subjects of different age levels. In each phase the students had to learn to identify the positive exemplar on each card, one of the two being positive and the other negative. There were many representatives of each card, and they were presented in a random order. Students responded by pointing to one or the other and receiving information concerning the correctness of their response.

---

*H. H. Kendler and T. S. Kendler, "Vertical and Horizontal Processes in Problem Solving," *Psychological Review 69* (1962): 1–16.

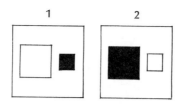

FIGURE 9.1

In the first phase the white or unshaded figure was correct: thus the concept was "white" or "unshaded."

After reaching criterion in the first phase, the second phase was introduced. Only one of the cards, the first one, was shown to the students; it was shown many times, with the placement of the two figures varied so that the students wouldn't learn the answer by using position as a cue (that is, so that the irrelevant dimension of position would not be redundant with the relevant one). In this phase, in direct contrast to the first, the correct figure was the shaded or black figure; note that this figure is also the smaller one.

After reaching criterion in this phase, the students were given the third phase. In this phase both cards were used again. The student was not given feedback as to his choice, but only observed to see what choice he would make. Most of the students responded to Card 1 as in the immediately preceding phase, Phase 2. The outcome of the experiment hinged on his response to Card 2, that is, on which figure he chose. It may be well to examine at this point the implications of the two possible choices.

In Phase 2 the student had two alternative hypotheses for his choice: he could have said, "The relevant dimension *was* color, but *now* it has changed to *size*." Since the correct answer was the smaller of the two, we might expect him to choose the smaller figure on Card 2 also in the third phase. On the other hand, the student might hypothesize, "The black or shaded figure is positive, instead of the white or unshaded one: this is simply the other possibility within the color dimensions." If he adopted this hypothesis, then he would pick the larger of the two instead of the smaller.

These two alternatives have been identified with two supposedly different learning strategies. The first strategy, wherein the student shifted from color to size, has been called *trial and error*; the second, in which he shifted from one color to another, has been called *reversal shift*, that is, a reversal within the formerly relevant dimensions. The latter approach has been considered cognitively more efficient and more representative of complex human cognitive processes, while the former has been identified with the learning of lower organisms. However, as a hypothesis to be tested, the reversal shift strategy may be considered to be trial and error also, until established as correct: it is simply a more sophisticated type of hypothesis.

The results shed some light on the operation of mediating mechanisms: preverbal children do not shift within the relevant dimensions as frequently as verbal children do, implying that the concept of "color" and the strategy of operating within the concept have both been learned previously. It is possible that this learning is made possible by neurological maturation of some type, but the age at which this maturation takes place is not well established if such is the case. Another way of describing the difference is to point to the greater vocabulary development, and assume that even though it is unexpressed, the vocabulary contributes to or mediates the cognitive process: this avoids the question of learning versus maturation, or rather subsumes them both under one larger developmental process.

9–3 Concepts in Other Learning

To many, the type of figure used in concept formation or identification research described earlier is rather limited and unlike the materials involved in most learning situations. However, one finds relationships between sophisticated learning and the behaviors demonstrated using the more basic types, if one makes allowances for generalization and reasoning by analogy, and if one applies the paradigms to the correct units of behavior. One such relationship is found in comparing concept formation to the development of what is called the *self-concept*, the concept or attitude that a person has of himself in one or a number of situations. This concept seems to be learned by exemplar as well as by rule, in that the learner forms an opinion of himself based on the behavior of others toward him as compared with their behaviors toward others. He also forms it through hearing others tell him about himself, directly or indirectly—Lucy's analyses of Charlie Brown in the comic strip *Peanuts* constitute an extreme example, but in a sense Charlie is fortunate, since many times a person never hears what others think of him. One phenomenon which supports this view of the self-concept rather dramatically is the so-called *break-off* phenomenon, where the pilot of an experimental jet flying at high altitude feels disassociated from both earth and plane, and imagines that he is looking at himself from outside of the plane. Long isolation has been observed to have similar effects. One explanation is that through past experience each person learns to "see himself" in this way, but suppresses conscious recognition of the image: if conditions are such that this is not repressed (as when no one is around), then the sensation of looking at oneself is allowed to come to consciousness. This has interesting implications for the operation of the subconscious in identifying forces that prevent conscious recognition of thoughts.

Another such phenomenon is the "phantom leg"; this is the feeling of an amputee that his leg is actually still there. It does not occur if the leg has been lost in early life, before the person learns what it is to have and use a leg, particularly a mature leg.

These phenomena lead to a hypothesis about imitative behavior. The sight of one's hand produces certain sensations which the sight of another person's hand may produce also, if one happens to view it from the same perspective. This enables one to generalize from himself to others, to see himself somewhat as others see him. It also provides the link between the behavior of others and one's own behavior. The feedback from one's own attempt to imitate another is differentially reinforced by others and by oneself, and thus shapes one's behavior. This process is imperfect, however, since one's view of himself is incomplete; thus one may shape a behavior that seems to him to be like what he is trying to imitate, but that is quite different in fact.

9–4 Frame of Reference and Variations in Attributes

What if the sample of positive exemplars of a concept was one in number. We could not vary the irrelevant dimensions of this one exemplar, nor use redundancy in presenting the exemplar. Could we "teach" the concept? The answer is "Yes, it is possible," to a degree dependent on a number of factors.

In the experimental approach to concept formation the use of words by the experimenter is eliminated in order to capture some of the flavor of concept formation where words are not available or entirely adequate. However, there are observing behaviors and learning strategies in concept formation, some already described, that can be put into words even though the concept itself is not easily describable or even though the particular student does not have the vocabulary for effective communication of the concept. For example, one might say to a student, "Color seems to be important," thus alerting him to this attribute in comparison with others, or one might say, "Notice that only one dimension has been changed, yet the feedback to your response indicates a change, that is, one was a *positive* exemplar but the other was *negative*." Or again one might say, "Look at the exemplar again; notice the color."

Such "guidance" or "hints" might be helpful when a number of exemplars is used, but what of the case introduced above where only *one* exemplar is available? Here one might still call attention to the various dimensions present, and, through knowledge of the concept which the exemplar represents, label the dimensions as relevant or irrelevant. In identifying a destroyer in a study of naval craft, one might point out that the particular exemplar had a certain pattern to its silhouette, that it had a certain arrangement of its guns, that its torpedo tubes and other equipment were of a certain size relative to its stacks, and the like. Without exemplars of other ships for comparison, one might have a more difficult time preparing the student to respond correctly to criterion tasks (identifying a destroyer in a series of pictures including other ships), but one might produce better results than if one did not teach at all. In some cases, where the relationships are fairly simple and already learned, one might even get the whole job done this way.

Another approach is to vary the frame of reference of the student: one can view a given exemplar in a number of different ways and thus learn a great deal from one exemplar, if one is led to do this or has been taught to do it independently. For example, one can look at a fish and note that it has a certain number of fins, a certain kind of teeth, and so on. If one has learned a number of categories that apply (mammal, vertebrate, etc.) one can classify the fish according to them and thus be able to identify a similar fish another time. Earlier discussions of memory imply that the more categories one has to use on a given exemplar, the better it will be retained, and this may well mean that the probability of correct identification of new exemplars will be higher.

9–5 The Title of the Concept

The title of a concept obviously serves as a "handle" by which one may manipulate it cognitively; it is an address in memory storage, a sign or symbol for the exemplars that make it up, a response given to each exemplar when called for in evaluating the learning, and a stimulus which makes the response to these exemplars probable; that is, which notifies the student that he is to look for aspects of the concept in exemplars to be presented. As the common verbal response to a number of experiences or exemplars, the title serves as a mediator for thought, facilitating recognition of common elements and eliciting the common affective response to the exemplars. It facilitates transfer in that relevant properties of a new concept will evoke both the feeling (classical response) associated with the concept and the title itself (as a response), and the title and the feeling in turn call up past experiences with exemplars of the concept.

One may look upon a concept from the point of view of paired-associate learning, where a number of stimuli have a common response, part of the response being the title. In paired-associate learning there is "backward learning" as well; that is, if in the list the stimulus BIX evokes the response NAV, then one will find that NAV also has some probability of evoking BIX. In the same sense the title, as the response term in a number of pairs with different stimuli, will work backward, and if one is given the title it will evoke as responses a number of different exemplars of the concept.

The fact of clustering in free recall in verbal learning and the phenomenon of concept formation, already discussed at some length, both imply cognitive processes which we describe as reducing or categorizing. One may look upon them as storage processes, where information for future reference is filed in common storage areas, so that when one retrieves something from an area, other things are likely to come with it. The sum of all experiences related to the concept "cow," for instance, is somehow accessible through the address "cow," through the perception of stimuli which have something in common with "cow," or through verbal statements such as "a creature with four legs, teats, a tufted tail, an odd lateral chewing motion, and a call that sounds like 'moo.'" These same experiences can be tapped in a different pattern, with a different outcome, when one addresses them with the word "horn"; other animals have horns, however, so some of the same storage is assessed, but is reproduced or reported differently. Another possibility is that the same term is filed in a number of different preexisting storage areas.

No model of the mind is proposed here to provide the necessary functions. If each perception or experience is indeed stored in many different places, it would imply that the greater the number of such places (categories) one can assign to a particular experience, the better the chance one has of utilizing them later on, and this seems compatible with previous discussions of memory and retention. Hypotheses, then, would appear to be combinations of categories or filing addresses which have some chance of fitting the situation, and transfer would be a matter of trying hypotheses until one fits and yields some kind of confirming result, that is, some result which is compatible with anticipated outcomes. This is still trial and error, and subject to reinforcement and shaping, but it is also "all or none" in that the trials involve complex patterns and when one fits, it is "learned" then and there in that one does not need to review the pattern or practice it in order to have it available or to use it.

9–6 Language and Concepts

Words in a language are ordered and patterned according to syntactic principles, with the help of additional words such as and, the, and such. The attributes or properties of concepts are ordered and patterned according to rules also. Grammatical rules generate word sequences that "make sense" in reference to past experience, particularly when a generative grammar is used. Concept rules can be used to generate stimulus groupings that have some background in learning also, and which can be described as positive exemplars as a result. A generative approach to concept formation has already been treated as part of Section 8–10 on "understanding" concepts. This is on the creative or discovery-oriented side of the curriculum spectrum and has implications for teaching concepts in any subject.

The ability to identify concepts increases with experience; the time required for identification is one variable used in exploring this ability. Similarly, the ability to perceive, memorize, and utilize word transformations and sequences is related to their conformance with semantic and grammatical principles, which are themselves concepts. Thus concept formation shows many of the phenomena of learning and of learning to learn, as previously noted in discussing verbal learning. The phenomenon of "learning to learn" will be discussed again in regard to problem solving.

9–7 Hierarchies of Concepts

To identify "white square" one needs to know "white" and "square"; there is obviously a hierarchy. The better one knows "white" and "square," the more probable the identification, that is, the more likely or quick the learning. Furthermore, the better one knows them the more likely the learning is to take on the pattern typical of "insightful" behavior as compared with trial and error; however, this also depends on previous experience with conjunctions. On the other hand, if one does not understand either "white" or "square" thoroughly, one will improve his learning of them while learning "white and square," although it may be more efficient to practice on each separately first: this relates to the *part* learning versus *whole* learning question, and some recent research has identified situations where the part learning is more effective.

Concepts generally are hierarchical, that is, based on previous concepts. In teaching concepts, then, one intuitively or consciously looks for the bases of the understanding, and evaluates the student's understanding in relation to them. If the student does not understand some of the bases of the concept, one teaches these first, or expects a slower learning process with the over-all concept, or both. It is true that this process of analysis of the learning task has been neglected in teaching for many years. It also seems true that overemphasis on such analysis may be to some degree self-defeating, in that intuitive and empirical methods of teaching have taken care of this problem in an optimal way as they have evolved through a number of years. On the other hand, even if one has a method or approach which has been developed intuitively or empirically to the point where it works well with groups of students, it may become obsolete; changes in teaching at lower levels may make some of the sequences of tasks unnecessary and also may make the inclusion of other tasks necessary where they were not before.

9–8 Learning Modes and Concept Learning

Exemplars of a concept are ordinarily given in the concrete or iconic modes, depending on the nature of the concept. Examples given from basic research were iconic, for example. One can present exemplars symbolically, in that one can describe them in words; for example, one can describe a physical phenomenon such as the interaction of a pith ball coated with metallic paint and a rubber rod rubbed with cloth, in giving exemplars of electrostatic force. However, one runs the risk of communicating poorly, due both to the possibility of ambiguity in language and also to the lack, on the part of the learner, of the previous experience needed to interpret the description. Thus a student may think he understands such a description, but when questioned, his answers may indicate he does not.

Iconic stimuli, that is, diagrams to go along with the text, can be used in conjunction with the word description, but these also can be ambiguous. Some research indicates that when the words-plus-diagram stimulus field becomes too complex, they even interfere with each other. This of course depends a great deal on the way they are presented and the way the student has learned to use such combinations. Some very difficult text materials are very effective because the students who use them have learned how to do so effectively through previous experience.

Related to this is a classification of concepts according to modes and types of stimuli within modes. In one category, exemplars differ in terms of length, width, weight, color, and such: blocks, spheres, and boats would be included here. Another involves exemplars which have a common property embedded in other properties: Chinese characters are used as an example, where the same combination of strokes may be part of a number of different characters and contribute to the meaning accordingly. Another category includes concepts which have attributes in common, either in their exemplars or in their titles: the words round, barrel, and doughnut, for instance, have some elements in common. This classification system would seem to be subsumed by the exemplar-title-rule relationship used previously; the first type classifies concrete exemplars, the second iconic ones, and the third defines a dimension through intersection of titles.

Some investigators of concept formation feel that lower organisms, including some animals, cannot form concepts; they feel that mediating verbal responses are a necessary attribute of true concepts. This in turn means mediating verbal responses that we associate with humans. Now the use of verbal communication itself implies the formation of concepts, since each word has a function that results from the set of experiences to which it refers. It may be more descriptive, then, to observe that animals show the ability to generalize from exemplars to other exemplars (one fundamental criterion of understanding) but have only rudimentary forms of titles and no rule-forming capacities at all to help them in this application or transfer process.

There has been some interest recently in the teaching of science in sequences based initially on interaction of the learner with concrete exemplars of concepts and processes in the environment. It is held that such interaction leads to meaningful learning, better understanding, and better retention, particularly when the students involved are led to generalize rules from the exemplars, that is, to render a general rule from the concrete exemplars, thus moving from the concrete to the symbolic mode, with perhaps some explanatory material in the iconic in the form of diagrams. This seems in part a reaction to the overemphasis on the symbolic mode in textbooks, which in turn results from the influence of cost requirements in publishing, as well as from the "flight from teaching" which separates authors from the students who use the books. This interest in concrete exemplars also recognizes disparities in student backgrounds; for example, the graduate student in literature may be at an elementary level in respect to concepts in physics. Such an unbalanced background may be in part the product of more "liberal" views toward student selection of content during his early education, partly due to chance biases in curriculum organization which result in all students taking certain subjects and not others (for example, most students take biology, few physics), partly due to arbitrary conventions of sequence of courses and the influence of college requirements.

The interest in the use of "concrete" exemplars also extends to the use of simulation in more complex concepts, that is, the use of games in teaching concepts related to political science, mathematics, and business processes. While the vehicles for such games are symbolic and iconic as well as concrete, the approach is similar in that there is an attempt to reproduce a larger percentage of the relevant attributes of the criterion situation in the learning phase. For example, in one game students are given the records of a fictitious "company," including sales forecasts, costs, and other relevant data, and asked to come up with a production figure that will minimize costs in relation to the sales for a given month or months. Often the computations are made using a previously derived formula and a computer, and thus the game can be played in an evening, with results from each student's decisions being given back to him quickly so that he can see the outcomes and alter his decision-making behavior accordingly.

9–9 Stimulus Sampling and Statistical Considerations

To learn a concept, one must learn or identify both its type and its relevant dimensions. For example, to identify "white circles," one must conclude he is working with a conjunctive concept (or make the assumption initially) and must also eliminate dimensions other than color and shape. Logically, there are four basic types or relationships, including conjunction and disjunction, as discussed previously, but there are other classification systems which are perhaps more easily applicable. For example, concepts have been categorized as analytic, relational, and inferential-categorical. The analytic type is identified by a common attribute or dimension; the relational is identified by use or function; the inferential-categorical is identified as part of a larger class. Consider a black circle. Analytically, it would be one exemplar of the concept "circle." Relationally, it would be an exemplar of a concept used in concept formation research. As an inferential-categorical concept exemplar, it would belong to the class "colored figures." This is one classification scheme; each student has his own, and it need not be any of those proposed here. One can regard concept learning as a process in which the student samples his store of possible types and subtypes. He selects one to test, identifying the exemplar as positive or negative according to that hypothesis, and then receives feedback concerning his selection.

This sampling of possibilities, be they dimensions of the concept or possible relations to other things or membership in another class, is similar to the stimulus-sampling process discussed in relation to conditioning. Some theorists have proposed the possibility that learners sample possible dimensions of the exemplars or possible relationships in a random fashion. This might be rationalized as a process of narrowing the situations down to a number of possibilities through use of past experience, sampling from them randomly, and attending to the feedback for information as to which is correct.

If this sampling process actually takes place in concept learning, one might expect that the percentage of right and wrong responses given before the responses are consistently correct might be that expected from chance processes. That is, there would be some right as well as some wrong answers, but they would be distributed as if the learner were guessing blindly and getting the right answer by chance. Some data from concept learning experiments show this kind of distribution. This "guessing" behavior in learning, if it is that, implies that teaching should involve a measure of repetition of the task. Some students will hit the right dimension or relation early in the game, others later, as one would expect from a chance distribution. Of course, this model predicts that the student who learns it first in one situation will be just as likely to be last the next time, which does not exactly match common experience with students. More sophisticated models of this type take that into account.

One particularly important question that relates to these ideas has to do with the function of errors in learning. Some say that students learn through errors, others that the making of errors only leads to making more errors. If one adopts a random sampling view of learning, then the making of an error gives easily interpreted information about the hypothesis one is using; namely, it is wrong. On the other hand, getting the right answer happens by chance, though one has the wrong hypothesis. Thus one needs to get several correct in a row before being correct is informative. This implies that one learns by being wrong as well as by being right.

This leads to a paradox. Making errors has an emotional connotation also, and if one reacts strongly to making an error, the reaction may interfere with the sampling process and make learning more difficult. Thus we can't do without errors, and we can't do with them either.

Perhaps the most important outcome of the application of the stimulus sampling concept to concept learning is the idea that in teaching, one will be more successful if he patiently presents a number of exemplars of the same concept without trying to make everything clear instantly. The fact that a student answers incorrectly is unimportant, since it means only that he is not one of those who has hit on the right connection or dimension early in the game; he will get it eventually.

On the other hand, one may be able to increase the over-all probability of getting the right relationship or dimension by limiting the number of possible ones to be sampled, as well as by making a presentation in which the correct one is featured or made more vivid, thus loading the dice, as it were. The inherent danger in this process is one of teaching the wrong thing, that is, making the learning situation too easy and thus rendering transfer to more realistic situations difficult.

Bibliography

GAGNE, R. M. *The Conditions of Learning.* New York: Holt, Rinehart, and Winston Inc., 1965.

HUNT, E. B., MARIN, J., and STONE, P. *Experiments in Induction.* New York: Academic Press, 1966.

KLAUSMEIER, H. and HARRIS, C. ed. *Conference on Analysis of Concept Learning.* New York: Academic Press, 1966.

KLEINMUNTZ, B., ed. *Symposium on Cognition.* New York: John Wiley and Sons, Inc., 1967.

Teaching Concepts 10

10–1 Understanding

Various alternative definitions of "understanding" concepts have been described, and also various means and modes and strategies of presentation. To review briefly, the learner may be given a set of exemplars, or the rule, or the title. If given exemplars, his task may be to identify them as positive or negative, or to give the rule or the title. If given the rule, he may be asked to identify positive and/or negative exemplars, or to create exemplars, or to give the title. If given the title, he may be asked to identify positive and negative exemplars, to create exemplars, or to give the rule.

The recounting of a rule may be evidence of "understanding," in that the sophistication of the learner may enable him to use the rule effectively in identifying exemplars or generating them, or to use the concept in learning other concepts. However, the recounting of the rule in itself is not *sufficient* evidence of understanding. If one presents exemplars for the learner to identify, one cannot always know whether they are "new" and thus constitute criteria for understanding; even the generation or creation of an exemplar can be in imitation of some previously observed model, a product of some extensive practice, and may not imply that the student could generate another example or identify other exemplars. However, in practice, the identification of new exemplars and the creation of them is usually a valid criterion for understanding.

For example, a student may be called upon to demonstrate that he understands the concept "electoral college." He may write a description of it, fairly brief but to the point: this description could have been memorized. If given a description of some aspect of the electoral college system, the student might not be able to identify it by title; even if he could, the recognition of some salient attributes might not imply an understanding of the role of the college in politics or how it goes about its functions. A "College Bowl" type question regarding the electoral college might or might not imply understanding. A final observation relevant here is that the author of this paragraph implies that he understands the concept by talking about it, but could not furnish a description of its function or role.

The requiring of criterion behaviors involved in previous discussions is related to the problem of "testing." It was observed previously that there are many different types of criterion behavior. Often, unfortunately, one mode or format is considered appropriate for testing where another is appropriate to learning: thus the testing mode is not always related to the learning mode. In fact, the only basic difference between teaching and testing is the presentation of feedback: if one presents information concerning the response of the student during a "test," then the test becomes a learning situation. Since the student provides his own feedback, that is, since he assumes his response is correct in many cases when he answers a test question, he will learn that response whether it is right or not. Thus "teaching" and "testing" are not different in nature, and divisions between them cannot help being largely artificial. Perhaps the most valid criterion for the learning of most school subjects is the learning of other subjects based on them. Unfortunately, the criteria most used are only partially valid in respect to the over-all learning process; that is, they only cover a portion of the behaviors important in this learning. The unreliability of test results stems partly from this fact. For example, a multiple-choice test in history can hardly be expected to indicate the ability of the student to discuss a current event in the light of related historical antecedents.

10–2 Redundancy

The population of exemplars which we used to discuss concept formation (that is, the cards with circles and squares) numbered eight: this reflected the fact that there were three dimensions (shape, number, and shadedness or color) and two values for each dimension. Had we introduced another dimension, say size, and had we allowed two values for this dimension, say small and large, then we would have doubled the population of exemplars; there would have been eight with small figures and eight with large ones, each set of eight having squares and circles one and two, shaded and unshaded. Consider identification of the concept "shaded square" (conjunctive) or "one or shaded" (disjunctive); either of these would be more difficult to learn if there were more dimensions, that is, if we added "small" and "large." This simply reiterates what was pointed out previously, that adding relevant or irrelevant dimensions to the task increases the difficulty. Thus, in the same way, "small shaded square" would be more difficult than "shaded square" was before the new dimension of size was added.

The effect of additional dimensions holds except when one introduces a particular teaching strategy which is generally called *redundancy*. For example, if we were teaching the concept "shaded square" and were using the new population, with size added, we might simplify the task by making all shaded squares small and all other exemplars large.

Now one may say that this is cheating, that one is really teaching "small shaded square," but this is not entirely true, because we are not using all the exemplars and thus we are not going all the way on this; we have basically "cut down" on the number of possible examples used. One may also say, "If a student says 'small shaded square' you should not call him wrong"; there is truth in this, but in more complex concepts of the type one deals with in practical situations, this verbalization of the concept does not often come in the early stages of the learning process, if one is using an inductive approach; that is, if one is requiring students to learn from exemplars by identifying them as positive or negative, one of the basic requirements for "understanding."

Redundancy is the process of eliminating some of the possible exemplars from the presentation. One may leave out exemplars in such a way that an irrelevant dimension aids the initial learning, as in making all shaded squares small; this is redundancy involving an irrelevant dimension. It is cheating, in a sense, but if it enables students to respond correctly earlier in the learning process, it *may* be worthwhile. The basic question is, "Does the student come to the criterion behavior sooner than he would without the redundancy?" This means that one must still keep as a criterion the task of identifying exemplars when all of the population is used; this is in a sense a transfer task, in that the student must progress from the simplified set to the whole set, and must learn that not all shaded squares are small. Can one make this transfer easily? Is the over-all learning process helped or hindered by the early use of redundancy? This is a basic question in education, and one that needs to be answered in many particular instances before any general conclusions can be reached. However, it is appropriate to note that teaching in general involves redundancy, in that it arranges the environment in such a way that it is more ordered and simple than the "real world" without the teaching. Thus, to a degree, teachers are committed to the use of redundancy, and the problem becomes one of identifying optimal degrees of redundancy for particular situations.

AN EXAMPLE OF REDUNDANCY

An example of redundancy may assist the reader in understanding this concept. In the teaching of reading there is an approach called "ITA," standing for "Initial Teaching Alphabet." In this approach, characters are added to the regular alphabet, in such a way that each character then has a particular sound; that is, no two "letters" have the same sound, and no letter has more than one sound. This makes the pattern of the "letters" correspond to the sound; that is, the pattern of the letters is "redundant" with the sound, and perfectly so. In our ordinary alphabet, this is only partly true; some letters have more than one sound when they appear in different words, and sometimes different

letters or combinations have the same sound. Thus there is partial redundancy in our normal alphabet as used in language, but not complete
redundancy.

Now there seems to be good evidence that the ITA system is easier
to use initially; that is, there is evidence that many children learn to
read adequately sooner using the ITA alphabet together with stories
printed in the ITA alphabet. The question is, does this early advantage
hold when one takes into account the necessity of transferring back to
normal alphabet? Is the over-all learning time different, compared
with children who have learned using the regular alphabet? Is there a
lower or higher incidence of failure to learn to read using the "real-
world" criterion, that is, reading with the lower-redundancy alphabet?
Is there a lower or higher incidence of frustration and behavior problems due to difficulties in learning to read? Do children using the ITA
approach read more "on their own," voluntarily, after learning to read,
or do they do this less? The answers to these larger questions are not
entirely clear. However, this is an example of the general problem,
which may be stated more simply as follows: do methods of making
things easier early in the game, that is, through irrelevant cues not
representative of the final task, help in the long run or get in the way?

One trivial problem which arises in this connection has to do with
the use of a degree of redundancy without subsequent *decrease* of the
redundancy. To put this less abstractly, it is the use of cues or hints
or guidance in the learning process without subsequent withdrawal of
these aids. For instance, in the ITA example, a teacher might mistakenly assume that having taught children to read using the ITA alphabet,
her task is complete. Another instance is the use of simplified examples
of a type of equation in mathematics, and the use of the same letters in
the examples, such as "$x + 5 = 10$" and "$x + 8 = 19$"; a student
drilled on such exemplars might not be able to handle a problem such
as "$-8 + @ = -4$," even though he was able to work with directed
numbers and thus prepared with the basic tools. Another example of
failure to withdraw cues, and thus of failure to reduce redundancy of
irrelevant dimensions in the concept formation process, would be a
learning sequence designed to teach young children to identify various
animals: the same picture of a fox might be used every time "fox" was
required as a response, but in a criterion situation children who had
been successful in learning might fail to identify (name) a picture of
a fox in a different position, or of a different size, or of a different
color.

While the problem discussed above is trivial in a conceptual way, it
is important in an instructional sense, because the error described is
committed so frequently. Indeed, it is in a sense unavoidable, in that
one can seldom reproduce the ideal criterion situation in an educational

setting. One obvious example is the reproduction of the college atmosphere and social context in a college preparatory course in high school
—one may approximate it along many dimensions, but one cannot
reproduce it entirely. But on a more limited level, there are many,
many examples of learning sequences in which teachers inadvertently
or intentionally use redundancy and do not reduce it in the process of
attaining criterion. They mistakenly assume that they have completed
the task and are subsequently surprised at the lack of transfer. This
they sometimes rationalize through allusions to the low innate ability
of their students.

An abstract example of redundancy may be given using the population of exemplars referred to previously. Suppose that the concept to
be identified by the student has the title "one." Thus cards numbered
1, 2, 5, and 6 are positive. Suppose the cards are presented successively
and thus the student has no control over the order or pacing. The
teacher wishes to make the task easy, so he omits some of the cards, possibly 3, 4, 5, and 6. This results in the presentation of cards with one
figure in the unshaded version, and cards with more than one figure in
the shaded version. The irrelevant dimension of shadedness or color
has been made "redundant" with the relevant dimension of number.

The simplification of the environment, which has been classified generally as "redundancy" and which has been identified as a basic component of all teaching processes, can be thought of as "sugar coating"
or "spoon feeding" or can be seen as "guidance" or "cuing" or "helping." To be useful, it must be used to a degree that matches the individual's ability to cope, and it must be reduced during the learning
process; that is, the student must be "weaned." It is also possible to
have relevant dimensions redundant with each other, and thus to make
learning easier by adding dimensions, whereas generally an increase in
the number of dimensions interferes rather than facilitates. Thus if
one has a more realistic portrayal of an automobile, say a photograph
instead of a line drawing, it will be easier to identify as an automobile
so long as all the photographs used show the same type of vehicle,
with the same body design, same color, same drivers, and so on. However, it may well be that to enable a student to identify different exemplars as positive, a reduced version of the automobile, say a line drawing featuring essentials, will be more effective.

The various forms of redundancy, or cuing, or guidance are legion.
This complicated area of concept formation and of teaching in general
holds the key to greater clarity and ease of communication of concepts.
It is interesting to note that in communication theory the term *redundancy* has a technical meaning in that it is the reciprocal of *entropy*,
which is the degree of order in a system. In thermodynamics it is shown
that entropy increases: this is a general law for the universe. Teaching

may be regarded as a process of changing the entropy or order of a system to make certain behaviors more probable, thus *de*creasing the entropy (increasing the order) through redundancy. After decreasing the entropy initially, nature is then simulated more closely in the learning tasks; this implies *in*creasing the entropy (decreasing the order), which in turn implies reduced redundancy.

10–3 Alternative Teaching Strategies

Once a task or problem has been chosen as the learning "vehicle," then the teacher has some latitude in the presentation or communication strategy. The teacher can choose the order himself, giving exemplars one at a time or simultaneously. He can give the rule and then the exemplars, or vice versa, or combinations of these extremes. He can present both exemplars and possible rules and allow the student to select from each, receiving feedback as to his choice. The teacher can set the pace, or he can allow the student to set it. The teacher can determine the difficulty of the sequence and the rate of increase of difficulty, assumedly meaning an increase in relevant and irrelevant dimensions in the exemplars or an increase in number of subconcepts involved in the rule. The teacher may also enable the student to indicate whether he wishes to stay at the same level or move on, and this indication by the student may be verbal or it may be based on the student's performance, as when he is moved ahead on the basis of a certain level of correct responding.

10–4 Guidance Versus Discovery

All teaching involves a degree of guidance; all learning has an element of discovery in it. This section should therefore be entitled "Degrees of Guidance." It is a sequel to and is subsumed by the discussion of redundancy, but there has been enough research under the "guidance-discovery" rubric to make it worth examining as a separate entity.

The fundamental objective of most investigations in this area is to determine which of two treatments results in greater transfer (that is, positive transfer), guidance or discovery. Some studies have favored one, some the other. Part of this lack of agreement is due to different definitions or interpretations of the term "guidance," part from the use of different experimental tasks.

Guidance is generally taken to mean either the involvement of iconic stimuli in basically concrete (enactive) tasks, or the use of symbolic adjuncts to assist with iconic or enactive ones. In the latter, previous experience is invoked through verbal mediators, using the titles of previously learned concepts in the form of rules or directions.

Discovery, on the other hand, often involves the solution of a task in one mode, for example, the solution of an enactive task such as aiming a gun to hit a target, without iconic or symbolic dimensions added to the stimulus (that is, without diagrams or words to help). In a sense this is related to the inductive versus deductive question, in that rules or parts of rules are used in the guidance treatment only. If one analyzes the basic possibilities, one may arrive at the following relationship.

Learning Task	Criterion Task
Concrete ————	Concrete
Concrete ————	Iconic
Concrete ————	Symbolic
Iconic ————	Concrete

Etc.

If for each of the combinations above one adds relevant stimuli from one or both of the other modes, (that is, adds guidance), then the number of variations is great, and the possibilities of different types of results are numerous. Also involved in comparisons in research are such factors as dominance of stimuli, intensity of stimuli, previous learning in the use of cues of various types, and previous experience with the particular relationship between learning task and criterion task.

Despite this complexity, results suggestive for instructional procedures can be found in research in the guidance versus discovery area. One is the relationship between comparisons based on immediate posttests and those based on delayed ones; in several studies differences between guidance and discovery groups have shown up on delayed tests, whereas they were not evident on immediate ones. This might be taken to imply that they differ in their resistance to subsequent interference, in a manner vaguely analogous to the effect of massed versus distributed practice reported earlier. Where such differences between immediate and delayed results have occurred, they have favored the treatment in which the guidance is reduced, thus implying that the more one can put the student on his own, the better the learning is maintained in the face of subsequent interference. This could be due to the coding system used, in that in learning with less guidance the student encodes the concepts and processes according to his own previously learned foundations and processes; since these are more familiar and meaningful to him, he learns to a higher degree in the given time, and his retention is thus better. This implies that although more time is involved in "discovery" learning, the effective hypothesis, when it is discovered by the student, is stored in an area containing familiar information, and is thus learned to a greater degree since it is related to overlearned material; the effect may be due to greater ease of retrieval, that is, knowing where to find it in the mental storage system. Since in the guidance treatment the hypotheses used are those suggested by the teacher, they are likely to be less familiar and thus less resistant to interference;

another way of saying this is that they will be learned to a "lower degree" than the others.

It should be pointed out that some studies fail to replicate this delayed–immediate comparison effect, and that the factors involved and responsible for the effect have not been adequately analyzed. In such research, unexpected results may come up also. In one study comparing "guidance" with "discovery," for instance, a control group was used which learned by what was called "rote." The control group, using this currently despised approach to learning, performed better than either of the other groups on the criterion test.

Some of the guidance versus discovery debate has to do with motivation. The possibility of exercising choice in the learning, of bringing personal history to bear on a problem, seems to relate to interest, and will be discussed in a later chapter.

10–5 Positive Versus Negative Exemplars

If the population of possible exemplars is not too great, one can learn a concept by being presented with exemplars that are negative, that is, by being shown what the concept is *not*. This implies a comparison with the entire population to arrive at what it *is*, even though one has not seen all of it. When the amount of information is controlled in such limited cases, the use of positive and negative exemplars seems equally helpful in furthering learning. In most presentations, however, the positive exemplar contains more information. Some research implies that students using negative exemplars tend to be more cautious and less likely to jump to conclusions. Certainly if the student has been presented with a sequence of positive exemplars he will come to expect *every* exemplar to be positive. This implies the formation of a "learning set" which may interfere with his ability to cope with the real world of mixed stimuli.

There are, of course, concepts which have no concrete exemplars. What is a "good poem" or a "nice guy"? While these are more complex, the basic principles are the same. A "good poem" is the set of poems that a given critic or poet feels is "good." This will not be equivalent to the set by the same title named by another poet or critic or layman, although there will probably be an intersection of the sets. To teach "good poems" one either presents a series of poems and labels some "good" and others "bad" and then tests by presenting the student with others, or one presents a good poem and analyzes it from many points of view before going on to another. A combination of the two would seem to be ideal.

10–6 The Relationships Between Examples and Rules

Concepts may be taught in many ways. One way is to present a rule and expect the students to be able to apply it, without actually giving them some practice in application. Another way is to present the rule and then to give them such practice. Still another is to present only positive exemplars, with feedback, such as, "This is an example; so is this . . . ," and so on, and then have the students "generalize," that is, form their own rule. Again, one could present exemplars that are both positive and negative, and have the student identify them, as in, "That *is* an example, that *isn't* . . . ," and so on. This has been done with feedback ("You're right" or "You're wrong") and without feedback. When he begins to respond correctly, the student has a different type of "understanding" than in some of the other approaches. An extension of this latter approach is to have the student identify positive and negative exemplars and then, when he can, give a rule to cover the relationship involved. As was pointed out, giving the rule often takes place *after* the student has begun to identify positive and negative exemplars correctly, not at the same time.

There has been extensive debate over a long period of time as to the best way to sequence experiences for optimal concept learning. One phase of relevant research has been done using different forms of programmed instruction which compared "Ruleg" sequences (rule followed by examples) with "Egrul" sequences (examples followed by rules). The results of such investigations have been inconclusive, and suggest that the optimal sequence is a function of both the previous learning and experience of the student and the nature of the subject matter. There are elements of the "inductive versus deductive" question here, as well as of the question of "guidance versus discovery."

How does one decide whether to present exemplars of a concept or to delineate it through the use of a rule or definition? One must first decide whether the concepts which relate to or subsume the one to be learned have been formed previously by the learner. This can be done by requiring the learner to demonstrate his understanding of such concepts and processes, and this process can be called "reviewing" or "diagnostic testing" or "checking the entering behaviors." The latter description implies that the student must have certain behaviors on entering the learning situation if he is to profit from it, and also that the teacher or designer of the learning sequence must analyze the content and identify those behaviors. When the student shows that he can provide them, then he may be judged ready to begin learning.

But can one adequately sample such behaviors? A pretest must be cast in some format, and must use some content as a vehicle. The student may not be familiar with the format, or the particular terminology, or the particular content used to sample his behavior, although he may understand the concept or process to some degree. This means that he may have formed the concept partly, but is unable to demonstrate his understanding adequately on the test of transfer provided. On the other

hand, there is the possibility that the criterion task given him is one he
has been taught to respond to previously, although he may not be able
to transfer this knowledge to *new* learning tasks. Thus one may conclude erroneously that the student does not understand when he does,
and on the other hand one may conclude that he does understand when
he doesn't. While such a test will be reliable in most cases, these two
extreme errors are possible and are probably present in any large group
of students sampled.

One cannot lay down a general directive on the use of rules and exemplars in teaching. One can observe, however, that a group of students
who learn well from rules—followed by examples to which they apply
the rules—may still benefit greatly from experience in learning by
example and forming the rule themselves, even though this is not their
strong point, and vice versa. One can also observe that generally speaking the presentation of a clear rule is not enough, nor is the presentation
of a carefully structured set of exemplars: the interaction of the two
is the crucial aspect of "programming" a learning sequence. Research
into this area of teaching has not been exhaustive and, indeed, is just
beginning to be carried out to any significant extent.

Previous discussions of the use of rule and exemplar can be summarized also in terms of telling and showing. Many teachers assume,
erroneously, that the one good way to explain something clearly is to
describe it verbally, and if one description doesn't work, another one
will. To paraphrase an old saw, one example is often worth many
words: two examples, where irrelevant dimensions are varied and relevant ones kept constant, are worth perhaps five times as many, if not
more.

10–7 Reception Versus Selection

The easiest way to teach, or to seem to teach, is by telling; the next
easiest way is by showing examples one at a time. More difficult to
arrange is a presentation of a number of exemplars simultaneously,
allowing the student to select and receive feedback on them. This process may be in some cases the most effective one, however, in spite of
the extra effort that must be put into arranging the presentation. A
compromise is to present one or several exemplars at a time, with verbal
description; a better compromise is to present one or several exemplars
and let the students comment on them and come to some conclusion
regarding the concept(s) important to the teacher. This is a sort of
"Twenty Questions" approach. It is hard for the teacher to stay out of
the action, but it is often better for the student. It is a "discovery" approach to learning, but as observed before, it is highly guided in terms
of the arrangement of the presentation on which the student discovery
process is based.

Students are often highly motivated to learn through such a discovery process, but only if they interpret the feedback they get from testing erroneous hypotheses as nonthreatening, that is, as long as they don't interpret wrong ideas as errors and feel that they are being or will be punished for them. They must instead interpret errors as information that tells them to try again; trying again, in turn, will occur if it is reinforced and not punished by the teacher. Such punishment can occur in a number of subtle ways, from a particular tone of voice to withdrawal from and ignoring the student.

10–8 Grouping of Exemplars and Distribution of Practice

What of the teaching of more than one concept? How should exemplars of one be presented in relation to those of another to minimize inhibition in later recognition and use of concepts? Intuitively, one might say that in the initial stages of learning, exemplars should be limited to one concept, so that the student may come to identify positive and negative ones reliably and to learn the title thoroughly, or to form the rule himself, or both. On the other hand, this is a form of "massed practice," and might be expected to interfere with other learning, just as in paired-associate experiments. Furthermore, the presentation of a number of exemplars of the same concept is redundant, that is, leads the student to expect *that* concept and thus constitutes an irrelevant cue. This can be interpreted in another way: one may say that the student forms a *learning set* toward this concept, and is likely to "look for it" in other exemplars; this *set* is itself an irrelevant dimension of the learning situation. Thus some variety must be introduced, in the form of other similar concepts, so that the student may learn to expect different ones and thereby vary the set or make it more complex.

For these reasons, one should not give exemplars of the same concept ad infinitum, either with or without the title. The learning of one concept should be interspersed with learning of other related concepts; the latter may involve new or old concepts, or both. The relative scheduling of exemplars of each cannot be dictated in advance, since few quantitative data are available for such a prescription, even in basic research. Some of what exists indicates that one should give several exemplars of the concept at each *stage* of learning when one has a sequence which becomes progressively more complex and which builds each stage on the previous one, but no general optimum repetition level has been identified.

10–9 Teaching Learning Strategies

It is the responsibility of the teacher to shape learning strategies on the part of the student. One example of this, discussed above, is the requirement of discovery or inductive learning by students who function more adequately in a deductive milieu. Another might be the shaping of a conservative focusing strategy in a student who is a compulsive gambler—and frequent loser as a result. Such a student probably learned this strategy through contingencies of his environment and is unaware of it; he needs to be shown the nature of the strategy and its shortcomings, as well as to be taught other strategies. All learning sequences favor one strategy or another, and the teacher should be aware of the nature of each of them.

The strategies possible in discovery learning are not the only ones that are valid, however. A presentation of successive exemplars, or a demonstration, or a lecture and demonstration can be an optimal teaching approach in many situations, and the strategies needed to cope with such a presentation should be learned. Through such a "lecture" approach the teacher may make sure that the students have the necessary information for drawing a conclusion or forming a concept. On the other hand, the student must adopt a relatively passive strategy in that he has no control over the sequence. A film characterizes such an approach also. A discussion, on the other hand, may exemplify a selection approach or situation, but only if the participants have something to select from, that is, if they bring information of relevance to the discussion. Laboratory experiences can be of either type, depending on the organization of the experience. There has been general complaint for years about the "cookbook" nature of most scientific laboratory learning experiences, implying that the strategy has been basically a successive presentation, with some manipulation of equipment standing for actual student-initiated learning activity. More recent views of the function of the laboratory experience in learning science and other subjects has the student in the laboratory acting as if he were a scientist, being presented with problems which, though they may have been solved years before, are still real enough to him that they bring out his research instinct and make the learning experience a productive and enjoyable one. This allows the student to make full use of his capacities, in contrast to the partial use which characterizes a passive reception of exemplars or rules. It also implies a certain degree of insecurity which is hard for many students to tolerate, so one must put a large degree of structure and planning into even the simplest independent laboratory experiment or small group involvement in a discovery situation.

This interest in discovery learning and laboratory-based activity harks back to Dewey's insistence on presenting a problem to the student, and to Socrates' method of raising anxiety in the student over his state of knowledge. It also relates to motivation theories to be discussed later.

10–10 Hypothesis Testing Revisited

In learning to identify exemplars inductively, a student may operate by trial and error initially, and then form some hypothesis which he tests, or he may start out with a hypothesis. As described previously, his hypothesis may involve a conservative strategy or a gambling strategy, and the strategy may be more or less effective according to the type of concept involved. These observations apply most directly to a selection situation. If a receptive learning situation is offered, that is, successive presentation by the teacher, then the student will probably have more difficulty forming and testing hypotheses because the pacing is not in his hands and the learning strategy preconceived by the teacher as most appropriate may not be used by the student, either because he does not know this strategy or because he failed to adopt it to guide his hypothesis. Thus it would seem likely that a presentation strategy would in many cases encourage a trial-and-error learning process, and discourage hypothesis testing and use of previously developed strategies, unless the student were told to simply take notes on the material and then try to form the concept later. On the other hand, if the rule were to be given initially, and also perhaps some idea as to the nature of the learning strategy that the teacher feels would be appropriate, then the presentation approach might well be the more efficient and effective one available.

In the selection phase of the learning, the student can be regarded as testing hypotheses, operating on the basis of the feedback received, and testing again, until the discrepancy between the present situation and the expected one (the outcome or solution) decreases to some acceptable point and the student finally exits from the learning situation. This implies some ability on the part of the student to recognize the final exit relationship, or some intervention on the part of the teacher (saying, "That's good enough" or "That's the right answer" or "You have gone as far as you can on this one for now").

Thus it seems that a hypothesis-testing point of view and a trial-and-error view can both be related to the foregoing discussion of concept learning, and that they have their places in the scheme of things. Perhaps too much has been made of the contrast that seems to exist between these two. After all, a trial may be based on a hypothesis, and the word *error* implies some feedback to the learner. A *hypothesis*, on the other hand, is based on previous concept formation, where the concept involved is one related to learning-to-learn or a learning set.

10–11 Concept Teaching and Developmental Stage

The ability to identify the intersection of two or more concepts verbally or cognitively without assistance from concrete or iconic exemplars is typical of abstract or hypothetico-deductive thought; it has also been called the *formal operational* or *symbolic* mode of thought. There is some evidence of a developmental relationship here, in that adolescents are often at the stage where this type of thinking attains a level of complexity and probability which makes it effective and, since it is more convenient, preferable. This is to say that adolescents like to think

verbally without reference to concrete or iconic exemplars. The cases that
they experience where this type of thought is effective and convenient
probably convince them that it is the only type of thought and that it is
always effective. Thus they often show a tendency to avoid checking
outcomes of such thought against "reality," and thus tend to become
divorced from reality at times in their thinking. Perhaps this also
implies an avoidance of situations which test outcomes against reality
in the classroom, as in physics or chemistry. This involves avoidance of
situations where their background does not support such abstract thinking and where, therefore, they must return to a more "juvenile" level
of thought in abstracting concepts from experience. Just as this kind
of mechanism is typical of their thought in regard to subjects in school,
so it is typical of their social interactions and their personality development, especially in the area of behavior mechanisms: these will be discussed in a later chapter.

10–12 Expectation to Transmit

In research in learning of all types, including concept identification,
the expectation of the student in the experimental (learning) situation
is a factor. Its effects on the learning process obviously depend somewhat on the nature of the expectation. One type of expectation which
is of particular interest to teachers has to do with expectation to communicate the concept (information) to others, that is, learning something with the intent of teaching it. There has been some limited
research in this area, and it indicates that there is probably an effect
of such an expectation on the "understanding" of the concept as measured by a transfer task. This effect is to decrease the performance of
the learner as compared with other learners who do not expect to transmit the knowledge. One hypothesis regarding this situation is that the
student who studies something with the expectation to transmit the
knowledge may limit the mediating vocabulary he uses in order to be
able to translate his ideas into understandable language. This would
imply that the person avoids using personal allusions and analogies that
would make the material more meaningful to him and uses only ones
which he recognizes as common to most teaching situations. Another
hypothesis is that in searching for some useful view or summary or
approach to the problem, prompted by anxiety over the impending
teaching situation, the student overlooks details of the concept and is
not as "intellectually curious" due to "overmotivation." This distracting effect of overmotivation has been noted in other investigations also.

Bibliography

GAGNE, R. M. and GEPHART, W. *Learning Research and School Subjects.*
Itasca, Illinois: F. E. Peacock Inc., 1968.

Problem Solving 11

The original "problem" for both animals and humans was survival; others are more or less closely related to that basic one. Of course, obtaining food and water and avoiding dangerous animals have become less important than avoiding cataclysmic wars that could end civilization. Nevertheless, evolution can be viewed as a long-term problem-solving process. Through natural selection, species developed in ways which helped them solve problems of survival. There are evolutionary advantages to be gained from a tendency to solve problems even where there is no pressing need. Such exploratory and investigative behavior can "pay off" in later problem situations. This primitive "R & D" tendency has been postulated as an innate motive in many organisms, particularly humans. When survival is relatively well assured, people still go on solving problems, perhaps due to this inherited tendency.

One may also postulate as a rule of behavior that organisms seek (or are reinforced for finding) easier ways to do things. This conflicts with the inclination to do what one has found effective in the past, regardless of inconvenience or inefficiency. Over long periods of time the tendency to take easier paths often seems to win out over that more conservative pattern or motive. Thus when the caveman solved the problem of heat by discovering fire, the difficulty of producing the fire became a problem, then the difficulty of controlling it, then of securing fuel. This ultimately developed into the problem of developing computer-based accounting systems to accommodate all the checks people write to pay their bills, beginning with their fuel bills.

11–1 A Definition of Problems and Problem Solving

The title "problem" has been used for a concept which, in a sense, defies definition, that is, a concept which almost everyone understands but which has no rule, or at least none which is well established and accepted. An attempt will be made to define "problems" in a relatively basic way that will be compatible with earlier learning paradigms and with later discussions of motivation as well. This is important since motivation is based to some extent on the perception of a problem by the learner.

DEFINITION

A problem is a pattern of events that is recognized as different from that which was expected by the learner, and which leads to anticipation that a desirable outcome will be blocked or that an undesirable outcome has become more probable.

Problem solving, then, is behavior reinforced by the restoration of the familiar or anticipated pattern of events, assumedly through decrease in anxiety over the possible frustration of expectations, or over the possible occurrence of the aversive outcome. Thus problem-solving behavior is reinforced by a desirable change in the problem situation. A problem, as a result, is a "motivating" situation.

Another view of problem solving sees the problem as eliciting a desire to control the environment, to be competent, to deal effectively with ongoing situations. This emphasizes the positive approach to problem solving, where success is anticipated. Still another frame of reference is based on hypothesis testing. Here perception is seen as a process of observing situations, searching for hypotheses to interpret them, and then adapting behavior to them. A "problem" will occur when no hypothesis is available to deal with the situation, or when the hypothesis adopted leads to some undesirable change.

In these views, problem solving is dependent on previous learning. Different people may find a given situation unusual enough or threatening enough to pause and consider it a problem, but their reasons may not be identical. On the other hand, what is a problem to one may be a familiar, nonthreatening pattern to another. A given situation may imply a positive, desirable outcome to one person, partly because he has previously-learned behavior that will "cope" with it, where another may see the same situation as implying a negative outcome because of past inability to cope. Thus the same situation where the same mechanisms are acting may be a challenge to one person and a threat to another, in that the past experience of the individuals leads them to predict different outcomes. One should also consider the possibility that both learners may behave in identical ways, but due to different perceptions of outcomes based on different backgrounds. One learner may see the result as positive since it has been reinforced in the past, while the other may see it as negative since it has been punished. Thus problem-solving behavior may have different emotional connotations.

When problems pose a threat, the process of behaving so as to reduce the discrepancy in the environment may take on other attributes. For example, one way to reduce the threat is to refuse to recognize the problem. Another way is to suppress it. One may rationalize it or avoid it in a host of other ways. These behavior mechanisms relate to personality theory.

11–2 Exemplars of Problem Solving

In order to assist the reader in appreciating the richness of problem-solving behavior, it seems appropriate to present descriptions of various kinds of activities involved in research in problem solving. The definition of problem solving admits many behaviors already discussed; the example of the dog whose foot rested on an electrified grid, given previously to explain avoidance conditioning, would be one. The examples of the cat in the puzzle box and the pigeon in an experimental space learning to bar-press would be others. Discrimination learning is also a problem-solving situation. The following exemplars are somewhat more complex, but still relate to this general level of behavior:

Exemplar 1: An animal learns to discriminate between flashing lights of two different frequencies; he is rewarded for pressing a button on seeing one frequency, but not when he sees the other. (This is discrimination learning.) Electrodes are inserted into the animal's brain to record electrical signals in various parts of the cortex. They indicate that "following responses" occur in the visual cortex when the light flashes, and these responses match the frequency which is being experienced at the time. When the discrimination-learning contingencies are invoked, following responses also show up in another part of the brain, called the *hippocampus.* While in one part of the hippocampus one gets these following responses, in another part one gets *anticipatory* electrical signals. Occasionally these anticipatory signals are "wrong," and when they are, the animal is observed to make an error in his response to the light. Some research reports that during the learning the phase relations between wave patterns recorded from the deeper and from the more superficial portions of the hippocampal cortex change as a function of task performance; early in learning while many errors are made the activity recorded from the deeper layers precedes that from the more superficial ones, while later when the performance involves many error-free responses the reverse is the case.

After learning, the signals disappear from the hippocampal area and are found only in the visual cortex once again.

Exemplar 2: If a repeated beep tone is sounded at irregular intervals, there is an orienting reaction on the part of an animal or person hearing it. The blood flow to the head increases, that to the finger tips diminishes. Electrical activity of the brain connected to the internal ear shows choppy activation patterns characteristic of alerting behavior. Other parts of the brain give altered records, such as in the theta rhythms from the hippocampus. After about five to ten minutes, these reactions disappear. This is called *habituation.* If one diminishes the intensity of the tone, the reactions reappear. This is a rudimentary problem-solving reaction, in which the organism responds to the existence of a problem, that is, a change in the environment which may imply the need for some behavior.

Exemplar 3: Animals, particularly rats, learn to run a maze at the end of which there is food; that is, they improve in their ability to negotiate the turns without error, and thus their speed increases (total time decreases also). Many early theories of learning were based largely on information acquired through maze-running experiments. For an animal to show *rapid* improvement in maze-running performance, he had to be deprived of food or water prior to the experiment, then find the appropriate satisfaction at the end. Some theories constructed to explain this behavior relied mainly on the idea of sequences or chains of responses, where each response acted as both reinforcer and stimulus—these have been discussed as behavioral *chains*. Other theories attributed the behavior to mental "maps" of the maze, postulating that the animal synthesized the pattern from his experience and then followed it in running the maze: this view was intuitively appealing as a model of human behavior involving higher mental processes. Some recent research has indicated that some rats learn primarily through the chaining process while others learn primarily through some sort of plan or pattern; it is, then, partly dependent on their heredity.

Some human behavior can be explained in terms of the reinforcements that exist as environmental contingencies; "plans" and other complex cognitive behaviors can have a foundation in these simpler paradigms of reinforcement learning. There is a developmental dimension to this, since humans of different ages show different approaches to problem solving. At some ages children demonstrate behavior which is primarily trial and error, while at later stages they show behavior which implies more complex mediation of behaviors more akin to the "cognitive mapping" view.

Exemplar 4: Several different animals have been taught to find food behind one of several doors when a light over the door is lit. There are three doors, side by side, with a light over each, and the animals are trained to go to the door where the light is on. Now suppose the animal is detained while the light is on, and then released some seconds after it is turned off. It is found that some animals can go to the correct door, in spite of the delay, while others cannot; that is, some can "remember" better than others. There is a hierarchy of species in the animal kingdom, ordered by ability to solve this problem over increasing periods of delay after the light has been turned off. Furthermore, there are differences among types within species. This is a type of problem-solving behavior and also requires prior learning of simpler forms of the problem.

These examples have dealt with learning that can be analyzed as trial and error for the most part, although one may postulate various degrees of mediating behavior. Another type of problem-solving experiment has received much attention because it deals with *insight*. This is where the learner seems to arrive at the solution suddenly, in an all-or-nothing manner, as discussed previously.

Exemplar 5: An ape is shown a pipe about a foot in diameter and longer than twice his arm-reach. He observes an experimenter place food in the middle of the pipe through a door in its side, which is then closed. There is a pole in the vicinity which can be inserted into the pipe. The ape tries to reach the food with his hands several times but the door is locked and the pipe is too long. He then loses interest, plays with the pole, rolls it along the pipe, then tries to reach the food with his arm again, then plays with the pole some more. By chance the pole becomes lined up with the pipe: the behavior of the ape now centers on shoving the pole into the pipe, ejecting the food from the other end. Thus the ape solves the problem, after some unsuccessful trials, and with the help of the chance hint in the lining of the pole with the pipe. There is an observable change in the quality of the behavior just prior to the solution, which is often termed *insight*.

Exemplar 6: An ape is shown food outside his cage. There is a hoe among the various implements in the cage, the hoe being long enough to enable him to pull the food close. When several different apes were put in this situation, some solved it; of these, some showed the type of abrupt behavioral change referred to as insight. Many of the correct solutions had observable antecedents in trial-and-error behavior.

Exemplar 7: A group of monkeys is confronted (individually) with a sequence of problems of the type described just above. If one of these problems is given to another group of monkeys, which has not had the same experience, that is, has not been through the same sequence of problems, they will have more difficulty solving the problem than those which *have* had such experience.

It is said, then, that the monkeys with the more extensive experience have "learned to learn" or that they have developed a *learning set*. This implies that there is a complex set of responses, not entirely dependent on the particular problem, which might be called *problem-solving responses*. If we consider these to be a concept, a *problem-solving concept*, then they are shaped as concepts are, with each of the individual problems involving both relevant and irrelevant dimensions. If we look upon this as a set of responses to a larger set of stimuli (one definition of *concept* or its relative, *process*) then it is subject to extinction also. Therefore, one must maintain this response complex by arranging conditions wherein it is reinforced. If on the other hand, a teacher uses only situations where problem-solving is *not* required and therefore is not reinforced, the learning set will be extinguished.

Such an analysis implies that if one gives a problem to a group of students, and then gives a set of subproblems designed to help in the

solution, one may be conditioning or shaping a problem-solving response complex, or a learning set, in respect to some of them (that is,
in some of the students, namely those who have not yet learned to solve
problems), while at the same time he may be extinguishing a more
sophisticated learning set in others (that is, those who have previously
learned to solve more complex problems). Thus one must choose his
strategy either to (a) reinforce the well-formed set (frustrating the
slower students) or (b) shape the simpler learning set (leaving all
better students to shift for themselves or, if they participate, extinguishing their more complex and sophisticated behaviors and thus doing
them more harm than good). While this analysis is somewhat pessimis-
tic and does not confirm the popular idea that an interest in the student's
welfare and a desire to do good in teaching are the main ingredients
of success, it unfortunately seems to be going on in all too many situations.

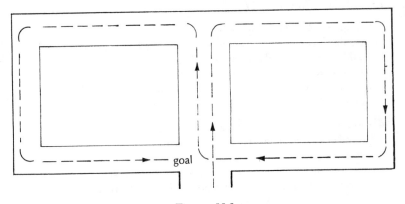

FIGURE 11.1

Exemplar 8: A double-alternation maze is one which requires animals
(or humans) to follow one path which turns to the right (see Figure
11.1) and then another which turns to the left, before being rewarded
with food or water. Thus the subject must go through the maze twice,
once one way and once the other.

This task is nearly impossible for rats. Raccoons, cats, and other animals can learn to solve it. Preverbal children (that is, children who
cannot yet talk) have difficulty, while verbal children do not. This
implies that words function to aid problem solving even where they
are not used overtly. Another hypothesis is that the neurological
maturation which enables children to learn to talk also aids in the
solution of this task.

As one views different examples of problem-solving behavior, relationships with concept formation and verbal learning both become
apparent. The following examples bring this out.

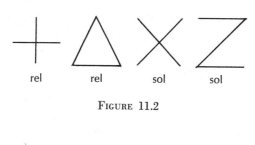

rel   rel   sol   sol

FIGURE 11.2

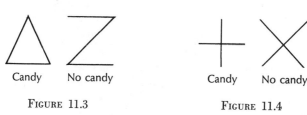

Candy   No candy   Candy   No candy

FIGURE 11.3   FIGURE 11.4

Exemplar 9: Very young children are shown a set of four boxes, each having a different and distinctive design on the top, and each being otherwise the same as the others. These children are taught one name for two of the boxes, and another name for the other two. For example, the designs and names might be as shown in Figure 11.2. One box from each pair is chosen by the experimenter and some candy is placed under one of these two (Figure 11.3). After each child has learned to find the candy under the box, the other two boxes are brought out, and the candy is hidden under the box with the same name as the one that covered the candy previously (placement is randomized so that the correct response is not always on one side). (See Figure 11.4.) The children are unable to find the candy on the first trial at better than chance accuracy. This is taken to imply that learning the common name does not facilitate finding the candy in the second case—the name does not aid in *transfer*, or to put it another way, the name does not *mediate* a solution.

The experiment above parallels one of the mediation paradigms described in Chapter Six on verbal learning, the one called *stimulus equivalence*. Think of the first pair in each set above as pairs in an A–B list, that is, the stimulus is the plus sign and the response is "rel" for one, and for the other the stimulus is the "X" and the response is "sol"; then the second pair of each set is the C–B list, where the stimulus C is the triangle for one set and the "Z" in the other, and the response is again "rel" for the first and "sol" for the second. Now it was asserted in the previous discussion of mediation that there would be an effect of stimulus equivalence, that is, responses "rel" and "sol" would serve as connectors for their respective stimuli, so that the plus sign should evoke the triangle and the "X" should evoke the "Z." If this is so, why doesn't the child find the candy under the plus sign after he has learned that it is found under the triangle; that is, why doesn't this stimulus equivalence mediate the learning?

If we carry the analogy further, the candy–no candy situation becomes another paired-associate learning situation: let's call it A–D. Now the question becomes, "Will the stimulus equivalence between A and C mediate the learning of C–D?" When this is tried with nonsense syllables there is no effect either. Evidently the strength of the "association" is not sufficient to do the job. Another hypothesis is that the learning of A–D brings about the partial extinction of A–B, since the response "B" is wrong and must be labelled so. Thus one might predict that if the students are given practice or review on the A–B relationship *while* the A–D relationship is being learned, then they will be aided by it and the list C–D will be learned more easily. In the case of the candy experiment, this would imply that one would have to review the relationship between the plus sign and the syllable "rel" and between the triangle and the syllable "rel" while one taught the child that the candy was under the triangle, if one wished to facilitate the learning that the candy was also under the plus sign. This has implications for the teaching of any concept or process that depends on other relationships learned recently: the basic relationships must be reviewed while the new links are taught, if the final solution is to be facilitated. Another way to say this is, "The mediators must be maintained through active practice."

Exemplar 10: In another problem solving experiment two groups of students were given the same puzzle to work out. One group was asked to respond overtly regarding their individual hypotheses or strategies while they attempted to solve it. The other group was not asked to respond overtly in this manner. The correctness of the verbal responses of the first group was not crucial. They were not rewarded in any way for correct responses or given any information on their correctness. The group which responded overtly was still found to solve the problem quicker on the average than the other group. Evidently, active overt verbal responding during the solution was facilitating in this case. Yet in another experiment where young children were asked to put together a number of known facts to solve a problem, it was found that giving hints during the solution process interfered with the solution in some cases; the verbal hint seemed to interfere with whatever mediation process they were using and to cause them to operate less efficiently.

There does seem to be a common element between these two experiments. In each case, there was a personal solution process going on: in the first, its personal and unique nature was emphasized by the overt verbalization, whereas in the second, the personal nature was to some extent interfered with. This seems to imply that students operate best in problem solving according to their own personal strategies and mediators, rather than using those of another, expressed in words which may not be entirely meaningful to them. Some investigators in the area of science education involving low-achieving students who often come from lower socioeconomic groups, have observed that understanding of scientific phenomena is more within their grasp if they are allowed and encouraged to apply their own language to the problem, no matter how unintelligible this language might be to the investigator. It seems likely that such an approach to teaching can be carried too far, in that students need some common language that is particularly suited to the subject if they are to progress beyond the elementary stages of under-standing. Thus the personal language must ultimately be translated into a more universal one, or to put it another way, the student must make the standard language his own. This may be a longer and more difficult process than we realize, however, and emphasizes that the importance of language teaching is not relegated to classes in French or German or Spanish. Mathematics, for instance, has a great many elements in common with foreign language teaching.

The Swiss psychologist Piaget has done extensive research in problem solving by children of various ages and has identified stages of learning which seem to shed light on the role of verbal learning and also on the nature of insight and transfer. The following examples illustrate some of the kinds of problems used in these investigations.

Exemplar 11: If one places a block beside another block of the same length, then pushes one of them so that its end projects beyond the other, then a child of age six will probably indicate that they are of different length. An older child is likely to indicate that they are of the same length, thus indicating an understanding that what is gained on one end is lost on the other.

Exemplar 12: Suppose one has a group of smaller blocks that add up to the length of a large one when placed end to end, and suppose that one puts the smaller blocks at angles to each other so that they do not reach as far as the larger (see Figure 11.5). A young child, when asked which of the two paths would be longer for a fly to walk, will probably say that the solid block would be, even though you initially presented him with the short blocks end to end to equal the longer one before rearranging them as shown.

First position   Second position

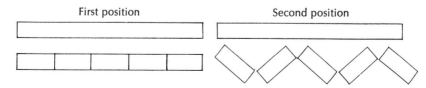

FIGURE 11.5

This is taken to indicate that the child has not developed the concept of *conservation* of length, part of the general family of conservation concepts which in turn are basic to problem solving in many areas.

Exemplar 13: A "gun" is used to shoot marbles; it is made of a plunger and a spring, as in a pin-ball machine. The gun is aimed at a wall constructed so that the marbles will bounce off it; as in other reflections, the angle of incidence to the wall equals the angle of leaving the wall, as shown in the top view of the game (Figure 11.6).

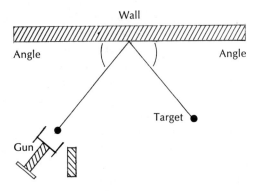

FIGURE 11.6

The objective is to bounce the marble off the wall and hit the target. Very young children do not master this task easily, if at all. Children old enough to master it may still not be able to describe the path of the ball accurately, either with an iconic representation or with words. Their descriptions may indicate, for example, that their concept of the path is as given in Figure 11.7.

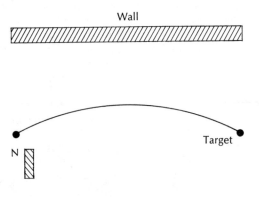

FIGURE 11.7

Children who master the task and who can also describe it accurately may still not recognize the equality of the angles of incidence and leaving the wall. This recognition, coming as an answer to pointed questioning designed to require the concept but not give it away, has insightful qualities; it is brought about in some instances by making the relationship between target and gun such that the ball bounces almost straight back from the wall, that is, so that the angles are approaching ninety degrees. This implies that the insight process requires some cuing, as noted previously in discussing experiments with primates. It also evidences a trial-and-error prelude to insight.

Problem-solving situations, both of the concept formation type and others, have been used to investigate the relative effects of guidance or discovery in learning, as noted in a previous chapter. In one such investigation, mathematical sequences were used as follows:

Exemplar 14: A problem was given of the following type: "Fill in the missing numbers: 0, 1, 1, 2, 3, 5, —, —, ..." Three modes of learning were used to bring about understanding of the process of completing such series. In one learning mode the learner was given the principle and asked to apply it to an example; in another he was given examples and asked to discover the principle; in the third he was given examples and provided hints to help him discover the principle (this was called *guided discovery*). In a test in which he was required to transfer this knowledge to other series of the same type, but new to him, students who had been exposed to the guided discovery approach performed more effectively than those in either the discovery approach or the guidance (given principle) approach.

It is appropriate to reiterate that the guidance–discovery question is one of *degrees* of guidance. Obviously, in the discovery approach, the nature of the series used for the learning tasks, their sequential relationship to each other, and the difficulty of the rule and the size of the numbers used all affected the "learnability" of the exemplars. The discovery sequence could have been tried, revised, and tried out again several times until it was so organized that students would learn more easily from it than from the guided discovery sequence. It is also possible that the guided discovery approach taught the students, by example, a more effective or powerful use of mediators, as well as giving them some of the useful mediators (words) for such problems. If this were so, it could imply in turn that the guidance group, which received the principles and was asked to apply them, received less experience in identifying the relevant and irrelevant attributes of the exemplars, and thus was *less* able to utilize them in the criterion situation.

Two other experiments in this area are worth mentioning as exemplars of problem solving related to a crucial problem in teaching.

Exemplar 15: Learners were exposed to a concept-learning task similar

to those described in the preceding chapter. In one treatment the subject was told the correct answer immediately if he gave an incorrect
response; in the other the subject was told to keep trying until he
"discovered" the correct answer. Conjunctive concepts were to be identified. Comparisons of outcomes indicated that there were no significant
differences in the number of concepts named correctly or in the number of presentations required to name them correctly, but that the
discovery group learned to recall and recognize significantly more definitions of concepts and also learned to recall definitions of a greater
percentage of the concepts that they learned to name correctly.

Exemplar 16: Two groups were compared in their ability to decode
unfamiliar cryptograms. One group had derived the coding principles
from examples, while the other had the principles given to them (both
groups had the same learning tasks and the same criterion tasks). There
seemed to be no consistent difference between the deriving and the
given groups on either immediate or delayed posttests.

These exemplars indicate that the final word is not yet in on the guidance–discovery question. Indeed, if one looks upon it as a matter of
degree and kind of guidance, then the possibility of different outcomes
in different problem situations seems obvious.

The examples given in relation to the guidance–discovery problem
concentrate on the interaction of students' and teachers' efforts to reach
problem-solving solutions. There is another type of research in problem solving which sheds some light on factors that affect difficulty in
relation to the interaction of previous experience.

Exemplar 17: Two ropes hang from a ceiling; the objective is to tie
them together. The problem is that they are so far apart that one cannot grab them simultaneously. However, if one ties something to one
rope and sets it swinging, then he can hold on to the other and grasp
the first when it swings toward him. This requires the learner to use
some object as a weight for the pendulum, often an object that has
been used recently for other things. For example, an ash tray may be
used which the learner has needed for his cigarette, or a screwdriver
which he has just used to fasten some object to the wall. In one variation of this experiment, subjects were previously given another problem
in which they had to use either a switch or a relay to complete an electric circuit (one group used the switch, the other the relay). When
they came to the string-tying problem, both a switch and a relay were
available for making a pendulum. Data from this experiment, when
tabulated, appeared roughly as follows:

Subjects	Used Switch	Used Relay
Group previously using switch	2	7
Group previously using relay	10	0
Group having no previous problem	3	4

Evidently proactive inhibition operated, in that the previous use of the component affected its probability of use in the new task.

Bibliography

SNYDER, H. I. *Contemporary Educational Psychology.* New York: John Wiley and Sons, Inc., 1968.

TRAVERS, R. M. W. *Essentials of Learning.* New York: MacMillan, 1963.

12 Some Analyses of Problem Solving

12–1 Dewey and Problem Solving

Investigation of problem solving has been less intense and thorough than investigation of conditioning, partly because of the complexity and the difficulties involved in controlling variables in problem solving. On the other hand, educators have viewed problem solving as a crucial aspect of learning and motivation. John Dewey, for example, set down five stages of problem solving, summarized below:

1. arousal of a state of perplexity or doubt;
2. identification of the nature of the problem;
3. search for facts and possible solutions;
4. testing of successive solutions, and reformulation of the problem where necessary;
5. application of the correct solution.

This analysis reflects strongly what is generally called the *scientific method*, which is largely a problem-solving process emphasizing observation, formulation of hypotheses, and testing hypotheses as a model of behavior for dealing with natural phenomena. One might note that the existence or arousal of a sense of doubt about something and the identification of the nature of the problem might be considered part of the same process. It is related to our previous definition of a problem as a situation that is not what is expected, or in which some discrepancy exists between the situation and the normal environment. However, what is a problem for the scientist is not a problem for the layman. Perhaps the emphasis on observation in the scientific method, and in Dewey's formulation, results from the need to focus attention on phenomena and processes ordinarily taken for granted. This implies that in ordinary problem solving the recognition of the problem is more or less forced upon one by his previous learning experience; the scientist, on the other hand, seeks problems in situations which we ordinarily accept, by adopting different frames of reference.

Some investigators of problem solving conclude that we solve problems in ways not immediately available for observation and dissection. Just as students come to an "understanding" of concepts in terms of ability to identify positive exemplars *before* they can identify the concept verbally, so scientists, mathematicians, and artists report that they "solve" very difficult problems without knowing how, or without being able to put the solution into words immediately. Sometimes it takes months after the solution (insight) occurs to put it into a formal statement, such that its relationships with other knowledge are clear to the person who has discovered it and to others in the field.

12–2 Computer-Related Analyses

One of Dewey's formal steps, the formulation of hypotheses or solutions to the problem, corresponds to the hypothesis-testing view of problem solving originally proposed in relation to concept formation. The conservative focusing strategy mentioned in that chapter was a simple hypothesis-testing strategy, one requiring little of the memory. A more sophisticated model of concept formation assumes that the learner is able to receive and interpret stimuli in terms of conceptual groupings and seeks to describe a repertoire of cognitive processes by which a computer can be programmed to do the same thing. The computer is instructed to "attend to" or "focus on" attributes of positive exemplars, and to build a "tree" of decisions to describe the concept. At each point where there are two branches to the "tree," the model chooses one branch if the attribute is present in the positive instance and the other if it is not. This is somewhat analogous to the generative grammar described in a previous chapter.

Another computer-oriented model of behavior which emphasizes hypothesis testing is based on a recognition by the problem solver of some discrepancy in the environment. When a discrepancy is found, the problem solver operates on the environment in order to reduce that discrepancy, then tests again to see whether it still exists. The learner continues this process until the discrepancy is reduced to zero, at which he stops. In the same way a computer can be programmed to read a difference between the existing value of some factor and a predetermined standard, to operate according to some process or "algorithm," to come up with a result, and to compare this result with the standard again. If the difference is other than zero, it will continue to operate, but when the difference reaches zero, it ceases to operate; that is, it "exits." One may substitute for a zero difference some optimal level of discrepancy, and arrive again at the "optimal discrepancy" model of human motivation; of course, the discrepancy is more than a numerical difference, but the analogy is clear.

Many investigators of problem solving have assumed that the hypothesis-testing model, in some form, is the most productive one, and have developed procedures and measures for evaluating the nature and power of the various hypotheses adopted and used by learners. Larger and more powerful simplifying concepts and processes are sought through more complex models based on computer operations. Here the process of storage and retrieval of information, of carrying out algorithms (standard sequences of operations), of heuristics (simplifying assumptions which make it possible to operate effectively in the face of an infinite number of possible solutions) have been utilized in solving problems through computers and subsequently constructing models of the process based on experience programming them. The assumption is that the brain works like a computer in some ways, and that we can begin to understand its operations by observing what happens when a computer is programmed to deal with these problems. In the process of such investigations, computers have been programmed to play tic-tac-toe, checkers, and chess, among other games. The chess project has not succeeded as yet in producing better than a class D player, but the checkers project has produced an unbeatable player (computer) by programming the computer to learn from its errors and thus to become better with experience.

Just as computers can be programmed to solve problems in order to investigate the problem-solving process, so computers have been programmed to guide human learners in problem-solving activities and to shape their problem-solving behaviors so that they become more effective. This involves both an information-providing capacity for the student to access in finding solutions and also routines which guide the learner and which reward certain strategies and discourage others. This kind of function has been extended into the field of guidance and counseling, where computers are programmed to provide students answers for questions concerning careers and personal difficulties. One interesting demonstration program simulates a detective story or mystery in which the learner takes the part of the detective calling for evidence from the "crime lab" and for testimony from various characters involved, such as the "maid." The detective–learner addresses the computer for information and can receive such answers as, "Yes, honey, I'm the maid" and "The crime lab is not ready with a report on the powder burns; call back in fifteen minutes." The analogy to problem solving in a number of different areas is obvious.

By observing the effectiveness of prepared programs and improving them step by step, some concepts have been reached concerning the functioning of the human brain in problem solving. The concepts are very incomplete and inadequate as yet, but some of the early results have indicated that the following are common strategies:

a. attempting to find the answer by substitution of facts at hand into a known relationship or theorem or equation, for example, "It is always the butler who did it, and the butler in this case is George, so George did it."

b. beginning at the end of the problem, assuming the answer, and working backwards to obtain some relationship which in turn implies the solution, for example, "To get across the brook one finds a stone close to the other side, then works backwards to make a path to the near side, then reverses the activity to cross the brook."

c. using a syllogistic form of reasoning in forming a chain of ideas from known facts to solution. This involves chains of behavior, including verbal chains which lead from one equivalence or relationship to another, for example, "Given the fact that the corresponding angles made by a line crossing two other lines are equal, and desiring to prove that the lines crossed do not meet, one may insert the verbal chain" (previously accepted); "if interior angles are equal then the lines are parallel" followed by the verbal chain "if lines are parallel then they do not meet."

d. forming a reverse chain such as that in (c) but starting at the end as in (b), for example, "What kinds of lines do not meet? Answer: parallel lines. What conditions make lines parallel: Answer, among others, corresponding angles are equal." Then reverse it.

Building on such approaches as those above one can arrive at very complex sequences of cognitive events; in dealing with such sequences in respect to *sets* of similar problems, many chains and processes are repeated over and over. These chains or processes become learning sets and demonstrate one meaning of the previously discussed phenomenon of "learning to learn."

12–3 Gestalt Analyses

During the First World War and for some years thereafter, a school of psychology developed which gave great emphasis to perceptual phenomena and their relationship to problem solving and cognition generally. This school explored extensively the relationship between designs and patterns and the "meanings" ascribed to them by learners, as well as the competence of learners to perceive the patterns in various contexts. They set down some principles of learning which are still considered in research involving problem solving. Some of their experiments in learning, while not rigorously structured and carried out, have shed light on aspects of learning and inspired extensive debate and further exploration. Many of them were designed to demonstrate that certain higher animals and humans learn in ways that are not adequately described by trial-and-error learning paradigms involving conditioning of various types. They indicated that learning occurred primarily through a process of insight, a sudden and complete understanding of the solution rather than a cumulative bit-by-bit process.

The investigations of Gestalt psychologists have been replicated in a number of different ways, partly using primates in problem-solving situations, and the results have indicated that while insight as a rapid arrival at a conclusion does occur, it is often preceded by the learning of elements of the solution and/or by manipulation of the situation in ways that make the insight more probable. Furthermore, animals and humans learn to learn in these situations, implying that there are basic processes being learned which are not hereditary and that the problem is not solved by dint of some innate intelligence which the person possesses from birth, except as that intelligence has made use of previous experience and is able to bring it to bear on the present.

Closely related to this matter of insight was the Gestaltist's assertion that the whole of anything, whether a perceived object or a concept or process, was greater than the sum of its parts. They would demonstrate this by examples showing that the parts in themselves were meaningless until put together in certain configurations, and that once the parts were so arranged (or so perceived), they conveyed a meaning beyond anything that any individual part could convey. A simple example is the letter A, whose component parts (three straight line segments) are meaningless until put together in this manner. This is obviously related to insight, which is achieved when one "sees" the parts in their proper configuration; knowing the parts is trivial as compared with knowing the proper configuration or pattern. This also can be taken to imply a perceptual hypothesis-testing process, where the pattern is matched against various previously experienced stimulus sets from memory until one is found which "clicks" or "jibes" with the context. Gestalt psychologists extended this part–whole distinction to learning generally by stating that one should always learn the whole first, that the parts were meaningless without it. This was offered as a contradiction to the familiar process, superficially related to conditioning paradigms, of giving practice or drill on limited examples of concepts and processes rather than discussing the processes in their most general form, that is, verbally and abstractly.

One example sometimes given is the learning of a language through studying a paragraph or a page of it, with assistance from the teacher, identifying cognates and such and gradually making sense out of the "whole," rather than proceeding to study vocabulary and grammar first and then reading passages which exemplify these words and rules. It is probably obvious to the reader that one can overdo this "whole" approach just as one can get lost in presenting the "parts" and never reach the "whole." This, and the additional trivial observation that everything is both a "whole" in respect to its parts and a "part" in respect to larger wholes, makes it fairly evident that the whole–part controversy is not a matter of absolutes: just as all "discovery" is guided, so all "wholes" are parts. What one comes to, then, is a search for the optimal learning unit in respect to the previous learning and experience of the student. It follows that some research will indicate that learning parts first is superior to learning the whole, and other research will indicate the opposite, and indeed this is the present situation. A concept as defined previously cannot be taught as a whole until the exemplars have been experienced; however, if they have been experienced previously, a statement of the rule may suffice to communicate the concept. Thus the part–whole method in concept formation is called for in one case, the whole–part in another. This is also the inductive versus the deductive debate and guidance versus discovery.

12–4 Developmental Aspects of Problem Solving

Problem solving by children has always been an area of interest and exploration, often with the objective of understanding their behavior and human problem-solving processes generally. Often investigators have carried an implicit conviction that the child goes through stages similar to those through which his evolutionary ancestors went, that is, that at a given age the child will approach a problem as did human beings at a certain earlier stage of their evolutionary development; thus there is also an archaeological component to such studies, although it is not often emphasized. Others feel that the human child goes through a series of learning stages which are determined by his greater capacity to learn relative to other organisms, and that this greater capacity implies that he will develop differently than organisms with lesser capacities, including perhaps his evolutionary ancestors. One obvious difference between the cognitive and physical development of the human child and animal offspring is that the human is slower, and thus relatively retarded in his progress as compared with animals; the wolf pack often reminded Mowgli of this. While these motives and others are present in investigations of problem solving in children, the most valid rationale seems to be one which aims at understanding more fully how to bring about and control problem-solving behaviors. As mentioned previously, the control of behavior is not an entirely acceptable concept or philosophy to most people today, but since it goes on all the time, it would seem best to understand the process if only to be able to limit it. Of course, such limitation is itself a form of control!

Piaget, in investigating the behavior of very young children in response to a situation related to the concept of velocity in physics, found as he had in other situations that children were apt to concentrate on one dimension of the situation at the expense of other dimensions. This might be described alternately as a demonstration of limited ability to consider more than one attribute or dimension of the problem or concept. In a situation described iconically in Figure 12.1, two cars are made to pass through their respective tunnels and emerge at the same

Initial   Final

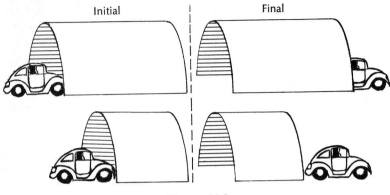

FIGURE 12.1

time (they start at the same time also). The tunnels are not the same in length. When questioned in such a way that the concept of "velocity" or "speed" is inherent in the behavior described in the question (so that the *title* of the concept of speed is not a barrier), children indicate by their answers that they assume the cars have gone at the same speed. For example, one might ask them, "If the cars continue the same way they are going, how far will each travel in the next three seconds—will the distances be the same or different?"

Piaget concluded that this indicated a human propensity to judge velocity on the basis of something other than distance and time; this implies an innate tendency rather than something learned from experience, or at least Piaget's wording suggests that *he* makes this inference. Piaget relates this simple and direct approach to speed to relativistic views of velocity and suggests that the Galilean solution to the problem of speed in terms of distance and time, which has been employed and taught for centuries, has been an artificial one which has *impeded* understanding in certain areas. Thus, according to Piaget, such research in primitive problem-solving processes can shed light on sophisticated scientific concepts, and can suggest new frames of reference or kinds of questions to be asked. Thus the study of developmental aspects of learning may contribute to our most advanced understanding of the world and the universe. This is certainly a broader rationale for investigating developmental aspects of problem solving than is customary.

12–5 Developmental Stages After Piaget

The preschool child appears to manipulate the world through action and to learn to represent this world through symbols established by simple generalizations; Piaget regards this as elementary concept formation. The child does not separate internal motives and feelings from external reality as adults do. When his behavior is ineffective, he reorganizes it through behaviors which are best described as trial and error, with little mediation or manipulation of symbols related to the variables. It is not clear whether *mediation* refers to iconic types of representations as well as symbolic, but it probably involves both.

The young child has yet to form certain concepts which enable him to deal effectively with his environment or world. One such concept is that of reversibility: this is the idea that what has been done can be undone. Thus if marbles are divided into subgroups for counting, one has to believe that they can be put back together again and that, when they are restored, there will be as many marbles as before. This last conclusion exemplifies another such concept, that of conservation, which says that although one changes the form of a substance, one does not necessarily change its volume or mass, that is, that something is conserved even though something else changes. In its most sophisticated forms, this concept can be very difficult and requires experience with phenomena which illustrate it. The concept of conservation of energy, for example, is a sophisticated form of the conservation concept. In its simpler manifestations, however, it can be comprehended by children. If one pours juice from a short wide glass into a tall thin glass, its volume remains constant—there is just as much juice as there was. Young children will conclude that the amount of juice has increased, indicating that they have not formed this concept, or that they are using height (one attribute) as a sign for mass or volume (that is, "how much").

As the child develops and matures, he is able to cope with more and more complex inputs. His operations on the environment increase in effectiveness, partly due to physical maturation and development, partly due to the development of a language with which to process events and experiences symbolically and thus more efficiently. This enables him also to carry his past experience into present events more effectively, and to furnish more and more refined hypotheses to deal with problems. Then he begins to be able to do more things "in his head" and thus to be less reliant on immediate concrete evidence from the environment. He begins to be able to predict outcomes. He can see two arrangements of the same blocks as being the same group of blocks and can rearrange things to be "as they were before." He can also predict the number of rooms in a building made of blocks if he knows that each room is a block, even before he has completed the whole building.

As this process continues, the learner develops concepts of area, length, and time, among others. He develops the ability to manipulate symbols of reality cognitively and thus becomes free of the immediate environment and able to perform symbolic acts and to predict outcomes from these symbolic acts. This stage of development, marked by freedom from the immediate environment and by the ability to deal with ideas and symbols and to come up with meaningful conclusions, is sometimes called the *hypothetico-deductive stage*; it has also been called the *formal operational stage* (by Piaget) and the *symbolic stage* (by Bruner).

The hypothetico-deductive stage is characterized mainly by a capacity to operate with images and titles of things and concepts, to manipulate them cognitively and arrive at some prediction regarding the present or future environment. This stage often comes to maturity during the adolescent period of the student, assumedly due to increasing experience with learning strategies and problem-solving processes. There may be some maturational elements connected with it also, but since such cognitive behavior is observed in preadolescents and younger children, its dependence on neurological maturation is not to be assumed lightly. When it does occur, it sometimes takes on aspects of intellectualism, a defense mechanism to be discussed later: in this sense, the student involves himself in abstract cognitive behavior in order to avoid recognition of any responsibility for concrete problems which face him. Some elements of the student culture reject this tendency toward abstract verbalization, and their distrust is partly based on the fact that such hypothetico-deductive processes often result in conclusions regarding the real world which turn out to be false or at best misleading and inadequate in solving problems at hand.

12–6 Some Implications of Piaget's Point of View

Problem solving in Piaget's view depends greatly on processing of information at the formal operational level of cognition. This implies a process not entirely unlike the "insight" of the Gestaltist: it stresses the complexity of human thought and, instead of attempting to analyze it into its component parts, treats it as a phenomenon of maturation. Thus the intellectual powers of the human species are emphasized, and the difficulty of analyzing the nature of these hereditary mechanisms is implied. Verbalization is central, as a code or language into which one translates concrete experience in order to classify it, interpret it, and act upon it. However, there is seemingly no intent to analyze this in order to achieve more effective problem solving, or in order to teach problem solving; instead, the intent seems to be to observe and analyze what exists and to assume that these facts reflect innate hereditary characteristics of the developing human organism rather than the vicissitudes and contingencies of the experiences that different learners have had.

One important developmental concept stressed by Piaget is of particular importance to teachers. It has to do with the difference between the learner's ability to perceive the environment and his ability to process or act upon or interpret that perception. A recent experiment clarifies this difference. Several children were shown a group of sticks of different length. Then some of them were asked to reproduce the perception, i.e. to draw what they saw. Some were asked to do this fairly soon after they saw them, others were asked to do so some months later, while still others did it a year or so later. In no case did they see the sticks after the first experience. Piaget and his co-worker, Inhelder, found that the reproductions increased in accuracy and complexity as time went on, indicating that the perception of the actual event was present "in the mind" as it were, but that the interpretation of the perception as evidenced by the drawings changed over time. This implies certain limits in the ability of children of certain ages to interpret what they see although they are able to perceive fairly accurately at an early age. It also implies that there is a cognitive mechanism whereby the learner processes or interprets or decodes his perceptions, partly in terms of his previous experience and partly in terms of his neurological ability to do so. The latter is assumedly determined in part by heredity (in an absolute sense) and in part by maturation (in a developmental sense).

12–7 Problem Solving as Interaction of the Learner with a System

In the science laboratory the feedback comes from the natural system being investigated. When the investigator acts on a system, examining the output given by that system as a result of some input of his own (that is, his manipulation), he must determine for himself which outcomes are relevant and which are irrelevant. The investigator (that is, the learner) may act upon the system as many times as he chooses, and yet information exchange between him and the system rarely has the clear two-valued yes–no characteristic of concept identification experiments. Thus the information necessary for responding is contingent upon events perceived to occur in the system, and the problem of assigning meaning to the events becomes an important determinant of behavior. Of course, this requires a deep faith on the part of the investigator in the regularity of the system, that is, of nature. This faith may be lacking in a student: it is an important element of what is called *motivation*. It also can be lacking in a culture or subculture generally, which would mean that most of the persons in the culture would lack motivation.

In concept identification research described previously, there was an implicit process which might be described as "progressive constraint". For example, if the concept to be identified was "blue circle," the learner would progressively eliminate number and shadedness as irrelevant, by finding that if he changed these dimensions while holding the others constant it would make no difference in the feedback. This can be viewed as finding or adding constraints to one's behavior which reduce the number of possible arrangements which give a certain kind of feedback. In that earlier research the input of the learner was limited to selecting an exemplar, and the output of the system (the system including the exemplars and the experimenter or teacher) was limited to "yes" or "no" (or a red light and a green light, or some other symbols for "yes" and "no").

In scientific investigations the feedback comes from the reaction of the system to the behavior of the investigator, and the input or behavior of the investigator in respect to the system may have a variety of forms. The investigator may heat the system, shake it, push it, drop it, weigh it, and so on. It may respond by blowing up, breaking, melting, rebounding, or rising, among other things. Thus the investigator not only tests hypotheses but forms additional hypotheses from the behavior or output or response of the system itself.

Progress in such a complex situation consists of reductions in the variability of the system. This may be seen as an increase in the number of constraints one *puts* on the system; it is another way of saying that one reduces the variability. An example of this process is found in a "black box" experiment in which students are given a box with something loose inside it. They cannot open the box, but they are permitted to do anything to it other than open it in order to deduce or induce what it is that is inside; for example, they can weigh it, shake it, balance it, turn it over, or give it numerous other treatments. From the responses of the system (the box and its contents), they can begin to form some idea of the contents. If one tilts it from side to side and it feels and sounds as if the object inside is rolling, one may conclude it is spherical or cylindrical. One may test this hypothesis by some input which would differentiate between them in terms of their responses. As one does this, one adds constraints to the situation; that is, it would then be a mistake to use a test designed to differentiate between a cube and a tetrahedron, unless it happens to be the same test.

Concept formation does not provide the only model for the process whereby one formulates hypotheses during this learner–system interaction. Concepts involve a large number of exemplars and a few titles, plus one or more rules: the converse of this is one or a few exemplars and many titles and rules. For example, if one has a brick as a stimulus object, a teacher may reinforce a learner for giving a large number of different responses to it, asking only that each response describe some appropriate use for the brick (though not necessarily a *common* use). This requires the student to respond to dimensions of the stimulus and relationships to other things which are not commonly responded to, implying that the responses themselves will be relatively weak, if present at all.

Where forming or identifying a concept is a *convergent* process, this is a *divergent* one. Yet such creative behavior leads to problem solving in many situations, and thus such creativity is to be fostered and shaped by the teacher. To what degree this should be done in various subject areas is a matter for debate, and will be for some time to come. Incidentally, if the convergent relationship is called a *concept*, it might be convenient to call the divergent one, where many responses are furnished for a given exemplar, a *dicept*.

An example of learning in science will serve to illustrate the importance of divergent thinking that emerges from tasks such as that described above. In analyzing or investigating certain physical systems, it often happens that more than one mode or pattern of relationships is found to conform to the data; that is, given a set of responses of the system to certain inputs or treatments, one may account for these by more than one set of assumptions or hypotheses. Any given behavior exhibited by the system might be produced by an indefinitely large number of combinations of relations in the system—there are alternate solutions. Thus, if one advances one hypothesis to account for the behavior of the system recorded through discovery processes employed by the investigator, chances are one will be employing only some of the known facts about this behavior; that is, the hypothesis may be based on only part of the responses of the system. Another hypothesis might account for another set of facts about or responses by the system. The facts which are taken into account by the first hypothesis may or may not overlap those covered by the second hypothesis; that is, some of the facts or behaviors may support both hypotheses. Then further investigation is constrained in one way by one hypothesis, and in another way by the other, and the investigator must make a choice before he goes on. While the choice is a convergent process, as is the formation of each hypothesis, the fact that more than one is formed and that a choice is required is due to a divergent process, and without this divergent process there would be no choice; one would converge along one path or possible route only, and thus one's choice would be more limited. This would imply a lower probability of success, as well as a lower level of sophistication of knowledge. Thus the divergent process appears as equal in importance to the convergent one; they complement each other.

In the case where the investigator or problem solver or learner is attempting to relate stimuli to a small set of responses, we expect him to generate a hypothesis or a set of hypotheses which reduce randomness and increase constraint. However, where he is attempting to explain the behavior of a more complex system, he is expected to generate a number of alternate hypotheses and to vary the factors involved on purpose in order to observe whether one or the other accounts for additional outcomes. Ultimately the objective is the same in both cases, to reduce randomness or induce order into one's symbolic handling of a system. In the second case, however, the situation is so much more complex that one must seem to "go the other way" at first before making progress; this process of "looking away from the problem," of acting as though one were not trying to converge on it too soon, has long been a strategy of problem solving. It is based on divergent processes, and these processes may not emerge if the learner has been too thoroughly conditioned to produce convergent solutions in his early learning experience.

12-8 An Example of Interaction with a System

In a problem-solving situation in science each student is given four containers. Each container has a different powder, and they are numbered one through four. In addition, each student has sixteen unlabeled envelopes of powders, distributed as follows: four soda, four starch, two sugar, two salt, two starch plus soda, two starch plus salt. In front of each of the four bottles of powder are placed three small plastic containers. Powder from each bottle is put into each of the three containers in front of it. The student is to test each of the powders with three things, water, vinegar, and iodine. Then he is given a collection of cups and directed to use the information he gained from this to sort the powders in the sixteen additional envelopes. He writes or draws his observations directly on the envelopes if he wishes.

In this problem of identification, the exemplars are the powders and their attributes are determined by chemical tests, for example, "gets cloudy in water," "turns dark with iodine," "fizzes or bubbles in vinegar." The envelopes containing the unclassified powders are mostly pure examples of the four types already tested, but some are ambiguous, that is, they could be classified in more than one way. In the unambiguous cases, the data does not overlap from the various tests; that is, when all tests are applied, there are not conflicting or confusing outcomes. For example, baking soda gets cloudy in water and fizzes in vinegar, but has no reaction to iodine, and no other powder in the experiment has either of these two reactions. Thus there is redundancy of relevant dimensions. Also, this is a conjunctive concept, and therefore we may expect that it is fairly easy to identify since the students have had previous experience with such concepts. The ambiguous cases are less redundant and are disjunctive in nature, and so one may expect that they would be more difficult.

In one investigation of this problem there was an interesting outcome related to the placement of the ambiguous (confusing, more difficult) cases in the sequence. If these were examined first, subsequent performance on the simpler cases showed high error rates. If the ambiguous cases were introduced in the middle of the investigation, errors were low; this would imply that they were absorbed in the hypothesis-testing procedure without too much difficulty or interference. Finally, if they were introduced later, errors were even higher than when they came in the first position. This unexpected outcome might suggest that the hypotheses developed earlier had become well accepted and were considered reliable by that point, and thus that the ambiguous cases upset a learning set already established (this is of course only one of many possible explanations). Such interactions of variables in learning systems need greatly increased exploration if better teaching strategies are to be discovered. They are part of what were previously called "mathemagenic" behaviors.*

*The experiment described was reported to the author by Mary Badd Rowe of Teacher's College, Columbia, in mimeographed form.

Bibliography

BRUNER, JEROME, ed. *Learning About Learning: A Conference Report.* Washington, D.C.: U.S. Government Printing Office, 1966.

KLEINMUNTZ, B., ed. *Problem Solving: Research, Method, and Theory.* New York: John Wiley and Sons, Inc., 1966.

13 Teaching Problem Solving

13–1 Some Teaching Strategies

One can teach concepts and processes related to problem solving at the same time he teaches algorithms for solving particular problems: this is part of "learning to learn." One way to accomplish this is to expose the student to a number of problems which are similar in nature, controlling the complexity (number of relevant and irrelevant dimensions), the redundancy, and the difficulty of the responses required as outcomes of the process. This has already been alluded to several times previously. Through feedback and discussion the student will come to be able to identify the relevant and irrelevant attributes of the problem, and to learn the sequence of events involved in the solution, and thus to increase his ability to cope with this type.

Another approach concentrates on one particular problem. This is more typical of the traditional tutorial function, where teachers are called upon to assist students in problem solving, and often need to furnish enough assistance to the student without being able to call upon a prior sequence of easier examples. This form of guidance, in which the tutor furnishes advice and hints and information to the student, has been treated in a number of books and papers through the years. Generally, the art of such tutoring consists of assisting the student on a general level (rather than getting into details of the particular problem), and thus paving the way for transfer to other problem-solving activities.

13–2 An Historic Precept

What are some of the general processes that are effective and can be taught? One of the most powerful was enunciated by the mathematician Pappus around A. D. 300. He said: "Assume what is required to be done as already done."* This is in a sense analogous to the divergent thinking requirement developed previously, because it releases the mind to conjure up various ways by which this as-yet-unrealized event might have been realized, and avoids overconcern with the problem of whether

*Gyorgy Polya, *How to Solve It.*(New York: Anchor Doubleday paperback,1957).

or not it will be realized. It also relates to the "looking away from the problem" brought up earlier.

13–3 Postulates of Heuristics

Another general postulate of *heuristics* (that is, the study of the solving of problems generally, rather than of a particular problem) is that one should look for the unknown. If one is presented a problem, particularly verbally, it may not be clear immediately what facts or tools are needed to solve it. In mathematics, this consists of finding the quantity to represent by the letter x. Finding the unknown may involve interpretation of words, or it may require the location of actual evidence of something missing, for example, "trouble-shooting" a piece of electronic equipment with a missing or faulty part. In the latter case, finding the unknown is a large part of the task; on the other hand, there are some problems where the unknown is obvious, but finding its value or nature is difficult. In other problems, one looks for some process to confirm a given fact; in one sense there is no unknown, in that the fact is accepted or is obvious from a number of examples. The problem is to find a logical process by which one can proceed from previously accepted postulates to the conclusion already known; the unknown in this case is the path or process one chooses.

Another general postulate of heuristics is that one should attempt to relate a given problem to others like it. This is another way of stating that one should have a graded set of problems of the same type, with several at each level of difficulty, in order to teach problem solving. In the absence of such a set, one can approximate the process by asking the student to recall others of its type, or by reminding him of others of that type when he cannot recall them. If one cannot solve the given problem this way, he can often solve a related problem, or a simplified version of the problem, and thus gain some insight into the handling of this type of task. This then becomes a special case of presenting a series of problems of a given type, where the initial ones are simplified in various ways; rather than starting at the first of such a series, however, one begins in the middle somewhere and works backward until he finds the type of problem which suits the student's ability.

Another principle of problem solving, related to the prescription of Pappus quoted previously, is that one should make some estimate of the outcome of the task, or the solution, before he gets into the details. For instance, if one has the problem of multiplying the numbers 8.100347 and 1.946328, one should be surprised if he comes out with the answer 158.032, since the final result should be around sixteen. Also, after one arrives at a solution that seems to be in the right "ball park," one should, if possible, solve the problem by another strategy or

method, to check the details of the result. Ideally, the solution will be
the same by both methods.

13–4 Further Discussion of Heuristics, or the Science of Problem Solving

Obviously the success of any of the approaches mentioned above, or to
be mentioned, depends on the motivation of the student (where motivation is a vague word used to describe the time and effort a given student
will put into such a process). If this is high, then one need not structure
the situation as much as when it is low. Furthermore, if the student does
this structuring himself, instead of requiring the teacher to do it, he
learns something about the structuring process. This is part of learning
to solve problems generally. Thus if he can "get it on his own," he will
often (not always) learn more about the problem, and solving problems
of that type. An exception to this is the case where the student applies
some previously learned strategy successfully and thus overlooks or is
unaware of some strategy which is more efficient for solving the problem; this other strategy may also be necessary in solving another more
complex type of problem, and if he does not practice it on the simpler
version, he may not be able to cope with the more complex.

In future teaching–learning systems, students may be brought to a
number of different solutions for each type of problem; their progress
will be measured in terms of the types of strategies learned rather than
the number of problems or level of problems solved. When the processes are better understood and the sequences of tasks required to learn
them have been programmed, students will be able to solve problems
which now cause great difficulty as a matter of course.

At the same time we will be able to teach the strategies of solving
problems; through analysis and programming of sequences of exemplars or tasks (thus teaching these strategies as concepts), we will be
able to shape the attitudes and behaviors that are subsumed under the
title *motivation*.

13–5 The Inventor's Paradox

There is a prescription or principle of problem solving which says, "The
more ambitious plan may have more chances of success." This does
not immediately fit into the views of problem solving discussed thus far.
It might be likened to a "wholistic" approach as compared with a "partistic" one: this matter has been considered already. Perhaps it is warning us that one can break any task down into so many constituent parts
that it is difficult to put them back together again, and that one can
make a fairly simple situation more difficult by treating it in a nitpicking
manner. Perhaps by focusing on a larger problem, one deals with behavioral units or general concepts that enable one to "see the forest instead
of the trees," to focus on the level of operation that is most suited to

the solution process, to identify the crucial aspects of the situations, to see what is relevant and ignore what is irrelevant. Also, since concepts, and thus problems, are hierarchical, depending on other concepts and other solution processes, one may, by choosing the more difficult task, bring into play more complex behaviors and larger units of behaviors, and these may be better able to support the problem-solving process. This is all speculation, of course, and much more exploration of the matter is called for.

13–6 A Problem-Solving Set

One final aspect of problem solving which is important to teach or condition is a habit or set or predilection for solving problems. Visitors to underdeveloped countries are often amazed at the lack of interest of the people in doing anything about problems, or their inability to believe that anything *can* be done about them, or their unwillingness to understand it is permissible or right to do anything about them. This has something to do with the perception of the world that the culture engenders and is related to motivation. However, to condition in students the desire to solve problems and the belief that problems *can* be solved is a necessary and important part of the teaching process. This is done through example, through experience, through shaping of problem-attacking and problem-defining behaviors over long periods of time. It is important to teach students to ask questions, and to ask the right kinds of questions; this in turn requires a teaching process that reinforces questioning and shapes it carefully. When followed to the extreme, this kind of behavior can be seen in the quest of mathematicians and scientists on the frontiers of knowledge, who have the conviction that they can answer any question, and are searching primarily for the right questions to ask.

13–7 Group Problem Solving

Most analyses and discussions of problem solving have to do with the way the individual processes information and comes to solve a problem. There is some research and theory related to the effect of a group on the problem-solving process. In some of the research it is evident that the effect of having several persons interacting in solving a problem is to increase the probability that the problem will be solved: several heads are better than one. There are a number of factors involved that may explain this.

Suppose a problem has five steps in its solution, and each step requires a different kind of operation—synthesis, substitution, or such. Suppose that one individual is able to perform three of the five, and that another individual can perform the other two. Then the probability of the two of them being able to solve the problem working together would seem to be higher than the probability of either of them solving it alone. This is an extremely simple case illustrating the idea that where there are several steps, a group of individuals is more likely to have the necessary expertise than any one individual taken at random. This is one source, then, of group superiority in problem solving. Obviously, in a group where one individual knows all five steps and has solved such problems before, the other members are no help to that individual although he is of great help to them—that is, he could solve it by himself but they could not. However, since one cannot usually tell in advance whether one person alone has the expertise, one may conclude that he has a better chance of having the problem solved by a group rather than by any one individual working on it.

If one's objective is to bring a number of persons to learn to solve a kind of problem, that is, if one's objective is teaching rather than problem solving per se, then one might conclude that the initial experience should be by a group, or better still, a group of two, where one of the participants is experienced at solving such problems and knows all of the stages or steps to be performed. This must be qualified, however, by considerations of guidance versus discovery, that is, by research that indicates some advantages to having the student discover solutions himself rather than having them shown to him by a teacher. This has already been discussed. Another factor involved in the individual versus group problem-solving comparison has to do with motivation (individual effort as compared with group support). This would seem to be at least partly a matter of background, that is, whether the persons involved had learned to work in groups and to expect and need the support of others, or whether they had learned to work alone and found interaction with others distracting and interfering with their cognitive processes.

Other factors relate to the nature of interpersonal interactions in the group. Some research has indicated that certain combinations of personality result in interference in the interpersonal sphere which upsets the theoretical advantage of group solving processes. In some cases, social power and status interfere, in that the less able person has more status or prestige than the more able one, and thus his hypotheses or processes are attended to and the other's are ignored. In other cases, heterogeneity of aptitude for a type of task has been found to interfere in rather unexpected ways: in one study, a homogeneous group of low ability performed better on a creative type of task than a homogeneous team of high ability (in this kind of task), whereas wholly mixed groups performed according to expectations derived from their mean ability.

13–8 Further Instructional Considerations

The teacher's role in problem solving has been discussed previously: it has been suggested that he should provide only as much guidance as is absolutely necessary to assure that the student will solve the problem. However, there are many factors operating in this process, and so the simple maxim just stated is really not adequate for practical application. First of all, one must consider the amount of time required. Perhaps the student eventually will solve a given problem at his present rate, but if the teacher does not have enough time to be present throughout the entire process, he may speed up the process somewhat by giving additional assistance. Second, one must consider the alternate strategies. Perhaps there is a strategy which the student will succeed with, but it is not as powerful a strategy as the one which the teacher wants him to learn. Then the teacher may set up requirements in the problem that prevent the student from using the simpler strategy, and may furnish additional cuing and help so that the student can succeed at least partially with the more complicated one. Then there is the problem of repetition versus variation, already discussed in respect to concept formation (remember, how to solve a certain kind of problem may be considered a concept, or in the terminology of an earlier chapter, a process which is itself a sequential concept). Once the student has solved one problem, he should be exposed to others of the same type, where the irrelevant variables are varied and relevant ones remain constant, and where the number of irrelevant and relevant dimensions may increase. But it may also be helpful initially to have the student repeat the solution of the same problem, by the same strategy, as well as by other possible strategies. There is little research evidence on such matters by which one can formulate instructional hypotheses.

13–9 Computer Simulation of Problem Solving

One way to study the process of problem solving is to make a machine that solves problems: in making the machine, one gains insight into what such a machine requires and indirectly discovers some mechanisms or circuits that might possibly be characteristic of the human brain. This is model making of the concrete kind, rather than of the abstract kind, which can also be devised to represent cognitive functions as well as mathematical relationships. One method of devising problem-solving machines has been to ask human problem solvers to report in detail their problem-solving processes when confronted by fairly simple, standard problems such as transforming expressions in symbolic logic, then translating this record into a computer program. The computer goes about solving the problem as described previously. It compares the current state of the problem with the desired final state, selects some operation which it has been taught (that is, which has been stored in its memory) to use on the current problem, and then compares the result with the final criterion state again to determine whether progress has been made. It continues to operate in this way until it achieves the criterion. Since the computer can perform the same operations over and over with tremendous speed, it makes up in speed for what it may lack in complexity of cognitive functioning; that is, it gets along with only a few simple operations (cognitive processes) repeated over and over at high speed.

One element of this problem-solving process which is not ordinarily emphasized is nevertheless of prime importance when considering problems of instruction: it is a problem that comes up very often in programming instruction for human learners. This is the recognition–comparison function required of the computer—the requirement that the computer compare a given state of the "problem" to the final state and determine whether there is a difference or not. This requirement limits the ability of the computer to solve complex problems; the more complex a problem, the more difficult it is to "read" the present state and compare it with the final one in many cases. This problem is met in attempting to set up learning sequences for students so that they can solve a problem, compare the answer they get to the correct one, and then interpret the difference, if any. One finds that students have some difficulty in simply comparing their own answer with the correct one, and of course they have even more difficulty interpreting any existing differences.

A very difficult problem can have quite simple "states"; that is, it may be very easy to recognize whether one has the correct answer or not but very difficult to determine what to do about it. A crossword puzzle may call for a simple one-syllable word, and it may be very easy to tell when one has the correct one—its letters fit with other elements of the puzzle, for one thing, and it makes sense for another. On the other hand, the description of the word may be very vague, and therefore when one tries a word that doesn't fit it is not easy to know what to "do" about it, that is, how to go about finding the correct one.

Thus we have isolated two elements of problem solving which are common to computer versions and to programmed learning sequences designed to help humans learn: one is the factor of comparison of one's answer with the correct one, the other is the factor of interpreting differences and choosing alternate answers (or alternate strategies in more complex cases). The reader is probably reminded by now of the discussion of strategies in learning concepts; obviously we are getting into some of the same matters here.

Clearly, the learning or solving strategies in the computer situation are the operations which are fed into or "taught to" the computer. If there are several operations possible, then there must also be some routine or system whereby the computer selects the operation to be applied. Perhaps there are cues in the problem itself that determine this, such as, "If the problem has an x in it, then divide by the coefficient of x first."

Perhaps instead, the instruction to the computer, built into the program, is, "Try operation one, and if this doesn't result in a desirable outcome, try operation two." Another approach would be to have the computer select from its possible operations at random, according to a table of random numbers, for example; this would then resemble a stimulus-sampling model of learning.

There is another aspect of computer programs for solving problems which sheds some light on teaching problems as well. In some such techniques there is a "planning" phase. Here the program can simplify the problem by omitting certain details of the original statement or description of it. Then it can rephrase the original problem according to the simpler version, find a solution for the simpler problem, and finally, apply this solution of the simpler problem back to the more complex one. This is a devious way of describing a process whereby the computer "sees through" the problem and views it as a simpler one which it can handle, then goes about the task of solving the more complex one as a simpler one. For example, the computer might take a mathematical statement such as the following:

$$(a + b)x - (rn + t) = c$$

and reduce it to the following problem:

$$fx - g = c,$$

then solve the simpler one and substitute the more complex notation into the solution for the simpler one, that is, substitute $(a + b)$ for f and $(rn + t)$ for g. The reader will recognize certain similarities between this process and elements of heuristics described previously.

The use of a computer to model problem solving becomes very complex and is beyond the scope of this treatment. However, there is another area where the simpler models and instructional concerns merge. One of the current uses of computers in schools is for motivation of students to understand and use mathematics. Students in grades as low as fifth and sixth are taught simple languages for communicating with computers and then asked to program the solution to simple mathematical problems on the computer. In "teaching" the computer to solve simple equations which the students themselves can do fairly easily, these students come to understand the broader nature of the solutions; that is, they are required to abstract the essential operations and relationships more completely and generally, and thus are more able to go on to more difficult problems themselves. There seems to be something about teaching these things to a "stupid" machine which is very motivating to some students: part of this is the control they have over the situation, part the great speed with which the computer can do simple computations and thus relieve the student of this task, and part the sheer enjoyment of the analytic process which this method of instruction requires.

From an analysis of computer problem solving, one can conclude that problem solving is not a rigid, programmed thing, but rather that it requires plans, means for getting out of cul-de-sacs, and ways to monitor one's own behavior so that the solution process does not go off on a wild goose chase.

COMPUTERS THAT LEARN

The ideal model of the problem-solving process would be one where the model derived from solving one problem shows how to solve other similar problems more easily. One obvious area for demonstrating such learning is in respect to simple games like tic-tac-toe or checkers, or simplified versions of these. In certain computer models of learning, the program not only analyzes the input and selects an operation and monitors the results to determine whether it has been successful, but it also returns the results of this process to a central pool of information about that kind of situation, and in such a way that it will react differently the next time it meets the same situation. This process of making current events alter the basic program so that future behavior is different is a basic learning operation, obviously. It also may be viewed as the missing element in elementary stimulus-sampling theory, which implies that a learner selects at random from his store of possible responses or strategies each time he meets a problem.

As work progresses on such programs, it becomes increasingly possible to teach a computer by secondary means, that is, indirectly rather than through actual experience with the situation. This requires a fairly sophisticated computer, one which has either had extensive experience with the problem (game) and thus has sorted a great many relationships and moves, or one into which such "experience" has been programmed in advance by the programmer (that is, a more "intelligent" computer). It is the expectation of investigators in this field that as machines are built to be more and more capable of profiting from experience and learning how to cope with the type of problem presented them, such matters as intuition, intelligence, creativity, and even consciousness will come to have concrete definitions in terms of types and degrees of complexity of circuitry and programming.

13–10 Teaching as Problem Solving

The problem of the teacher is how to bring about learning effectively for one or several or hundreds of students. Whether dealing with one or more than one, an initial task is the analysis of the behavior to be learned and of the behaviors which the students are likely to bring to the task, that is, of their initial or entering behaviors. The more students involved, the greater the variety of entering behaviors. If one deals with one student one can diagnose the present state of learning and deal with it flexibly, within limits, during the tutorial period. This in itself, however, is not a trivial problem, since we do not have theorems of teaching that prescribe the best approach given different degrees or kinds of preparation. If one is dealing with a large number of students simultaneously, however, one must make the diagnosis on the basis of past experience or give tasks that indicate the variety of ability and learning within the group. How one applies this knowledge to the teaching of the group as a whole is a highly complex matter, and one which we will only begin to cope with in later parts of this book. One might assume that the group situation is far less productive because it is inevitably Procrustean in nature, but there is evidence that some teachers can handle large groups with unusual success in reaching individual members, while others have difficulty in adjusting their methods to one student at a time.

Teaching as problem solving can be divided into two general areas, one the cognitive and the other the affective. In the former, one hypothesizes concerning the nature of the difficulty a student or group of students experiences in respect to a given subject; in the latter, one hypothesizes concerning the sources of difficulties one observes in respect to behavior, attitudes, relationships with each other, relationships with the teacher. The two areas are both based on similar learning paradigms, with the classical component of responses perhaps more important in the affective domain. Personality theory and theories of motivation contribute to the formation of hypotheses in both areas. The object of this chapter and this book is to furnish information for the formulation of hypotheses in the problem-solving process called *teaching*, through discussion of personality and motivation in the next chapter as well as through treatment of learning paradigms in previous chapters.

One example of analysis of teaching may clarify the point of view. Suppose a teacher has a class of students at Grade X, and there are N of them. They are about to study Subject A. The class has a mean I.Q. of I, and the previous year they had a mean of P percentile on a standardized achievement test in that subject. C percent of the class intends to go to college and is therefore competing for grades and preparing for college boards; of those, Q percent will take boards in the subject of this class. The students for the most part operate well with the symbolic mode of thinking, at least in this subject, but some are still in transition from the earlier stages. Some are able to deal with concrete operations but are unable to formalize these into general theorems. Of course, this is a relative matter, since their ability to deal with theoretical matters is at an early stage of development. Finally, this class has had a rather authoritarian teacher in this subject during a previous year, and shows the effects: they are withdrawn, not apt to volunteer answers, work well under direction, do not take initiative well and do not work well with each other in groups. Obviously this is a problem situation where a number of parameters must be handled simultaneously. The teacher will be attempting to optimize his treatment of the class and the individuals in it by formulating a course of action that will best take into account the various factors considered important. He will weigh these factors differentially according to his own biases and according to their relative importance in respect to this particular class and its future.

One difficulty encountered by the teacher-as-problem-solver is that feedback is often long delayed and indeed may never appear. Decisions which he makes to meet immediate requirements will have delayed effects that are difficult to assess. As a result, teachers (and others in our culture) seem increasingly prone to base their behavior on more immediately evaluable responses, such as attitudes of the students and social behavior toward each other and toward the teacher, rather than on such outcomes as ability to cope with problem situations in real life and ability to meet the demands of college courses. Some of this is realistic: it is probably both futile and unreasonable to base one's behavior on abstract principles like, "Spare the rod and spoil the child" and the thought that discipline is its own excuse for being. On the other hand, teaching in such a way that students enjoy the subject can be carried so far that the behaviors learned are largely irrelevant to the future needs of the student. More realistically, the success of a teacher is a function of a rather complex set of variables, including the impact of his personality, the relative difficulty of the course, the relevance of the subject matter to student expectations for the future, the requirements of the course in terms of study time, the nature of student–teacher interaction during class. There is some evidence that these are related to the cognitive outcomes, but the relationships are by no means well-established or sufficiently analyzed. Some elements of these relationships will be discussed in Chapter 17.

Bibliography

POLYA, GYORGY. *How To Solve It*. 2d ed. New York: Anchor Doubleday paperback, 1957.

Personality Development and Learning 14

Learning involves emotional as well as cognitive and operant responses. One never teaches without feeling something and, as important, without conveying a feeling to the learner. Thus in any discussion of learning and teaching one must consider the emotional components of behavior as well as the mechanisms by which people adjust to stress and conflict.

The patterns or styles with which a person carries out his adjustment process or the resolution of conflicts make up that person's *personality*. Personality is integrally involved in learning and teaching, since it is a complex of learned behaviors by which the person has come to terms with his environment. While a treatment of personality and adjustment may be seen by some as out of place in a treatment of learning such as this, it cannot be omitted if one is to lay a foundation for decisions concerning teaching. One does not teach a brain or a machine or a set of cognitive abilities; one teaches whole students, and one cannot ignore the person in teaching if he is to achieve satisfactory results.

14–1 Conflict and Adjustment

When a child is young his parents demand certain forms of behavior for acceptance of certain social values. They enforce these by rewards and punishments, often in the form of approval and disapproval. Through these and through the "hard knocks" of other experiences, the child learns complex patterns of behaviors. Some of these show consistency across many situations and thus become typical of him generally. These constitute his behavioral "style" or his personality. Such behavior can be viewed from many frames of reference. For example, in one such view behavior is classified as either *approaching* a situation or *avoiding* it. In another a person is viewed as either an *introvert* or an *extrovert*. In still another he is seen as *tradition directed, inner directed*, or *other directed*.

However one classifies behavior styles, they can be viewed as the result of many problem-solving experiences in which the person has attempted to resolve the conflicting demands of his environment. His ways of solving these problems, his strategies if you will, are part of his means of *adjusting* to his environment. This term implies a reaction to the contingencies of the environment, and implies some reward and punishment system. However, it also implies that the person is seeking a match or a comfortable relationship between the environment and his own internal state, and this in turn implies that the adjustment process is very much dependent on the inner events or conditions of the person himself. Thus it is a very personal kind of thing, and often difficult to observe or report objectively.

Analyses of internal *needs* or *drives* make up a great amount of literature generally referred to as *personality theory*. Some aspects of this theory will be discussed here, but the discussion will not be complete or even deep; the reader will have to seek elsewhere for that. Such a discussion is needed, however, because personality theories for the most part emphasize a view of the learner as one who seeks to find satisfaction and security in a complex environment, rather than one who reacts to contingencies of the environment: the former, more personal point of view is important to an understanding of learners, although it is not as incompatible with a behavioristic frame of reference as is often assumed. To understand learners, then, one should understand them to some degree from both points of view.

Conflicts occur when two or more demands are incompatible. A person adjusts by reducing the number and intensity of these demands. Two general ways of adjusting are accommodation and assimilation. If one accommodates he accepts situations as they are, compromises, and makes the best of things. If one assimilates he tries to satisfy both conflicting demands simultaneously, to "have his cake and eat it too." An example is the basic conflict between the need for security and the need for individuality (assuming that both needs exist, which most theorists do). One wants to be one of the gang, yet one also wants to realize one's own potential as far as possible. Some assimilate by becoming leaders, that is, by making their own objectives those of the group, while others resolve the conflict by accepting some lesser role and thus accommodating to the situation. A third strategy, of recent importance in relation to younger persons in our society, is to accept neither solution, but to opt for individuality and self-direction no matter what the cost. These are of course oversimplified overviews of adjustment, and are only for purposes of initial classification.

Resolution of conflicts is a relative thing: there are many conflicts inherent in living, and different people see different degrees of threat or have different amounts of concern over any particular situation. Some persons are unable for various reasons to resolve a reasonable portion of the conflicts presented by life, and are made anxious by this fact. In extreme situations they may become *maladjusted*, in that they demonstrate one or more symptoms of psychological discomfort. Among these symptoms are physical discomfort, where there is no identifiable physical problem; cognitive inefficiency in the face of rather simple problems; damage to body tissues resulting from worry (usually internal damage); hypochondriacal symptoms (symptoms of ailments that are not present), and certain odd behaviors that seem to represent attempts to adjust to or avoid the problem by acting out unrealistic solutions. It is suggestive to note that when animals are subjected to unavoidable punishment they develop one or more symptoms similar to those just listed. The similarity suggests that failure to resolve a conflict successfully may result from past experience where a person has received aversive treatment no matter what he did or tried to do to avoid it, that is, no matter what solution he attempted.

In discussing avoidance learning, that is, learning reinforced by avoidance of punishment, it was noted that there were negative side effects of such learning due to the fact that punishment was involved. Some of the behaviors of persons who are referred to as *maladjusted* resemble such avoidance behaviors, and as noted earlier, such persons also show some of the side effects of punishment. Thus it seems reasonable to treat such behavioral disorders as if they were avoidance responses. This is an important point of view, since one may regard many of the contingencies of learning that exist in our schools as avoidance contingencies; too often students learn in order to avoid failure and its resultant punishment (primarily social rather than physical), rather than to achieve understanding and thereby gain the rather vague goals which learning has traditionally been supposed to achieve. On the other hand, most of us have learned to learn under this system, and it will take a great deal of relearning if another system is to be substituted successfully.

14–2 Adjustment Mechanisms

People use a number of basic behavior mechanisms to adjust to their environment, particularly to avoidance-related situations. These are sometimes appropriately called *defense mechanisms*, implying that the person sees the environment as threatening and tries to build up defenses against it. In understanding the relationship to conditioning paradigms, it might be well to review avoidance learning. Just as a signal such as a bell can elicit fear in an animal if it has been followed previously by punishment, so certain *response-produced* stimuli can come to elicit fear in humans if those responses have previously been punished, either by physical blows or by social disapproval. *Anticipation* of a punished response will also elicit fear; then the response may be *suppressed* in order to reduce such fear as well as to avoid the punishment. There is some evidence that one can avoid thinking about making such responses; there are such suppression mechanisms in the brain, and also, one can think about something else when cues arise that are signs for the response to be avoided. This seems to be at least part of what is involved in the mechanisms described below.

If one misses a shot in golf, he may blame it on the fact that he had a bad "lie" or was using the wrong club or that someone made a noise while he was swinging. He will thus suppress the feeling (or use the feeling as a cue to suppress the thought) of personal inadequacy. This misplaced blame also may serve to avoid adverse comments from other players, or covert opinions they might hold but not express; such opinions and expressions may originally have been the source of the feeling of inadequacy that he is trying to avoid. This process is called *rationalization*, wherein one recognizes only those associations that do not threaten one's self-concept.

Another adjustment mechanism is *projection*, wherein one avoids conscious recognition of certain aspects of his own behavior or appearance by "recognizing" it in others. This avoids the aversive effects of recognition of or concentration on one's shortcomings. Avoidance is also present in *reaction formation*, where people behave as if they felt the opposite of their true feelings: a child who has strong aggressive tendencies may guard against expressing them by acting in an overly friendly way. In another such mechanism, *regression*, one acts as though he were at an earlier stage of development and thus avoids the conflicts which are present and which are facing him in his present stage. Adolescents can regress at odd times and act in a completely infantile manner. This is sometimes due to adult behavior that does not recognize their age and responsibility, sometimes to chance stimuli that generalize to earlier behavior. Part of the reinforcement is the security remembered from being at that earlier age.

One can withdraw from situations mentally, through fantasies, or by removing oneself from situations physically. Another way to avoid meeting obligations and resolving conflicts is through *intellectualization*, wherein one builds theories about problems or conflicts and thus escapes dealing with them. One can achieve a similar escape or avoidance by simply labeling the problems and acting as if finding an appropriate description or title for them in some way constitutes a solution. Activism on college campuses reflects in part a feeling that college faculties use this defense mechanism to a large degree to avoid grappling with serious problems in our contemporary society.

Sometimes people avoid the punishing outcomes of responding aggressively to an authoritarian, punitive person or group by submitting to such treatment at the time, and then expressing their pent-up reactions against another object in some way resembling the person or group responsible. Thus students sometimes take out resentments against parents on teachers, or resentments against teachers on parents. This is called *displacement*. In an institution such as a boarding school or prison, complaints about the food often represent such displaced resentments toward the institution as a whole. More generally, one may be angry at certain persons and take it out on others less likely to fight back: "scapegoating," where students pick on one of their peers, is an example of this.

One may deal with failure in a given area, such as athletics, by devoting oneself to other pursuits; this is called *compensation.* One may also substitute an activity that is reinforced for another (usually sexually based) that is punished, as when one substitutes artistic endeavor for sexual behavior not allowed by society. This is called *sublimation.*

Teachers must deal with adjustment mechanisms under classroom conditions involving groups as well as individuals. It is therefore more difficult to be entirely objective due to the fact that there is an audience. If a student denies to himself and others that he is at fault in a certain situation, the teacher may find it necessary to prove that he is to blame, since prestige is at stake. It is difficult to take into account that the student may not really be aware of the true causal relationships, yet in many cases of defense behaviors the person is *not* aware—that is the value of the mechanism. On the other hand, if a student uses a particular defense process too frequently, to the point where it becomes a habit, this self-delusion prevents objective, clear thought necessary for good scholarship. Thus the use of defense mechanisms can interfere with cognitive functioning.

If a teacher feels that a student or many students are using defense mechanisms too frequently, and that as a result, cognitive functioning is not what it might be, he or she should consider two possible approaches to remedying the situation. First, the possibility that the environment is too threatening, thus causing defense mechanisms, should be considered, and something done about the threats if possible: the classroom should be a place of security from threats both without and within (should be, but sometimes cannot be). Second, the teacher should consider the possibility of discussing adjustment mechanisms with the students, and leading them to discover more about themselves from this point of view, so that they may see the difficulties and avoid them where they threaten to interfere with their ability to function effectively. This last is being called by some *psychological education,* and will probably gain acceptance in schools in the next few years. Generally speaking, however, the main value to a teacher in understanding defense or adjustment mechanisms is in viewing them objectively and thus not reacting to them as to a personal threat or as if the child were in some way attacking the teacher or being evil. Less threatening examples of such defenses can be altered by suitable nonpunitive comments by the teacher over a number of situations where they occur. This preventive kind of therapy is helpful since it does not allow such habits, where potentially harmful, to gain strength and become deeply ingrained. In some cases, on the other hand, the teacher may decide that a particular adjustment mechanism is needed by the child to get him over a particular developmental hurdle. Generally speaking, an accepting and encouraging attitude on the part of the teacher will reduce defense mechanisms and help students view themselves realistically and objectively.

Where a defense mechanism needs to be eliminated, conditions can be arranged to bring it out and then not reinforce it, that is, to extinguish it. This usually means arranging for the person to be successful in situations where he has come to expect failure, thus reducing the fear component. For children in whom certain inhibitions are very strongly developed, this may be a difficult state to bring about, however.

14–3 General Anxiety

A history of failure and punishment in many different situations often causes anticipation of negative outcomes from a variety of environmental contingencies more or less closely related to them. This fear is called *general anxiety* or *free-floating anxiety*. It implies continual stress, not unlike that which occurs in a conflict situation, but with no particular cause. Stress interferes with the solution of new problems or conflicts, in that it narrows one's perceptual field and makes it more difficult to take a number of variables into account. It leads to defense activities that eliminate the stress at the expense of a realistic appraisal of the conflict. These activities may also lead to maladaptive behaviors. Of course not all conflicts can be resolved satisfactorily, and a certain amount of psychosomatic symptomatology or neurotic behavior is inevitable in any normal person.

Anxiety as generalized fear cannot be alleviated easily, partly because it is not practicable to extinguish fear to all of the stimuli that elicit it. It often leads to psychosomatic disorders, symptoms of insomnia, nervousness, difficulties in concentrating, fatigue, exhaustion, irrational fears, unreasonable preoccupations with bodily health and imaginary symptoms. These are conditioned responses, and they receive negative reinforcement by some reduction of the anxiety, possibly because a recognizable symptom or problem gives one something to be anxious about and the known is less threatening than the unknown. On the other hand, even though the original causes of the fear have generalized to a number of stimuli, one might still expect some limited success with extinction procedures because extinction (as a type of response) also generalizes from one stimulus to another.

14–4 Personality and the Self-Concept

Personality can be regarded as a concept about a person which others develop by observing him in a number of different situations. His behavior in these situations becomes the exemplars of the concept; consistencies become relevant dimensions, inconsistencies to some degree irrelevant. If we call a person an *introvert,* for example, we are saying that generally speaking his responses imply that he is more concerned than the average person about his own reactions and responses and thoughts, and less concerned about those of others. This contrasts with an *extrovert,* who directs his responses and thoughts to other people and their behavior; the latter's concern for others may be an indirect expression of his own concern for himself or it may be more complex than that, but his behavorial pattern leads one to expect more attention to others and more overt verbal behavior regarding others.

A person also forms a concept of himself. This concept is sometimes quite different from that formed by others; that is, a person does not necessarily see himself as others see him. One's self-concept (concept of himself) can be affected strongly by early experiences; for example: the child who is relatively small initially may feel small all his life, though he grows to be more than six feet tall. Adults have a tendency to respond to their parents (and teachers) as they did when they were still children.

Generally one's concept of himself is formed from the responses of others to him, since he cannot observe himself well otherwise. If one is persecuted and rejected, he forms a concept of himself as of low value. If one is treated as if he were handsome and attractive, then he sees himself in that light. There are cases where people with very low opinions of themselves have been treated by their acquaintances as if they were much more sociable and attractive and able than they think they are. This has in some cases had striking effects on the person's self-concept and resulting behavior; that is, the person forms a new concept and behaves differently toward others as a result.

One's self-concept to some degree determines what he tries to do and succeeds in doing, and previous successes and failures determine one's self-concept. However, previous experience may not apply to a present situation, although one thinks it does: in this case one is perhaps identifying irrelevant dimensions of the situation as relevant, that is, misidentifying a concept. People are not notably objective about themselves and sometimes act as if they are trying to confirm their low self-concept and prove that it is correct by making sure that things come out the way they would if it *were* correct. In such situations, the self-concept becomes a self-fulfilling prophecy. This can be seen as problem solving in which the feedback (outcomes) is not interpreted accurately or in which the situation is not sampled thoroughly by the learner: erroneous solutions thus persist.

Since the self-concept develops from the interaction of the person with his environment, it can be changed on the basis of new experience that brings out relevant dimensions from the past. The self strives for consistency, either through hereditary predispositions or through past learning of rational processes, and so inconsistent experiences threaten it. By examining one's own behavior and past record objectively, one may perceive inconsistencies in his concept of himself and develop an improved self-concept. This sometimes requires personal confrontation of memories that are threatening or uncomfortable. Since words are the tools by which we deal with past experience, one way to confront the past is to put failures and guilts as well as successes into words and express them. This is easier to do if one has an audience, since there is a certain cultural taboo concerning talking to oneself, and that audience must obviously be an accepting, nonpunitive one or else the person is not going to do that much talking about things that are uncomfortable anyway.

Thus what is needed is an audience that will accept some generally unacceptable revelations without reacting negatively or punitively. Such acceptance allows the expression of the thoughts so that they may be examined objectively, also so that the fear component conditioned to them may be extinguished. Now if the audience (perhaps an audience of one) responds selectively to those elements that are potentially most helpful for the person to examine, reinforcing certain types of responses while remaining neutral in reaction to the others, then the process of bringing out the past and discussing oneself may be even more helpful. This is what is done in what is called *nondirective* therapy, although the language for describing such therapy does not ordinarily use reinforcement theory terms. Contact with a person who is genuine, internally consistent, acceptant, and empathetic can help one reorganize one's perception of himself and his environment. This can then result in one's becoming more realistic in his self-perception, more confident and empathetic himself, more self-directing, more valued by himself, and also less repressive of disturbing memories. This then results in more mature socialization and adaptation, less upset by stress, and quicker recovery from such upset. Generally it can result in a more healthy and well-integrated personality structure.

This process can be regarded as a problem-solving one, where the therapist provides selective reinforcement of hypotheses and tests of hypotheses that are potentially helpful to the learner in making his self-concept more realistic and positive. What goes for conflicts and anxieties in therapy also goes for difficulties experienced in academic pursuits. A teacher who provides an accepting, encouraging, and selectively reinforcing audience to one or more students engaged in attempting to understand some concept or process in some subject is in a similar position, except that the subject matter is a little less personal and potentially threatening. However, one should not assume that any subject matter or any attempt to understand is devoid of personal involvement or threat, because it does not work out that way. All learning situations are also personal and social, and all learning is threatening in that the person feels insecurity and threat of failure, and gropes for adaptations of old strategies and concepts that will apply to a given situation. The self-concept of the learner as a learner is at stake as well: too many failures, too many blind alleys will "turn him off" and he will reject the learning process. He may continue to do what is necessary to avoid failure, but the entire process then will be tinged with the negative side effects of avoidance learning, and he will not operate as effectively as he might (this does not, however, imply that the threat of failure should be entirely absent, or that some degree of risk is not helpful to learning). It seems appropriate to assert, then, that many teachers misconstrue the degree of threat and risk in the typical classroom situation by underestimating it, and misconstrue adjustment mechanisms of students as motivated by a desire to attack the teacher. Their negative reactions, some of which add to the threat, therefore increase this kind of behavior and make the situation worse. If, on the other hand, the teacher has a well-organized course with consistent and reasonable demands both cognitive and behavioral, this in itself represents more than enough pressure or threat, and the teacher can then assume that his role becomes one of alleviating the effects of such threat in respect to those students who are least able to cope with it. Among these will be students who from another point of view would be classed as "behavior problems," and while they are still problems, the teacher may regard them objectively as such rather than defending against them as a threat to his or her person.

14–5 A Developmental Analysis of Personality

Perhaps the most famous theory of personality development, that of Sigmund Freud, employed among others a three-fold model of internal structure guiding behavior. While this model is now part of history, some elements of it are currently used and also have interesting relationships to behavior paradigms already discussed in this book.

The basic component of this model is what is called the *id*, an inherited source of energy that seeks to "discharge" itself immediately through reflex actions, to gain physical pleasure and the satisfaction of basic needs. If thwarted in this it will discharge its energy in the form of fantasies which create a direct or disguised image of those things that would remove the tensions it has caused.

Another component is the *ego*; it develops as a result of the infant inability to reduce tension by primary processes (that is, fantasies, creation of images of things which remove tension) and is useful because it acts on the environment to predict and bring about behaviors that will satisfy the needs of the id. Thus it is a utilization of cognition to satisfy the needs, rather than a blind behaving inspired by the id itself.

The *superego* is the third component, and it develops out of rewards and punishments that come to the child, usually through the parents. It is an internal representation of values and ideals of the culture. It includes the conscience as the sum total of those things which are "wrong," and the ego-ideal as the sum total of those which are "right."

One can view these three components in terms of basic learning paradigms as well. The id can be viewed as a force which acts continuously, and in this sense is equivalent to a state of deprivation in that it is reinforced by stimuli related to pleasurable and desirable outcomes of behaving, in a very basic way (food, water, sex, comfort—the "primitive" or "basic" needs). The conscience-like component of the superego can be viewed as the sum of all punished behaviors, or the anticipation of negative outcomes based on past experience; this anticipation is elicited by the initial stimuli in the chain of behaviors which led to the undesirable outcome, and this anticipation is felt as fear or a "twinge of conscience." The *ego-ideal* is probably less an outcome of direct experience than a concept of what "works" in personality, formed by observation of successful and unsuccessful exemplars (other persons) in important situations. The ego then can be viewed as the "problem-solver," which applies the dictates of the id and guidance of the superego to effectively cope with reality. The ego is based on operant conditioning relative to successful strategies of coping with conflicts and threats, on classical conditioning which results in generalizing and discriminating stimuli according to their relative effects on the emotional structure of the personality, and on verbal learning and concept formation. It effects some balance between id and superego; it makes behavior effective and productive.

When the energy of the id is blocked, for example, by social mores, energy accumulates and flows into various psychological systems. An object that permits the discharge of this energy is said to be *cathected*. Energy has then become *invested* in an image that serves to motivate behavior by increasing the person's sensitivity to particular objects. The force or energy which activates life instincts or survival instincts and permits them to perform their work is called *libido*: sex is the most important of these. The blocking or channeling of these basic forces results in anxiety, then, which is of three general types: (a) objective anxiety, resulting from actual traumatic experiences in early life which are generalized to other similar situations; (b) psychotic anxiety that relates the ego to the id, where the ego fears loss of control over the forces of the id and to prevent this instigates some behaviors that are harmful to the organism itself, much as if it were trying to put out a fire and in the process harmed property not actually threatened by the blaze; (c) neurotic anxiety, where the ego is combating overactivity on the part of the conscience (superego), which results in what we feel as "guilt." One way such tensions are reduced is by displacement, where the blocked energy is turned into other channels that are not threatening. Another way to reduce tension is through repression, where the tensions and their causes are avoided by not recognizing them. These were involved in the behavior mechanisms discussed previously.

14–6 The Psychosexual Stages and Adolescence

One contribution of Freud to the developmental aspects of personality, which has particular implications for adolescence, is his classification of early development into stages. He postulated that the child goes through three major stages before school age. The first is the oral stage, where the main concern of the child is with oral behavior, sucking being the original one. The second is the anal stage, where the preoccupation is with defecation. In the first, the behavior is primarily the operant one of taking in liquid through the mouth and the classical accompaniments have to do with the warmth of the mother or nurse and the timing of reinforcement in response to demands. In the second, the operant behavior has to do with restraining natural reflexes related to expulsion, with classical accompaniments resulting from parental concern over bowel control. While both of these have implications for later behavior, the most important stage in relation to adolescent behavior is the phallic stage, the period of the famous—or infamous—Oedipal conflict. Here the preoccupation of the child is with genitalia, either male or female, and with the father–mother–child relationship. For boys, there exists competition with the father for the mother's love, and ultimately the compromise occurs where the boy identifies with the father and postpones his need for sole possession of the mother. For girls, there is the competition with the mother for the father's love, and ultimately a similar identification with the parent of the same sex. The guilt and concern which the child feels over his love for the parent of the opposite sex, or perhaps even for the same sex, evidently causes relatively minor problems in the years immediately following these early ones: social concerns, adjustment to peers and the like may interfere, or there may be a period of physical *latency* in relation to such feelings. However, during adolescence the increase in sexual drive results in reawakened fears concerning incestuous love, and causes the adolescent to turn away from his parents (as a defense mechanism against his love) to peers and other figures for relationships and identification objects. Some are less successful than others in achieving satisfaction in this way, and those who are less successful may call upon other less acceptable defenses against these urges, such as hostility toward parents or outright aggression against them. For those who are more successful, there are still dangers in this period because of the adolescent's need for substitute figures and the possibilities of having this need filled in ways that will cause difficulty and guilt later on.

This kind of analysis confirms the popular view of the adolescent as a unique form of human being, and also views that adolescents are generally uncooperative and unpleasant. However, some investigations of adolescents in suburban types of cultures contradict this myth of the "adolescent subculture" and make it apparent that the adolescent's social behavior is carefully structured through cooperative planning between them and their parents, and that there is very little of the *"Sturm und Drang"* that traditionally has been seen as characterizing this age.

14–7 Sexual Versus Social Bases of Personality

This original developmental theory of personality was preoccupied with sexual tensions and repressions; subsequent theories have emphasized the social bases of human behavior. An early one, that of Jung, looked toward racial origins of personality development, seeing in the realm of the mind of which a person is not conscious the latent memories that are his ancestral heritage. He classified these into "archetypes" such as the universal mother. He assumed that humans understand each other through such common inherited concepts: for instance, man understands woman because he has in himself the feminine archetype. These might be viewed as the evolutionary inheritance of man which determines what things are most easily learned by him. Perhaps the four types of concepts mentioned previously are also such archetypes for learning, and there are other types which might be discovered that would enable us to cope with our complex culture more effectively!

Jung was also responsible for introducing the concept of extroversion (orientation toward others) and introversion (orientation toward self) as classifications for personalities; in this he represented the trait-type school of personality study. Since Jung, theorists have emphasized the role of social structures and types even more. Man is seen as a creature whose principal motivation comes from social needs. He has a self (ego) which organizes and interprets experiences, and which searches for experiences that fulfill a unique life style. The way he is treated in early life determines his expectations and his behaviors: for example, if he is pampered or spoiled he will have a faulty life-style and will be unable to delay rewards sufficiently to achieve what he wants. Sociability, individuality, and creativity are proposed motives or needs, all related more or less directly to his early conditioning.

One classification of such needs emphasizes their hierarchical nature. After basic needs for food and water are satisfied, then there are needs for belongingness, transcendence (creativity), rootedness, identity, and frame of reference (something to identify with). There is also a central struggle involving all these needs; this reflects a sense of aloneness that we all have, the struggle between the fear of isolation on one hand and the desire for personal growth on the other. This is the existential problem discussed previously.

Modern theories regarding social bases of personality probably reflect the increase in socialization and organizational behavior which characterizes our culture. Recently, however, there has been emphasis on the need for people to realize their potential, to feel at home with themselves, and to emphasize the inherent goodness of man. This view sees aggressiveness and destructiveness as motives brought on by unfortunate contingencies of the society or the unique history of the individual, particularly by rejection and punitiveness on the part of others (mainly parents). This in its extreme would imply that if everyone treated everyone else properly in this world, there would be no aggressiveness and destruction, and that these characteristics or traits of individual or collective personalities are artificial, not inherited.

The opposite view is that aggressiveness and destructiveness are inherited traits that have been of evolutionary value. One must provide ways of channeling this aggressiveness for the good of society. It does seem possible that neither is completely right, each partly so, and that we have latent aggressive tendencies that even the most careful and considerate handling cannot avoid touching off occasionally. For example, the complexity of relationships even in a small group may inevitably lead to situations where aggressiveness is brought out in one or more members. On the other hand, it may well be that in trying to avoid aggressiveness we keep it repressed so that it gains strength from being dammed up: this implies that the result of such repression is more serious aggression. Some investigators point out that such traits as friendship and love occur only in those species that show intraspecific aggression; friendship and love are protections against inherent tendencies toward destruction of one's own species, perhaps even of oneself.

In addition to aggressive tendencies there probably exist tendencies toward maximum use of one's potential. The need for realization of one's potential, for competence and control of the environment, for success in what one does has been posed as a basic motive. Persons who demonstrate this kind of motivation in the extreme are called *self-actualizing* persons. They are people who are generally more simple and natural than others, more spontaneous in their behavior, more concerned than most over showing such traits as laziness, thoughtlessness, loss of temper, prejudice, jealousy, envy, as well as shortcomings of the group or culture with which they identify themselves. Their motivation seems to stem from a desire to expand, to express themselves, to grow rather than to overcome shortcomings or make up for lacks or acquire things they need. They tend to focus on problems outside themselves, and in this sense are extroverts. They are generally no problem *to* themselves, accepting themselves pretty much as they are. They can be alone without being uncomfortable, and actually like a degree of solitude and privacy. They can experience again and again the basic things of life with the same degree of appreciation, including art, music, children, and sexual pleasure. Such people seem to have deeper relationships with others, but also maintain fewer of them.

14–8 Extreme Environmental Effects on Personality

If an individual is exposed to an environment in which he is punished without possibility of escape and thus sees the world as a threatening place, then he will have to handle his anticipations of aversive outcomes somehow in order to maintain some semblance of normality and security. One way he can do this is by imagining situations that restore the balance, that make him able to cope with his environment, that reduce the threat. Children often find themselves in such situations, where it seems that no matter what they do they will end up being punished and reproved: it does not help them that the adult sees it as a case of not knowing how to behave to avoid it, and adults do not always act in such a way that these behaviors are learned easily. Most children use displacement, which is the transfer of aggressive tendencies due to punishment or frustration to some object which is less threatening than the authority figure. Many use "acting out," that is acting parts that symbolize the authority figure(s). They use these in an unconscious way, as if they were daydreaming. They find in them a source of security. They cling to fantasies of power, force, indestructibility, or omniscience. However, in extreme cases where the outside danger is too unpredictable to cope with, or where the inside conflict is based on a feeling of guilt because they have been punished for things which are essentially normal, ordinary children will resort to a complete denial of reality. For example, if a child loses the love of an adult who is important to him because he has expressed some thought about sex, he may subsequently repress such thoughts far more completely than other children do, to defend against the threat. This is obviously avoidance behavior. It results in behavior that is nonrealistic; this behavior can be described as insufficiently mediated by the ego, or one can say that the ego is poorly equipped to reduce the fear or anxiety reactions. The child may resort to total avoidance of threatening situations, or to destructive attack to reduce the threat (as if he were a cornered and wounded animal). The behavior of such children has been studied extensively, notably Redl and Bettelheim (separately). Redl has labeled this problem the "pauperized ego." For example, where a normal child may demonstrate a disgusted withdrawal from an unpleasant situation, the child with a poor ego will flee in panic; where a normal child will engage in an obvious but harmless display of aggression, the poor ego will allow destructiveness, and afterwards the superego will inflict its punishment in the form of high anxiety. Such children have trouble waking up, getting out of bed, getting dressed; they have lost out too often to meet the new day with confidence. Such children find it difficult to resist temptation in the form of playing with gadgets, snitching food, and the like. They find it difficult to use playthings for other than throwing or breaking. They sometimes have difficulty taking care of things they like since this implies some dependence on the regularity of the future.

In relation to learning, such children often show a lack of exploratory and questioning behavior; this results from their rejection of the adult world and all that it implies. Similar lacks are found in low economic status groups, perhaps from a similar rejection of society in general. Low ego children have also learned to observe the actions of authority figures and discount the words; this reflects the differences between the verbal behavior and actual behavior that has been characteristic of adults they have known. Similar differences exist in the behavior of teachers, who say one thing about rules and about important aspects of a subject, but act otherwise in terms of approval and disapproval or in terms of what appears on tests.

Included in the function of the ego is the mediation between immediate wants and reality, which requires postponement and intervening behavior. A poor ego cannot enforce these requirements on the individual, and such children are less able to postpone rewards, or in other words to work for delayed rewards. This too has been observed as a problem in working with students from low economic status families.

14–9 Intelligence

Intelligence is a factor of personality just as it is a factor of cognitive behavior, although it is more frequently associated with the latter in relation to academic achievement and its prediction. The ego must be "intelligent" in that it must match the demands of the id and cautions of the superego to the requirements of reality. It must bring the organism to achieve its ends without frustrating the one or violating the other or both. Success in this function may not be reflected in the kinds of behavior required on intelligence tests, which can be thought of as tests of generalized achievement emphasizing response to symbolic stimuli and, to a lesser extent, iconic and concrete stimuli also. As research in intelligence becomes more sophisticated, more and more factors of intelligence are identified. Furthermore, intelligence is a cognitive functioning that develops beyond adolescence, in increasingly varied and specialized areas, rather than remaining static after the age of fourteen or thereabouts. While intelligence is usually considered an innate characteristic, a hereditary aptitude, it has become increasingly clear that the task of separating the hereditary part from the environmentally and experientially determined part is a very complex and delicate one. Some possible successes have been reported, but the issue is still in doubt; that is, it is not completely certain that such an hereditary factor has been identified. This emphasizes the environmentally determined aspect of intelligence, which is a function of the past experience of the child from birth on (perhaps before birth as well).

"Intelligence," as it is used most frequently in institutions of learning, is a rather verbally oriented cognitive ability reflecting general achievement in a variety of tasks, none of which are identifiable with common subject matters beyond the sophistication of arithmetic, reading, and common history. Attempts have been made to separate out the factor of socioeconomic level, through tests which do not use words for example, but success has been very limited. Intelligence, or more generally "aptitude," has fairly strong correlations with most of the academic subjects taught in schools, less so with vocational subjects such as home economics, shop, and the like. One can predict academic success on the basis of "intelligence" as measured by common tests used for this purpose; this prediction is statistical, however, and should be stated as such. One should not, for example, talk about the so-called *underachiever*, that is, the student with high intelligence but low achievement in one or more subjects, without qualifying his statements by observing that the general achievement measured by intelligence does not necessarily overlap the particular achievement required or measured by the subject(s). Thus one should not assume that the achievement or ability required on the intelligence test is a prerequisite for understanding the subject or is a factor involved in the conceptual hierarchy of the subject. Statistically, most students who have one have the other also, but a particular student may have one but *not* the other. On the other hand, a student who lacks general achievement as measured by an intelligence test is *likely* to lack the basic concepts and processes needed to understand a given subject, whether or not these concepts or processes are evaluated by the intelligence test itself.

Research has yielded evidence for a number of factors of intelligence where each factor related to a type of task or type of response. Among these factors are two basic ones which have attracted some attention: they have been called *convergent* and *divergent* thinking. The former is exemplified by the problem, "The product of the difference between five and eight and the sum of three and negative four is ———," while the latter is exemplified by the problem, "How many ways can you have an operation involving two numbers that yields a result of forty?" This dichotomy is analogous to that discussed in the chapter on concept formation, where the converse of a concept was called a *dicept*. Convergent thinking is prevalent in our culture and possibly more prevalent in the tasks we require of students in school; divergent thinking is being considered of greater importance than formerly, and has been of interest to educational researchers under the general title *creativity*.

14–10 Creativity

Creativity is a factor of personality characterized by unique yet appropriate responding to familiar stimuli, and also by fluency of such responding. It may be explained through reinforcement paradigms as a response set or learning set shaped through unidentified contingencies which reinforce such responses. Such responses are often controlled by dimensions or sets of dimensions of concepts ordinarily considered irrelevant or neutral; that is, the creative person gives responses that others are not likely to think of due to different past experience. He may then build a set of defenses against the type of reaction that such responding elicits in his audience. Part of the uniqueness of his answering is due to his greater fluency; that is, he gives all the expected responses and then goes on to others. Such "brainstorming" type of behavior, in which unusual responses are allowed or encouraged to come to the surface, is important in problem solving. While inappropriate responding also comes from brainstorming, it should not be too quickly or heavily punished lest the creativity of the responses themselves suffer and the creativeness be suppressed.

Creativity has been measured through special tests. In one such test a student is given a brick and asked how many different uses he can give for it. His responses are analyzed for fluency (number), uniqueness, and appropriateness. To be measures of creativity such tests should correlate highly with each other but not highly with batteries of tests measuring intelligence in the traditional sense.

Students who score highly on tests of creativity have been found to achieve grades as good as slightly more "intelligent" counterparts, even though their teachers find them more difficult to cope with and favor them somewhat less. Students with very high creativity but quite low intelligence have been found to be unhappy and maladjusted in their social environment.

Creativity can be taught through sequences of experiences where creative responses are exemplified, then encouraged and reinforced. Creative responding is a concept and a process, and can be taught by example as well as rule. In part it involves an awareness of limitations on ordinary responding, as well as understanding of different strategies of responding. It also involves discrimination between ordinary stimulus control and unique yet appropriate stimulus control, that is, a discrimination between those properties of the stimulus which ordinarily control responses and those which *can* control responses although they do not usually do so. This in turn implies a flexibility of learning set. It may well be that tolerance of confusion or misunderstanding by one's audience may be necessary for a person to become effectively creative, since in learning the processes involved he will make errors and these will be punished in a social way. That this punishment exists is evidenced by studies which show that the creative student is not always held in highest esteem by teachers or peers.

It seems likely that tendencies toward creative responding are limited by evolutionary processes, just as the tendency to form new concepts rather than using old ones may be, as speculated upon in a previous chapter. The reason might be that creative responses are high risk ones; the probability of their being effective is lower than "tried and true" ones. On the other hand there is an evolutionary advantage to creative responding, as an ingredient of effective problem solving. Creativity in all subjects, particularly in the fine arts and literature but also in science and social sciences, is highly prized by intellectuals, at least verbally, although it is not universally reinforced. While creative behavior may be a good thing, it may be well to "take it with a grain of salt," since indiscriminate reinforcement of creative responding may not be best for the student or class. As discussed previously, it seems possible that the preponderance of our shaping of behavior in schools is toward convergent thought processes; creativity, being divergent, then needs some gesture toward "equal time," lest in our quest for order and control (the *effectance or competence* motive!), we create a society so controllable that it succumbs to totalitarianism. Creative behavior, based on thorough understanding of concepts and processes (which in turn are based on exemplars, or "facts") should be encouraged and reinforced to a greater degree than is currently the case.

Bibliography

LAZARUS, A. A. *Personality and Adjustment.* Englewood Cliffs, N.J.: Prentice-Hall, Inc., 1963.

REDL, F. and WATTENBERG, W. *Mental Hygiene in Teaching.* New York: Harcourt Brace Jovanovich, 1951.

ROSENBLITH, J. and ALLANSMITH, W. *The Causes of Behavior II: Readings in Child Development and Educational Psychology.* Boston: Allyn and Bacon, 1966.

Motivation As Learning 15

15–1 Historical Views of Motivation

Primitive man was controlled by "good" or "evil" spirits or demons. Later in his cultural development, man came to feel that the "soul" was the animating part of each self, and was separated from the body in death, thus resulting in everlasting life. Descartes, the philosopher and mathematician who lived in the 17th century, postulated a *bête machine* that implied that motivation came from physiological characteristics of the person; that is, he said there was an animal aspect of humans that could be viewed as a very complex machine. Where Descartes only *implied* that humans functioned as machines (and thus did not go so far as to risk the displeasure of the church), Lamettrie, in his *L'Homme Machine*, asserted explicitly that most physical and mental problems were due not to evil spirits or malaise of the spirit or to the condition of the soul, but rather to malfunctioning of the person's inner "mechanical" works. Lamettrie was hounded out of France, and later out of Holland, for his views; such views in other form are still unpopular today. We accept now the tinkering of the medical doctor with our insides, and respect him for his science, but an analytic view toward human behavior is frequently damned as "mechanistic." Darwin's theories, implying that animal behavior could be used for clues to human behavior, were likewise proscribed in a manner not too different from the accusations leveled at behaviorists today, and Freud was ostracized from the medical community for practicing what to many of his contemporaries amounted to witchcraft.

If one accepts an evolutionary view of human behavior, one can either concentrate on the biological–neurological development of the organism as a source of motivation, or one can concentrate on environmental influences, or one can look for motivational forces inherent in ideas themselves, as Herbart did. Instincts epitomize the biological frame of reference, while ethics carries out the last-named ideational view. However, the fact that very weak stimuli can lead to vigorous responses, and the fact that similar stimuli lead to different responses in different individuals, imply that there is more complexity to human motivation than can be explained by instinct and biological maturation.

It leads, of course, to *learning* as a source of behavior, as well as to the concept of the role of *drives* in directing learning and other behavior.

Drive theories assume that the motivation of behavior comes through the existence of drive-establishing conditions that release energy coming from the metabolic processes of the organisms: this is essentially the Freudian view of personality, already discussed. There are many ways in which such drives can be controlled, disguised, and transformed by the mental apparatus. The ego is the integrator in this process, learning through conflict, but it does not account completely for the urge to master one's environment.

Post-Freudians have observed that development is not entirely a consequence of conflict. Some functions mature without conflict, others developed through conflict become ends in themselves when conflict ceases. Many investigators observe that an urge to manipulate and general restlessness are characteristic of organisms, and that play is a way of learning to deal with the environment. Successful, gratifying experiences lead to increasingly integrated action. Monkeys have been observed to solve problems when there is no point in it, when it gets them nothing, and when they are satiated. Brain centers responsible for control of basic motivations have been identified, and it has been observed that some signals excited action and other signals inhibited it. This implies that inaction is not a state of euphoria, but rather one of balance between opposing forces. Investigators have begun to postulate that growth itself, whether physical or cognitive, is motivating. This means that one does not have to live or teach by the goad, nor even offer a carrot. Rather, one can present a problem and then simply get out of the way while the organism operates on it. Young children are being viewed as special kinds of organisms who operate on problems in their own way, not in the way of the adult. Each sequence of behaviors is being viewed as having its own intrinsic motive, its own purpose. The astonishing inefficiency of early learning is seen as an expression of the tremendous complexity of the human brain and its great potential —rather than as stupidity. As a parallel, investigators have begun to recognize that *very* high motivation, perhaps resulting from some deprivation, *interferes* with learning in many cases; *strong* drives do *not* lead to the most rapid problem solving, nor do they appear to create maximum familiarity with surroundings.

It has also been observed that if some task, say a verbal chain, were learned to the point of mastery and beyond, then this task itself will take on secondary reinforcing characteristics. Learned responses, or acquired predispositions to respond, then become secondary sources of motivation.

Fear has come to be seen as a drive also, in that its decrease furnishes a reinforcing situation (negative reinforcement), as long as the fear is not too intense. It begins to be clear that generalized fear, based on experience in many aversive, punitive situations, interferes with some learning and facilitates others: this anxiety has already been discussed.

One outcome of these various changing views of motivation, such as the increasing complexity seen in the sources of motivation, has been an emphasis by educators on a concept of learning as something that takes place spontaneously and naturally, in a self-fulfilling kind of activity that is its own reward and does not need to be motivated through aversive contingencies such as threat of failure or even through the promise of extrinsic rewards. Some describe this as a fantasy of a non-repressive civilization in which all work becomes libidinal pleasure. These continue to view work as a stern necessity for survival, whether it be to procure food or to avoid atomic warfare. Neither view presents the final answer, the complete picture.

15–2 Drives, Needs, and Reinforcement

The power of a need or drive theory in explaining behavior lies largely in its extension to what are called *secondary drives* or *acquired drives*. If an animal is placed in an experimental space and administered an aversive stimulus, say a shock, from which he escapes by leaving the space, then when placed in the same space again he will leave it again. He will also learn to open a door which has been placed between the space and freedom, after the initial learning (that is, after he experiences the shock). This has been taken to imply that the animal has learned a drive, in this case, one called *fear*. It is fundamental to avoidance learning, where animals and humans learn to avoid punishment in response to some signal indicating that punishment is about to occur that is, some signal that regularly precedes the aversive stimulus.

If one accepts the concept of drives—not all theorists do—then one may relate reinforcement to the reduction of some drive. This gives a common direction to all behavior, namely, that which results in the reduction of some primary or acquired drive. Drives do not explain all behavior, however. Some experiments show that animals and young children are often frightened by stimuli which represent a novel arrangement of quite familiar things: these cannot be attributed to earlier conditioning. For example, a chimpanzee in a laboratory may be quite unafraid of a stranger approaching his cage but may cower in fear when a familiar laboratory worker approaches wearing a mask or some unusual clothing. Thus there seem to be some behaviors which cannot be accounted for in terms of acquired drives or reinforcement stemming from the reduction of them. Other experiments have shown that the reinforcing effects of certain "foods" which have no nutritional value do not extinguish when they are used again and again, yet they satisfy no need. Still other experiments demonstrate that stimulation of certain brain areas (through implanted electrodes) can reinforce behaviors; no deprivation is involved, and no drive is reduced as far as is shown. It is also found that animals and humans will learn responses in order to achieve an *increase* in stimulation, rather than a decrease in some drive state.

One theoretical view of some promise postulates that there is a normal, customary level of stimulation (or state of awareness, or arousal, or readiness), and if the actual level of stimulation drops below this or climbs above it, behavior is initiated which tends to restore the accustomed level. If it drops too far below or rises too far above the normal level, then the organism avoids the situation, or seeks to escape. Thus with moderate departures one gets approach behavior, or problem-solving behavior, but with extreme departures one gets avoidance behavior.

While the examination and discussion of various views and theories concerning motivation is a fascinating intellectual exercise and eminently worthwhile, there is also a great need to synthesize and apply theories of motivation for the improvement of teaching and learning. Each theory has its implications for practice, and each could be discussed from this point of view. However, it may be worthwhile first to consider the concept "motivation" and analyze it, so that it will be easier to find points of agreement and disagreement among the various points of view about it.

15–3 What is Motivation?

If someone does something, others will conclude that he was *motivated* to do so; the word implies some driving force that makes him "go." The force itself is hypothetical or assumed, just as Renaissance scientists assumed that when an object was thrown through the air the particles of air removed themselves from in front of it and got behind it and pushed, thus keeping it going. We know by common experience that an automobile is "motivated" by the engine, as governed by the throttle; practically speaking, this is a useful point of view. However, the physicist and engineer use laws based on the assumption that the car will never stop, once set in motion, unless some opposing force slows it down. In a similar way one might assume that humans and animals behave or act continuously unless something slows *them* down or diverts them (we have already advanced the hypothesis that living beings remember everything except as other memories interfere). While the concept of motivation is a common and useful one, a view of behavior which emphasizes factors that *impede* progress or *slow down* behaving and learning may also be helpful for understanding human learning.

Retention was discussed as a function of interference from previous and subsequent learning, instead of as a trait depending on the nature of the material learned or the meaningfulness or importance of that material. In concept formation, redundancy was related to this interference also; that is, certain properties of given stimulus sets (the *relevant* ones) were made less subject to interference by having them repeated in the context of different exemplars of the set, while other properties (the irrelevant) were varied and thus exposed to interference. Here one might regard redundancy as a process of preventing the "friction" of continuous experience and perception from "erasing" the associations which one wishes to maintain, rather than a process of repeating or "stamping in" that relationship. One may also regard the recommended process of bringing out old responses as one of removing obstacles to learning through extinction of avoidance behaviors, errors, and interfering concepts.

15–4 Motivation in Previous Chapters

If one conditions an organism to respond to a stimulus in a certain way, either through classical or operant procedures, one has *motivated* it to do so. If one presents a serial or paired-associate list to a student and he learns it, one has *motivated* the student by presenting the list—the student would not have learned it otherwise. If one reinforces this behavior by subsequently paying the student, and other students hear about the reward, then there will be a higher probability that they will participate: this is *motivation* also.

Presenting a problem is a form of motivation if a learner attempts to solve it: he would not have exhibited that behavior if the problem had not been presented. Refinements of this behavior involve posing the right problem, or the right sequence of problems, to maintain the behavior and at the same time shape it to meet the demands of the environment.

15–5 Competence as a Motive

Some educators and psychologists have postulated that there is a basic human drive or need for competence which is shown in situations where the environment has to be controlled or poses a problem to be solved, and which is demonstrated even when no serious problem related to survival exists. Such a basic need would contribute to evolutionary survival, since the organism that persists in problem solving even when it is not motivated by hunger or thirst will assumedly learn to cope with the environment in ways that might be useful later. Another way to explain such behavior is to say that it is a generalized version of that required for finding food, water, and shelter, something so necessary so often that the organism comes to do it for its own sake; that is, it becomes self-reinforcing. This kind of secondary conditioning, where a behavior comes to be reinforcing in itself, has been discussed in relation to conditioning paradigms (reinforcement by response-produced stimuli) and is also related to the phenomenon of learning to learn.

There are behavioral phenomena involving both humans and lower organisms that imply that behavior that is effective in controlling or ordering the environment is reinforced when all other controllable needs have been satiated. This has been interpreted as indicating a need for competence or *effectance* as one investigator has termed it. Monkeys have been observed to store food in their cheeks while solving certain puzzles; they were not hungry, and yet their behavior indicated direction and persistence. Interestingly, they were also observed to eat some of this unneeded food at times when they had been unsuccessful with a problem, possibly indicating that frustration had introduced a state that resembled food deprivation.

Such experiments have been interpreted to imply that humans learn best under conditions where their desires for exploration and competence have been harnessed: this is done by facing students with a task which involves them in the process of solution. Extensive curriculum changes have been proposed based on this kind of research and partly on faith in a discovery approach to learning which is analogous to the selection strategies of concept formation research. Since a problem-solving or concept-attainment or selection-strategy approach to learning requires availability of materials for presenting systems with which the students can interact, and since it also requires teacher behavior which is less directive and authoritarian (nonpresentation strategy) and more tolerant of confusion and ambiguity (hypothesis formation and testing), inquiry or discovery learning approaches are slow to be adopted. Comparisons with conventional methods are difficult because of the number of variables involved. There seems to be little doubt, however, that these approaches are motivating, but this motivation can be attributed to many elements, including activity, variety, problem orientation, availability of choice in activity, friendliness and personal involvement of the teacher, and others.

15–6 Desire to Achieve and Fear of Failure

One approach to motivation views human behavior as an algebraic sum of a positive desire to achieve results (competence motive) and fear of failing (anxiety). The outcome of this hypothesis, after some development of it which will not be presented here, is that the tendency to participate in an activity will be greatest when the probability of success (and thus the risk of failure) is neither very high nor very low, but somewhere in between. Thus, if given a choice of difficulty level, successful students will choose a task of medium difficulty. Students in a conventional class do not always have such a choice, so one must be careful in applying this model. However, it does tell one something about the mode of operation of the achieving personality and suggests that if a choice is given and a range of difficulties is available, the achieving student will pick something that is not too hard and not too easy. It also says something about the motivation and behavior of the student who has failed frequently and fears failure, and about the student who is highly anxious due to parental pressure or other reasons: such students are likely to aspire to too high a goal, or to one so low that they cannot miss. These behaviors are demonstrated in many ways in the classroom and on assignments and projects.

15–7 Conformity

One powerful source of motivation is a desire to conform, to be like others, to reduce the discrepancy between one's behavior and that of one's peers. This can have interesting and significant results on cognitive as well as social behavior. In one classic study, a number of students were shown two lines of obviously unequal length side by side, and asked to compare them. This was done in a small group situation where all participants but one had been prepared ahead of time to say that the lines were the same length. The experimental subject, in the face of opinions conflicting with his perception of the situation, was apt to conform by agreeing with the opinions of the others. A number of replications and related experiments have shown that the opinions of others have a significant effect on the cognitive perception of the student.

15–8 Cognitive Dissonance

One variant of the type of study described above casts some light on the perception of students regarding past events in the light of subsequent experiences and thus relates to retention and interference, though on a rather complex and sophisticated level. One might introduce it by saying that if it is possible for students to "change" their minds about what they see before them, under the influence of the behavior of others, might it not be possible for them to change their minds about what they have seen or experienced in the *past*, in the light of subsequent events? There is some research which indicates that it is indeed possible and actually happens. This has led to a theory that deals primarily with assumed mental or cognitive conflicts between differing or incompatible points of view or emotions.

According to this theory, if a person acts in a way that is incompatible with his own feelings or attitudes, for instance if he tells a lie, then he will experience a mental or cognitive dissonance which is like a drive. Thoughts, attitudes, or changes of these which resolve the dissonance will be reinforced; that is, the person will actually think in that way in the future. For example, suppose a student is sitting in class and wishes to be outside playing; this creates a dissonance in his mind, a cognitive dissonance, in that he is acting in a way that does not agree with the way he wishes to act. Now if the teacher is very strict and deals out punishment for misbehavior, then he can anticipate this punishment, and it provides the resolution for the dissonance, that is, "if I do it I will be punished." If the teacher on the other hand is not very strict or is not a threat, then the dissonance may not be resolved this way; perhaps the student will actually leave, or perhaps he will misbehave, since that misbehavior is a substitute for leaving and helps resolve the dissonance. Or perhaps the teacher is very well liked; in that case, the difficulty may be resolved by thinking that leaving the class would threaten the teacher, and the student would not want that to happen.

Another example that may be given relates to the harmful effects of cigarettes. A salesman who is selling cigarettes acts as though they are not harmful; so does the advertising executive and the cigarette company executive. However, the salesman is not as well paid as the executives: as a result, he must resolve the cognitive dissonance by actually believing that they are not harmful, or defending against thoughts that indicate that they are, while the executives may resolve it by thinking of the high salaries they are getting and thus explain their contradictory actions on that account.

One possible application of cognitive dissonance theory which ought to be tested is the following. Suppose a group of students is asked to write papers expounding views that are not their own—for example, a group of conservative southern students may be asked to write a paper expounding the virtues of desegregation or miscegenation. Then suppose that part of the group is given A's for the paper and the other part is given C's. Cognitive dissonance theory might be used to predict that the students who get A's will be less likely to change their minds about desegregation or miscegenation than those who receive C's, because the high grade can be used to resolve the dissonance caused by writing in favor of a view that is not their own, while the lower grade cannot be used that way and so they will need some other way to resolve the dissonance—that is, by changing their minds.

15–9 Environment and Motivation

So far, motivation has been discussed as a function of the learning situation. To the extent that learning situations and teaching processes (or experimental processes) can be considered environmental in nature, these situations have been functions of the environment. The sociologist, however, has treated motivation as a function of the number and kind of behavioral "settings" that students can take part in. Examples of settings are membership in a club, leadership in a club, sitting at the corner soda fountain, participating in a pajama party, sitting in class, attending assembly, speaking in assembly, acting in a play, and the like. One important determinant of behavior is the number of settings that exist in relation to the number of students available to take part in them: if, for instance, a play is given with fifteen parts in it, then the probability of a student being given one of the parts (or asked to take a part) is a function partly of the number of students in the school. If the school is small, there is more likelihood that a given student will be asked to take part in a number of things, or that he will be accepted if he wishes to take part.

This probability is one aspect of motivation. In a large school, there is more emphasis on competition to gain admittance to the relatively fewer settings; in a small school, there is more pressure on individuals to take part in a variety of settings. In the latter, taking part is the "thing" to do, regardless (relatively) of talent, while in the former, the main approach is competition based on various factors, including talent. Such research also points out the possibility of variation in number and type of behavioral settings from school to school, given equal numbers of students in each.

15–10 Social Facilitation

Another source of influence on the direction and nature of learning and thus behavior in general lies in what is sometimes termed *social facilitation*. It has been found that subjects *learn* more quickly *without* the presence of passive spectators, but that they *perform* better (once having learned) *in the presence of* passive spectators. One explanation for this is that a student makes many wrong responses early in learning; assumedly these are partly related to proactive influences, and to the fact that the wrong responses need to be extinguished. The presence of an audience may be considered to invoke punishing contingencies for wrong responses, leading to their suppression and thus preventing their extinction. For the same reason, the presence of an audience is facilitating when a task already has been well learned because it introduces possible punishment and possible reward, increasing the relative desirability of a correct response and assumedly focusing the attention of the learner (now performer) on the relevant stimulus patterns.

In addition to such audience effects, there is a factor called *coaction*, which is somewhat more complex. Here individuals are simultaneously engaged in one activity, in view of each other. Animals will eat more and work harder in the presence of other animals than they will alone. If this is to be compared with the previously discussed audience effects, one might predict that group learning would be less efficient than individual learning; this has been confirmed in some experiments with animals (birds, cockroaches) and humans. In the latter case, subjects worked either in separate cubicles or sitting around a common table. When working in isolation, they did the various tasks at the same time and were monitored by common time signals. In chain word association, vowel cancellation, reversible perspective, and multiplication tasks, students working in groups learned more quickly; in problem solving and judgment tasks, they learned better individually. We may relate these results to previous ones by assuming that the tasks learned more quickly in groups represented those where the components of the task are already well learned, where those learned better in private did not. Indeed, in another experiment where the word association task was more complicated, the presence of others interfered with performance; in this the subjects were ones who also had trouble with fluency of speech (stutterers).

Other experiments also illustrate interfering effects of the presence of others in a learning situation. In one, rats learned to avoid shock more quickly when alone than when in groups. In another, human subjects received one-half second of electric shock every ten seconds unless they pressed a red button; each press delayed the shock ten seconds. When subjects were used in pairs, if one pressed the button the shock was delayed for both. Isolated subjects required eleven minutes on the average to reach criterion (less than six shocks in a period of five minutes) : paired subjects usually quit the experiment before reaching criterion.

The reader should note that in the cases of coaction and audience effects related above, no information was received by one subject by watching others. In some experiments, where such information is relevant to the solution of a problem, the presence of others has been found to facilitate learning.

Some investigators have found that adrenocortical activity is a reliable symptom of arousal (that is, activity of the endocrine glands). Adrenocortical activity has also been found to be a function of population density: crowded mice, for instance, show increased endocrine manifestations. This implies that the effects discussed previously may be partially a function of physical changes induced by the presence of others: these changes generally inhibit learning but facilitate performance of behaviors already learned. Where the presence of others gives relevant information regarding a problem or regarding effective behavior in a given situation, however, these effects may be secondary.

15–11 Familiarity and Strangeness

One other view towards human behavior in general may be related to two basic paradigms, reinforced behavior and avoidance behavior. It has been observed that situations one meets in his environment may be generally (and obviously not very accurately) classed as "somewhat similar to those met before" and "very dissimilar to those met before." It seems possible that for most people, situations of the former category have turned out to be characterized by reinforcing stimuli more frequently than situations of the latter category. Thus it is concluded that situations differing only slightly from usual experience will be explored or entered into, while very different ones will be avoided. It seems unlikely that there is an absolute zero here, where no behavior at all is recorded; rather, one may postulate the existence of a relative zero, which is the accustomed environment. Then if conditions depart from this slightly we assume that behavior will be *approaching* or *exploratory*, while a large departure will occasion behavior which is *avoidant* in nature.

15–12 Group Effects

Certain mechanisms discussed previously, involving the interaction of ego, id, and superego, as well as the defense mechanisms discussed before that and the competence theories as well, all have had implicit in them the idea that much of learning is done in reference to other organisms and groups of organisms. Thus the study of human behavior in group situations has much to contribute to the study of motivation. If, for instance, a person feels that he belongs to a group (due to the fact that the objectives of the group are similar to his and the members of the group are in some ways similar to him), his perception of what is reinforcing will be altered somewhat by the common perceptions of the group—that is, the group as a whole comes to have points of view and objectives in a collective sense. One simple example is that of the football team whose objective is to score. In a sense, then, the norms of the group become those of the individual, and these norms establish relative zeroes for behavior along certain dimensions. For instance, the nature and variety of modes of dress among teenagers is such that they dress to maintain that degree of variety (which many parents look upon from another point of view, as a degree of conformity). As another example, a representative from a group who may be sent to another environment to learn a skill or an improved way of doing things may, on returning to the group, find it impossible to maintain these new skills or ways because they deviate from group norms. The norms do not change in their absence, and to relieve the dissonance they feel, the returning persons are likely to change. This probably includes not only revising their new behavior, but seeing their recent experience in a new, less positive light (cognitive dissonance). Thus attendance at workshops and institutes (including T-Group sessions) does not always

result in changes in behavior "back home," and the problem of maintenance of behavior in the future continues to trouble those who design
such programs.

15–13 Success and Motivation

"Success breeds success," so the saying goes, and this conclusion can
be derived from a number of basic views of motivation involving task
difficulty, guidance, and conditioning to tolerate failure. There has been
some research with lower organisms, mainly by associates of B. F.
Skinner, which indicates that if a task is learned without error the
learner emerges from the experience with a different personality and a
different approach to learning than demonstrated by those who have
made errors in the process. For instance, pigeons who have been taught
to perform fairly complex discrimination behaviors, without ever
making an error during the learning sequence, behave in a way which
is observably different from other pigeons who have learned the same
task by a cruder sequence of experiences. They seem a bit cocky in
their behavior and are less distracted by interfering stimuli. This ideal
of learning without error is one primary concern of many behaviorists,
who see in it the most likely alternative to the unfortunate prevalence
of avoidance learning in education. Avoidance learning implies suppression of responses due to authoritarianism, which in turn contributes
to the general use and expectation of the use of force and violence in
our culture. Behaviorists look to errorless learning, involving only *positive* reinforcement, as a means of achieving a more utopian society.

This concentration on errorless learning and the avoidance of punitive contingencies in the environment has an interesting similarity to
the nondirective counseling described previously. In such counseling,
the therapist provides a nonpunitive audience for repressed responses
and reinforces attention by the client to aspects of his thoughts which
the therapist feels will be most productive. This is in a sense *error-free*
learning, in that no responses are punished and the verbal behavior is
shaped by the therapist. There are limits to this of course, involving
the "congruence" of the therapist, who must react at times in a negative
way so as not to be considered a "phony," but even this negativity is
couched in a manner and tone designed to be nonpunitive. This in turn
is analogous to the problem of discovery learning, where the student
must be taught that negative outcomes of hypothesis testing are not
errors in the conventional sense, that is, implying social or physical
punishment and thus evoking fear and anxiety responses.

Another aspect of error-free learning which should be considered is
that of avoidance of errors as a means of avoiding *learning* errors. This
is based on the possibility, considered very significant and real by some,
that if one responds incorrectly to a situation he will to some degree

learn that erroneous response. This in turn is based on the assumption
that one reinforces himself to a degree for his own correct responses,
and that if one responds without seeing the response as an hypothesis
to be tested one may reinforce himself for responding in that way, even
though later information indicates that the response was incorrect. Thus
one will *learn* his incorrect response. The author experienced this problem in trying to determine the point at which students began to "understand" a concept presented through programmed instruction; he did
this by inserting brief quizzes in between the early frames of the program, so that he could see *where* they began to understand. Although
no feedback was given on the quizzes, there was evidence that the students were learning their responses to the questions, even where the
responses were wrong, and that the quizzes interrupted the learning
process and changed it.

In another experiment with first-grade students, a fairly complex
matching-to-sample task was learned through a carefully developed
sequence of tasks presented mechanically. Students who used a later
version of the sequence were able to achieve criterion without the errors
demonstrated by students who used an earlier version of the sequence
(that is, the sequence went through several revisions). Now when students who had used the earlier version were given the later version subsequently, they still made errors, even though other students who had
never seen the material made *no* errors on the same sequence. This
suggests that one learns to make errors just as one learns to make correct responses; it also suggests that giving the correct answer is not
sufficient for correcting an error after it is made, but rather that one
must go back and bring the student to make the correct response in the
same situation.

15–14 Motivating by Removing Inner Barriers: Therapy

In analytic psychotherapy the therapist attempts to bring his subject
or "patient" to retrieve from his subconscious memories of experiences
that trouble him, and that may be affecting his current behavior. According to the theoretical foundation for this approach, the patient has
to expend considerable psychic energy to keep these memories repressed,
that is, to keep them from coming into the conscious mind, and this
prevents him from dealing as effectively with his environment as he
could otherwise and sometimes results in very obvious maladaptive behaviors. If the basic causes are not accounted for in this way, that is,
confronted by the patient and recognized so that the patient can somehow come to terms with his troubling past, then maladaptive behavior
will continue. One might succeed in "curing" one symptom, but the
basic difficulty will crop up again in some other form. In this approach
to helping others, the therapist probes the subconscious of the patient

at the risk of having the patient transfer some of his suppressed aggressions and resentments (that is, some of his blocked basic urges, or id forces) to the therapist himself, and indeed this transference is part of the therapy process. Ultimately, the therapist attempts to put the patient on his own, by bringing him to such a state of confidence in his ability to handle things himself that he rejects the therapist as an aid and thus becomes a free and independent person again. The relationship between this process and motivation can be seen if one uses the frame of reference where behavior is seen as ongoing and natural except when held back by some forces: this process releases the patient from forces that are holding him back.

In recent years another approach to therapy has become very popular, one based on similar tenets but placing less emphasis on the basic survival forces and more emphasis on the need of the individual for social competence and for a sense of satisfaction with himself. This approach to therapy is generally defined as *nondirective* and has been described previously as providing an accepting, nonpunitive, warm atmosphere for the patient. The effect of such unconditional acceptance on the part of the therapist is to improve the patient's opinion of himself, that is, to improve the patient's *self-concept*, as well as to lead him to discover by himself the nature of his difficulties. This in turn often results in a change in behavior resulting from this improvement, or at least it is claimed that such changes occur. One difficulty experienced in this and other therapy is the collecting of data that show that the improvement in cognitive response to the environment and to the self is reflected in improvement in the behavior of the patient in everyday life.

An important factor in non-directive counseling is the behavior of the counselor or therapist. He is continually trying to provide an accepting audience for the patient and at the same time avoid acting like a "phony" by pretending that the thoughts and reminiscences of his patient don't affect him—indeed, if there were no effect the patient would probably become suspicious of the honesty and candor of his therapist. This leads to a search for what Carl Rogers, the founder of this approach, has called *congruence*, that is, behavior on the part of the therapist which is at the same time accepting of the patient as a human being and yet representative of the therapist's honest reactions to the patient.

An interesting development arising from psychotherapy and more immediately from nondirective therapy, via group therapy, where some of the advantages of individual therapy have been sought on a more economical basis, is a movement that has been called *sensitivity training* and *T-Groups* (*T* for *training*). Here groups of "normal" individuals, that is, individuals *not* notable for the fact that they have been institutionalized or are seeking help for mental or behavioral disorders, are brought together with the objective of improving their sensitivity and understanding of other people, and particularly their understanding of the behavior of others in a group situation. These groups are often handled in a nondirective manner, and brought to confront each other with statements concerning their inner feelings as evidenced by their verbal expressions in the group. Verbal behavior here is taken as data, and one looks for what the person is "saying" *beyond* or *behind* the words he uses. Since the sessions are carried on over periods of many hours and through over-all workshops lasting a matter of several days or a week or more, the group eventually comes to discuss very basic feelings of one participant toward another and becomes more sensitive to the possible and probable meanings of statements that seem quite devoid of emotional content to the untrained. This kind of training has implications for teaching, both in relation to sensitivity to the feelings of others and in relation to the effective communication of subject matter, as will be seen in the next chapter. Since human motivation is in a large part dependent on the perceived motives of others, this is a motivational matter as well.

15–15 Behavior Therapy

Another approach to therapy for maladjusted behaviors is based more directly on conditioning paradigms. It assumes that a behavior or emotion that interferes with effective living is not necessarily the result of some inner problem that has to be worked out in therapy. If it *was* caused by such a basic problem, the basic problem may have long since disappeared, leaving the behavior problem as an unfortunate habit with no basic cause. On the other hand, it may be a *superstitious* behavior, one conditioned through chance contingencies of the environment, not recognized by the person himself but still effective in producing a behavior that interferes with the person's life. In either case, the problem is not to locate some central source of the behavior but rather to remove the behavior itself, that is, to take care of the *symptom* and not worry about the *cause*.

There are a number of ways to do this. One way is by identifying the unknown controlling stimulus or stimuli, for the person may know what the behavior is and not be able to produce it because the controlling stimuli are not known. An interesting example of this was that of a boy whose writing "disappeared"; that is, his writing became smaller and smaller and finally became too small to read. The cause was identified finally as a habit of making all his *T*'s capitals: he had been taught to follow a capital letter by smaller letters, and when he made a *T* he made it in the form of the capital letter but did not make it larger —then he followed it with smaller letters.

Another approach is to extinguish the response by having it given without reinforcement. Here the nature of the reinforcement must be identified and withheld (if it comes from within the person, he must be brought to recognize the fact that he *is* reinforcing himself for this response). This approach is called *negative practice*; it has been used to cure a number of problems, from spelling errors to stuttering. It is characterized by practicing of the wrong or unwanted response.

Still another approach is called *desensitization*; it is related to extinction but is not exactly the same. In desensitization, the stimulus which controls the response is given in very weak form, or a stimulus similar to it is given, in such a way that the stimulus is too weak to evoke the full response. The person is given repeated experience in such very weak responding until the response to that intensity of the stimulus extinguishes or dies out: this is a classical paradigm rather than an operant one, where the stimulus is given without the original unconditioned stimulus. Ultimately the stimulus used in the therapy can be brought to approximate the actual problem stimulus more and more closely, until finally the person can be given the full "treatment" without giving the maladaptive response (often a response of fear).

This process is exemplified in a form of treatment that can be administered to students who become highly anxious in test situations, that is, who have "test anxiety." Such a student is first trained to relax thoroughly, through a series of exercises which he practices many times with the help of the therapist. While the student is being trained to relax, the therapist also evokes from him concerns about schoolwork and tests with which he forms a list of things about which the student is anxious. This list is hierarchical in that it begins with things that are only mildly anxiety provoking and gradually works up to things that are highly anxiety provoking for the student. Then, to begin the treatment, the therapist brings the student to relax very thoroughly and asks him to imagine one of the things or situations that are only mildly anxiety provoking for him: the student is asked to signal the therapist if the thought causes anxiety. Most often, in such a relaxed situation, perhaps with music playing or other background stimuli that elicit feelings of security, comfort, and pleasure, these mildly threatening stimuli will not cause anxiety—the total environment is incompatible with that anxiety. Experience shows that such a pairing of unpleasant thoughts and pleasant surroundings have the effect of diminishing the anxiety elicited by those thoughts.

Once this has been accomplished with a mildly threatening or anxiety-provoking thought, the therapist moves on to thoughts or images higher on the list in terms of anxiety arousal. By this process, the student eventually comes to be able to entertain thoughts about tests without anxiety. Thoughts about testing situations of various kinds or thoughts about tests being more and more closely imminent (three weeks away, one week away, one day away, and so on) can be used to bring the simulated situation closer and closer to the "real thing."

This kind of treatment has been used successfully on a variety of fears or anxieties. It is interesting to speculate on the effects of removing such fears in respect to learning behavior. If the anxiety is so great that it interferes with any effective coping behavior on the part of the student, then desensitization will be beneficial in terms of studying and obtaining better grades. If on the other hand the anxiety is the only source of motivation, that is, if the study behavior is reinforced only by the decrease of anxiety (negatively reinforced), then one may predict that with the desensitization of anxiety may come a decrease in study behavior. This implies that other contingencies will need to be brought into effect if study behavior is to be maintained. Some research needs to be done in this area. There is evidence from experimental education programs that indicates that some such effect may be occurring, that is, when the threat of grades or examinations is removed in experimental curricula, one finds an increase of involvement and interest in various aspects of the subject matters involved, but one also observes an inability of the students to bring themselves to concentrate on and study the same subjects or others of their own choosing. This is not to be taken as anti-innovation or a criticism of desensitization: rather, it is to point out that if one removes one source of motivation, then one may have to consider replacing it with others if the others are not present. Generally speaking, however, the level of anxiety in many students under our present system is so high as to be considered debilitating, and desensitization—either in the form of individual therapy or through adaptations of this process by teachers—will more often than not improve performance rather than lower it.

Another important approach in behavior therapy is in building responses which are needed but not present, since maladaptive behavior is often based on the *lack* of appropriate responses as well as the presence of inappropriate ones. Here one must *shape* approximations to appropriate responding through careful schedules of reinforcement. Children who appear to withdraw from society and who are maladjusted as a result can sometimes be treated through such approaches: behaviors which they do *not* exhibit and which normal children *do* exhibit are shaped through special contingencies, so that they ultimately function more adequately. Many cases where children lose control and show tantrums and aggression may be approached on this basis, that is, by teaching other responses that are incompatible with the undesirable ones, and which provide some alternative when the undesirable ones are extinguished. Another important group of behaviors treated under this approach are study behaviors, by bringing students to behave in such a way that certain particular situations achieve control over their study behavior. For example, a student may be told to go to a certain place at a certain time each day, to study a particular subject in that place at that time when he gets there, and to have no other interfering materials present. He is to study only as long as he wishes, whether for thirty seconds or five minutes. Then, after deciding to leave, he is told to do one more paragraph or page carefully, close the book, and leave; thus the study behavior is reinforced by the more desirable behavior of leaving. Gradually, through this process, the *special situation* gains control over the study behavior, and the student finds himself able to spend longer periods of time with the subject.

Other simple applications of reinforcement can be found, some of them surprising in their identification of the reinforcing stimulus. In one, for example, the behavior of sitting still and paying attention (involving very young children) was reinforced by allowing them to run around and make a lot of noise: the former behavior increased in frequency by being reinforced by the latter.

Bibliography

KRUMBOLTZ, J. D., ed. *Learning and the Educational Process*. Chicago: Rand McNally, 1965.

Using and Teaching Motivation 16

"How do I motivate a class to learn?" This question, so often asked by teachers, implies that there are ways of bringing a class to want to learn. In fact, there are such ways. However, one should not assume that this is like eliciting a classical unconditioned response, that if you find the right button then motivation will result. The response of *trying to learn* is a very complex operant response which results from many kinds of learning; it is therefore a response which can be and must be taught. Furthermore, one should not accept a class or an individual as it or he is, that is, with the learned desire to learn that he possesses when he comes into a learning situation, without attempting to shape this motivation and bring it to a higher level. A teacher is or should be responsible for increasing the motivation of his students, just as he is responsible for finding the best possible uses of the motivations that they have to begin with.

The title of this chapter, then, is chosen with full realization of its implications. Motivation can be taught. Furthermore, we are beginning to find some very effective methods for teaching it. Some of these have to do with the *way* the teacher teaches, some have to do with the way the materials or tasks are *structured*, and some have to do with the *interaction* of the various approaches to teaching and the *variety* of them.

16–1 Shaping

To motivate a student is to bring him to do something he has not done or is not doing. One way to bring a student to do something he has not done before is to reinforce some response that is similar to the one desired, thus increasing it in frequency, and then differentially reinforcing those aspects of the response that most closely approximate the one desired. For example, if one wishes to teach a student to write a clear and interesting account of some event, one first reinforces writing about anything, to make sure the response is strong. If it is, or becomes so, then one reinforces any parts of the writing response that are descriptive in nature. As these become more frequent, one reinforces them only when one asks the student to write a descriptive paragraph—thus bringing this kind of writing response under particular and predictable control. Gradually, one reinforces selectively (and perhaps on increasingly high ratios of reinforcement) those aspects of the descriptive writing that one wants to build or increase, and extinguishes others that one does *not* want. One must be careful, incidentally, to continue to maintain responses that are desirable while building other more complex ones: if one ignores certain aspects of the writing that one finds good, in the process of concentrating on others that are lacking, then one may find those already-learned aspects are decreasing or breaking down, and this may be because one ignored them (extinguished them). More often, however, the good behaviors become parts of larger units that are built through reinforcement, and do not extinguish because the larger units are reinforced.

Shaping is a simple concept in theory, but difficult to manage in practice. It requires patience, careful observation, and most importantly a very clear idea of the nature of the behavior that one wishes to produce. It is much easier by far to decide what one does *not* want from a student than to decide what one *does* want; it is also much easier to tell a student which responses are incorrect or undesirable than it is to note which are good or close or on the right track. This relates to previous discussions of learning through positive and negative exemplars in concept formation: if one wishes a student to form a concept of what good descriptive writing is, one can furnish him with examples of good descriptive writing, and one can also identify those aspects of his own writing which most closely approximate the ideal. On the other hand, if one only points out what is wrong or bad, one is asking him in effect to learn from negative exemplars alone.

Why is it, then, that teachers so often concentrate on the negative? It is partly because, as teachers, they are not primarily practitioners and therefore are not primarily concerned with how *to* do it. It is partly because it is safer to say what is not right than to proclaim what is right —and to show the right way by doing it oneself or by finding it in another's work leaves one open to criticism from other teachers. This negative approach is evidenced in much of society outside of teaching: one finds criticism and having reservations about things and finding fault more frequently than one finds constructive criticism and showing the way.

There is another aspect of shaping that causes difficulty when teaching a group rather than individuals. In shaping one begins where the student is and reinforces responses that are most like that desired, no matter how crude they are. This means reinforcing responses that are "wrong" by certain standards. If an individual student is functioning below grade level, then a shaping paradigm implies reinforcing responses that are below grade level, responses that are "wrong." Some teachers find this difficult to do ethically, that is, they feel it is unfair to the other students who are at a higher level; other teachers find it difficult in practice, in that one cannot arrange for such reinforcement on an individual basis when one is teaching a group.

16–2 Learning to Want to Learn

Conditioning paradigms imply that whatever is associated with reinforcement becomes reinforcing in itself. If reading a book becomes associated with reinforcement in many and varied situations, then reading a book will become reinforcing in itself. On the other hand, if it becomes associated with a punishing situation, it will become associated with punishment, and reading will elicit a degree of anxiety in the student even though he does read under the influence of particular environmental conditions such as a reading class. This does not imply that if one teaches students some ability through threat of punishment that they will not practice that skill in the future. It does say that if they do (for various reasons), they will experience a certain amount of anxiety in conjunction with the activity, and this anxiety may interfere with learning or it may facilitate it by increasing their attention to the task. Some anxiety is debilitating, some is facilitating. As in the case of social facilitation described in the last chapter, a particular environment facilitates behavior in one situation and inhibits the same behavior in another. Finally, one must keep in mind that if two students, *A* and *B*, are both studying for an examination, they may be doing the same things but for different reasons. They both may have the same strategies of learning, but one may be studying in the hope of getting a good grade and thus some anticipated reward, either long or short range, while the other may be studying to avoid punishing contingencies resulting from getting a low grade. Furthermore, their aspiration levels may be different, and thus they may regard the same grade, should they get it, in different ways.

The foregoing discussion has a negative tone which belies some of the positive aspects of learning to learn. Therefore it should be observed that if one learns in a certain way under conditions that are reasonably interesting, challenging, and rewarding, then one learns to like to learn under similar conditions and to learn in general. In other words, students come to study for the sake of studying to some extent. Furthermore, if the conditions of learning are such as to give experience in independent work and in striving to understand for the sake of understanding itself, striving to solve problems for the sake of the solution rather than the reward that comes with it, then chances are very good that these students will continue to study and learn because it is a pleasurable behavior, something associated with positive and desirable things. In this sense, motivation to learn is a conditioned or shaped or taught motivation; however, in order to teach it or condition it one must arrange the environment so that the natural, inherited curiosity or tendency to order and control the environment, which every student possesses to some measure, may be brought to bear. This implies that one must structure the learning environment to avoid extinguishing this natural bent or urge. There are many ways to extinguish it: one may force students to listen to explanation rather than presenting them with problem situations and urging them to solve them and giving them encouragement; or one can present them with problems which are far too difficult, which teach them that their efforts will be to no avail and that they must depend on the teacher; or one can leave them to choose their own behavior course completely, and thus allow chance contingencies of reinforcement to operate and produce a variety of behavior patterns, most of them ineffective.

16–3 Control of Difficulty

Think of a learning task or a concept to be understood as a barrier or step to be taken, so that the learner arrives at a different level or in some way increases his ability or complexity or state of being by some degree. One way to picture this is as if there are two states, an initial state and a final state, and they are at different heights, as below:

_____State F (final)

_____State I (initial)

How can one go from State I to State F? There are two categories of journey or steps which we will consider; they are pictured in Figure 16.1. In (a) the student proceeds quickly from I to F; the rate of

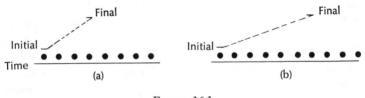

FIGURE 16.1

climb or rate of improvement is high, or the path is steep. This implies difficulty, however: the faster you make the trip, the harder it is. In (b) the same trip is accomplished in more time. Will there be any difference? It seems likely, from personal experience in teaching, that a greater percentage of the students will be able to negotiate path (b) than will be able to reach the final state by using (a). For those students who can "stand the gaff," path (a) is preferable because it tries their ability and motivation, and because it is quicker. However, for those students who cannot tolerate such a pace, (b) is the better course.

Thus it is possible to say that path (b) is the more *motivating*, because a greater percentage of the students were successful after they had used it.

What of the situation where all students must take the same path? This is a problem which is ever present; we may contrive a "homogeneous group" so that one path is more closely fitted to them all, but this group will inevitably turn out to be heterogeneous when we come to know it better, and we still have faster and slower students within it. Furthermore, "fast" and "slow" are crude terms, and should be discarded as soon as possible, to be replaced by more specific and helpful ones such as "identifies concepts in few trials," "verbalizes concepts more adequately," "repeats behavioral chains more readily," "transfers more adequately," and the like. Many years ago Ascham commented on the fact that the "quick wits" were likely to be less effective in using what they had learned than the "hard wits"; this a crude statement, but based on experience. Classification of learning abilities in the future should compare with that of the present somewhat as the Eskimo's classification of snow types compares with ours: he has about thirty-two of them, and obviously because differences are important to him.

Thus it is necessary to have a number of students taking the same path from A to B merely because we never have truly individualized teaching, since teaching implies arrangement of the environment, and we can never arrange the environment perfectly for any one individual —we can only approximate such arrangement in varying degrees. Suppose then that there are N students, and that by some criterion a given path (sequence, program, method) brings X percent of them to acceptable achievement. Assuming that we can adjust the path so that X is either 0 or 100 or some number in between, what figure should we set? An automatic answer illustrating a humanistic bent would be "One hundred percent, of course." But what does this imply? It implies that the path will be optimum only for the "slowest" student (of course, it is to be hoped that there will be several dimensions along which we can define this "slowness"). This means that we are requiring all the rest of the "faster" students to slow down. On the other hand, if we set the goal at a lower figure, some one or more students will fail to reach criterion. One answer to this is to accept a lower criterion or a different criterion. It is not the intent of this discussion to emerge with a prescription; rather, it is to point out that the *success level* or *productivity* of the path used is arbitrary, and more importantly to point out that our present means of handling this matter are crude and inadequate. There are many dimensions along which we can rate students as fast or slow, there are many paths that can be used, and there is the important matter of interaction among students if they are learning in a group.

16–4 Size of Group

Implications of modern approaches to individualized learning are that the ideal "group" is one: however, we need much more experience and research in this matter. Perhaps two students can learn more quickly than one, and three more quickly than two. Perhaps a class of one hundred is more effective in certain instances than a class of twenty. Consider the following hypothetical situation, as an example of what might turn up in such research. Suppose it is found that in order to achieve understanding of a certain concept in, say, political theory, the most productive approach is through presenting the problem and having a discussion. Then suppose that the discussion turns out to be most productive if a small core of students is briefed ahead of time to play roles demonstrating conflicting interests, with others observing.

Suppose then that unbriefed students are brought into the discussion at a certain point and, further, that one wants the most intelligent students possible to enter this. Suppose one also finds that other students not participating actively in this situation are still so involved that they learn well from it. Then it could well turn out that the ideal learning situation is one where there is a class of two hundred students, that one can pick good representatives for the role playing more conveniently if this is the case, and that there is a higher probability that there will be more intelligent students in the class to join in the discussion later if the class is large. Furthermore, since the participation by the inactive students is intense though vicarious, one can have any number of them learning profitably, the only possible limitation being in the inability to hear and perhaps see what is going on. This is determined in part by the environment, the classroom. On the other hand, it may be that as the number of students increases over a certain figure, due to sociopsychological processes not as yet understood completely, the involvement by the passive spectators will decrease accordingly (concentration on football games being variously a case in point or a contradiction depending on one's view of its nature). There is then assumedly an optimal range in class size which will be a function of the topic and of the type and structure of the presentation. It will also be a function of the heterogeneity of the class.

While still involved in homogeneity, among other things, it seems appropriate to reiterate that some research indicates surprising outcomes from grouping, in spite of the previous observation that no class can be completely homogeneous. For example, in one study a group made up of students of "low creativity" demonstrated higher creativity than a group made up of students of "high creativity." Thus there are complex interactions involved in group performances with different ability levels and different degrees of homogeneity.

16–5 The Meaning of "Errors"

If one ignores the heterogeneity of a group and attends to the difficulty of the learning sequence alone, we come to other relevant concerns regarding motivation. As described in the preceding chapter, a group that learns without errors or with relatively few errors may show different motivation on other tasks than a group that learns with more or many errors. This depends in part, as mentioned, on the "valence" of errors, that is, on the perception of the meaning of making an error. If the student sees error-making as threatening, then he will avoid it: for that student who does so, an errorless learning experience will probably be beneficial, just as the errorless sequence was beneficial to the pigeon. On the other hand, the nondirective therapy analogy implies not that one should teach without errors in the cognitive sense, but that there should be no errors in the emotional sense. This might be translated into conditioning terminology as follows: the making of errors should not result in punishment. However, one must be realistic in his appraisal of the usual situation, where error-making *has* been punished, and provide an accepting environment for discovery learning, so that the fears which errors elicit can be extinguished. Perhaps this should be qualified: one does not want errors to become reinforced, and one actually wants to have some *mildly* punishing outcome; the anxiety produced, therefore, should be the type that is termed *facilitating* rather than *debilitating*. This is probably an expression of the *degree* of anxiety, and is based in part on the rate of error-making in the learning experience as well as on the degree of punishment experienced (lack of reinforcement is itself, in a sense, punishment, so if one tries to extinguish error behavior he is to a degree punishing it). The affective reaction to making errors is also a function of the confidence of the student in the learning situation, that is, his confidence in the teacher. If he feels that the teacher "knows what he is doing," he can be induced to take greater risks than if he does not feel that way: thus the confidence of the teacher, even if to some degree a sham, is a factor in teaching. Prestige studies indicate that students learn more from a given presentation if they assume that the person making it is an authority.

16–6 Using Group Dynamics

The influence of a group upon its members is considerable. If students feel that they belong to a group, their behavior will be controlled by the principles and rules and ethics and interests of that group. The degree of this control will vary with the individual. Each individual belongs to a number of groups. Thus each student has group sets that can be altered. If he is thinking in terms of one group of which he is a member (or wants to be) he may act one way, and still another way if he is thinking of another such group. Thus students are seen to change their behavior at times in seemingly inexplicable ways. The influence of a group is partly a function of its attractiveness, partly of the relevance of the group's attitudes toward whatever problem or situation is current. The classroom, as a necessary and inevitable part of the environment, is often a relatively neutral aspect of the functioning of social groups in the school, and the teacher has a certain amount of leeway and choice in determining the relation of the class to various school groups (as well as its relation to the individual, as will be discussed below).

The teacher has two approaches at his disposal in motivating via groups: first, the establishment of the class as a group, with common aims, interests, rules, ideals, and such; second, the relating of the class and the individuals in it to other groups to which they belong, both individually and collectively, to derive positive motivation from these toward the class. The latter approach will be discussed first.

The students in a class belong to a number of groups; the higher the grade level the more numerous and important these groups become, with a maximum being reached in high school and perhaps a submaximum in college, depending on the nature of the college. The teacher will find that certain activities in relation to the course, particularly those carried on outside of class (homework, projects, papers) will be affected by group activities involving clubs, social cliques, and the like. Assumedly, however, these activities will have been structured so as to make a place for studying and projects, especially if the environment is such that study for college entrance and later success are considered important and relevant. If such is the case, then the scheduling of assignments and the nature of assignments should take into account this environmental structuring, if optimal effort is desired. Now the scheduling may not be adequate in the eyes of the teacher, and it may be mishandled in terms of study behaviors (with TV on, in groups, and so on); in this case, an appeal to the group leaders may be effective if the teacher presents a sensible and logical case and backs it up with his or her prestige and concern. This will be particularly effective if the teacher is seen as a "good teacher," and this is one behavior that a good teacher exhibits, that is, concern over the place of studying in the extra-school environment.

The appeal to group leaders and group codes may be more effective if carried on through the students themselves. While some studies indicate that the alienation of students from parents, which is particularly a concern at the high school age, is not as great as it has been made out to be, the students may be effective advocates of a better environmental arrangement for studying if they are convinced by the teacher that such an arrangement is necessary and will pay off in better under-standing and mastery—however these words are defined by the teacher.

Another source of identification of the class with positive aspects of outside groups is a continual awareness and informed position on the part of the teacher concerning these groups. The teacher will profit from knowing what is going on in the school; which groups are consid-ered important in and out of school; who the leaders are; what their interests and objectives are; and where they stand in relation to the subject being taught as well as in relation to academic work in general. The teacher also needs to be aware of individuals who are not members of groups, who are to a greater or lesser extent isolates or rejects, so that he can avoid difficulties in interpersonal relations with them, that is, so that he can take this into account and understand the concerns that may be interfering with performance or that, on the other hand, may be motivating overachievement on the part of some individual.

While the teacher need not pander to the interests of these groups that influence student behavior, if he shows an awareness of them, he will to some extent appropriate some of the positive influences of the group on his class, particularly if he is a person whom the students identify as an adult version of the type the group wishes to attract. Some teach-ers go a long way toward functioning as partial members of groups in such cases, but it can interfere with their functioning in their profession if not handled intelligently, and has implications that can be dangerous.

Generally speaking, an awareness of the nature and norms of groups outside the classroom enables the teacher to avoid asking for behavior that deviates considerably from group norms (or to realize that he is asking for it, where necessary); to make his objectives obviously rele-vant to the attitudes and interests of these groups or to explain the reasons for a lack of relevance or a conflict; to appreciate the influence of certain members of his class in terms of group leadership (though not to kowtow to it or treat such an individual differently as a result); to relate the changes which he attempts to bring about to group objec-tives where possible; and to realize that certain objectives of the class will produce a strain on the group, and to anticipate and allow for this where possible. It will also enable the teacher, as a counselor and guide, to assist the individual in adjusting his behavior to that of a group or to steer him toward membership in groups that are more likely to pro-tect his self-esteem and make him feel adequate and needed.

Another aspect of group dynamics, and a very important one, relates to the class itself as a group. Studying a new subject can be exciting because it is different. Learning something new, if it isn't initially too threateningly difficult, is motivating: this is another expression of the competence–curiosity–exploration motive. Furthermore, there are in-herent in classroom study of a subject, elements that make for group cohesion and that can be used to bring group dynamics to bear. For instance, if each member of the class can identify himself as the member of a group studying a new subject, in a kind of clubby way, then he is more likely to change his behavior in a manner consistent with the best interests of understanding the subject. In any class, there will be attractive members, and there will also be certain topics and characteristics of the course that make it attractive in competition with other courses. One should consider this competition with other courses as the important comparative element, rather than competition with out-of-school freedom, since the students do not expect such freedom during school hours. If the attractive elements of the class, including the individuals in it, particularly the teacher, and the unique and interesting facets of it, plus a warm atmosphere and a consistent set of ground rules are all evident and used to advantage, the class will exert an influence on the behavior of the students. Furthermore, if one can make the learning experiences relevant to these attractive features, that is, make them bear out the most positive factors of the attractiveness and not contradict them (for example, if one can make the speaking of French in simulated French culture situations part of the learning experience in a French class), then the influence of the class on the behavior of students will be correspondingly greater. Another source of influence is the development of group norms, things that are and are not done in the classroom, particularly things that are highly relevant to the subject (saying certain types of things only in French in a French class; qualifying statements in a careful way and stating one's conditions and postulates clearly in a mathematics class; reasoning from observed phenomena and quantifying one's reasoning in a physics class; and the like). These are most easily established by the teacher in the beginning, on the basis of past experience indicating which norms the group is most likely to accept, as well as by taking advantage of spontaneous group norm-setting if it occurs, or by setting up discussion sessions aimed at dealing with norms and perhaps at altering them. If these norms are compatible with the types and natures of norms established by other groups of which the students are members, then these norms will be even more influential; for example, if the norms are simple and behavioral and easily observable, then the younger students will be able to conform to them more easily, whereas older students will require a more subtle and sophisticated system of norms for behavior and interpersonal relations and learning success.

Other aspects of group influence will be covered in the discussion of achievement motivation; they include an acceptance by the group of the need for behavioral change, and some perception of the reasons for strains resulting from learning in relation to norms and codes of other groups to which they belong or to within-group feelings (in relation to grades, for instance).

16–7 Modeling

Modeling is an important and basic approach to bringing about behavior in a student, and thus a means of bringing about learning, and therefore a way of motivating someone to learn. It means providing an exemplar for the behavior of the student. It is a quicker way to bring about a new behavior than shaping is, since it offers a complete or partial version of the final behavior and makes it possible for the learner to imitate it fully. This is more efficient than building solely on behaviors resembling the criterion which the learner engages in by chance, as in shaping.

To take advantage of modeling, the learner must be able to imitate. The crucial role of imitation in learning was discussed previously in respect to verbal behavior, but here we refer to imitation of all kinds. It is worth noting that each modeling exemplar has relevant and irrelevant dimensions or attributes, and that the success of the learner in imitating an example is partly dependent on his ability to identify the most relevant ones. On the other hand, imitation involves reproduction of both relevant and irrelevant dimensions to some degree.

The criterion behavior need not be modeled completely in the early stages. Successive approximations to the criterion may be modeled in the manner of shaping, and the process will still be quicker and more efficient than shaping. Such a process is called *graduated modeling* and exemplifies the general direction of teaching, i.e. going from simple to complex or toward decreased redundancy, as discussed previously in relation to concept formation.

Modeling is surprisingly effective in a number of situations. For example, in the desensitization of test anxiety, it has been found experimentally that students who observed another student going through the desensitization process become desensitized themselves as a result. In another vein, one often hears that young people have a need for teachers with whom they can identify, i.e. who represent desirable models for their future behavior in social as well as intellectual situations. In Freudian terms, this represents an "ego ideal," or an exemplar of positive, effective behavior which the learner's ego can use as a standard to measure his behavior and modify it accordingly.

In another field, the author himself found when teaching tennis that his actions spoke louder than his words in that he achieved better results by exemplifying the strokes being taught than by describing them in words or telling the student when he was "on the right track." This seemed to extend even to a strategy of demonstrating a forehand left-handed when facing a right-handed learner, so that the learner saw in effect a mirror image of the criterion behavior.

In a more general sense, teachers set an example of learning behavior by their own approach to and attitude toward their subject. Unfortunately it is not unusual for a teacher to complain that students are not interested in the subject and then to exemplify a similar lack of interest in the teaching of it. A teacher can model "motivated" behavior and thereby bring about "motivation," i.e. similar behavior, in students.

16–8 Scheduling of Reinforcement

In the section on reinforcement paradigms it was noted that responses that were reinforced on a variable intermittent schedule, for example, every third response on the average or every three minutes on the average, were much more resistant to extinction and also showed greater frequency or probability. Reinforcers were defined as stimuli which reinforced, that is, which resulted in the preceding response being more frequent. Reinforcers are where you find them. A test, or quiz, for example, results in an increase in the behavior that precedes it, namely, studying; thus it is a reinforcer for study behavior, although the reinforcement may be negative (i.e., release from concern over a grade). The kind of study behavior which is successful on the particular type of quiz is differentially reinforced also. Thus, one can put quizzes on an intermittent schedule, either regular or variable, and achieve correspondingly high rates of responding. If the schedule is regular, say a quiz every five days, then study behavior will increase to a maximum just before the quiz and drop off to a minimum immediately following it. If, on the other hand, a quiz is given every five days on the *average*, study behavior will tend to be more regular between quizzes. Another implication of reinforcement scheduling has to do with the amount of reinforcement; one might predict that since the amount is not crucial, one will get the same level of study behavior with a short quiz as a long one. More research in this area is certainly called for.

Quizzes are fortunately not the only reinforcers that a teacher has to use. Teacher approval is the most convenient one and is also very effective if used sensibly. One would hope to put students on a reasonably high ratio here, perhaps every fourth or fifth response either individually or collectively as the situation allows; for anxious students a lower ratio, for overconfident ones a higher one would seem to be called for. Since the amount is not crucial, one need not overdo it; certainly the success and rapport of some teachers with a notably bland personality, even in some cases an overtly sarcastic or aggressive one, indicates that this is true. The secret then seems to be in knowing the students, attending to them, learning them as it were, and then treating them each according to his needs. One answers these needs by reinforcing differentially according to the behavior one has in mind, always maintaining the basic positive regard for the individual which implies that the teacher is behaving this way for the student's benefit, and that these negative responses are part of the game rather than a basic value judgment of the human being involved.

16–9 Small Group Processes

Recent developments in teaching and in therapy seem simultaneously to tend toward the employment of small groups to achieve their ends. In teaching, there have been several experimental demonstrations of the ability of a small group structure to involve students in cognitive matters and to bring them to a more thorough understanding of the subject; at the same time there are indications that this kind of process results in more lasting involvement with the subject, beyond the course itself. On the other hand, individual therapy, an expensive and time-consuming process, has been supplanted to a significant degree by group therapy. The most publicized version of such therapy is the *T-Group* or *Encounter Group*. Whether for cognitive gain or emotional therapy, there are themes which are common to small groups relative to motivation. One characteristic of the small group is involvement by each participant; the fewer the people, the more the individual feels compelled to participate and become involved in the process. Another characteristic is greater communication; since there is more participation, there is a higher level of interaction of ideas and feelings among the participants. In the basic encounter group it is assumed that people do not accurately identify the motives of others and the sources of their own feelings; in this sense it is a concept-identification process. When such groups are turned toward more conventional cognitive goals, the process is not dissimilar, but there is one major difference. In the encounter group the subject matter is known to all, that is, it is what the participants know and have experienced, by definition. In the learning of particular subjects typical of school, the subject matter is determined more from without and may not be part of the experience or preparation of the participants. When this is true, the group experience may not be as productive as it can be if the participants *are* well informed. On the other hand, the existing information of participants will be better and more thoroughly utilized in such a situation if the participants are accustomed to small group processes than it will if a conventional lecture-demonstration-discussion process is the strategy.

16–10 Warmth, Clarity, Task Orientation

Motivation is increased by having a warm, accepting teacher. The atmosphere created seems to promise the reinforcement and guarantee the security that the student needs in order to concentrate on the cognitive task. Another motivating factor is the clarity with which the teacher communicates objectives and processes to the class; regardless of warmth or reinforcement or other such dimensions, if a teacher is very clear about the requirements of the task and the behaviors expected of the student, their behavior will be more productive, and more of them will engage in this behavior. Communication, then, is an important facet of motivation. Finally, if the teacher is task-oriented and sets an example of working toward solution of the problems that are presented, then the behavior of the children will be more motivated, that is, they will accomplish more and do so with less fuss and difficulty. This task orientation submerges some of the personal idiosyncracies and momentary difficulties in the quest for the goal and in a sense is less personal and humanistic but in another sense is less reinforcing of concern over minor personal problems and therefore extinguishes minor personal concerns in the course of learning.

16–11 Curiosity, Intrinsic Motivation, Discovery, and Inquiry

Curiosity, a need to understand and control the environment, and freedom of choice are all used as explanations for the evident concentration and energy with which younger children carry on investigations of natural and artificial phenomena that interest them and "turn them on." While the claims for such approaches may have been overpublicized in the past, and while the students involved in such programs may have learned to learn this way previously through some extensive conditioning in the past, the successes achieved in certain programs using such approaches cannot be dismissed lightly. Beginning with such programs as the Montessori system and "progressive" problem-oriented approaches, and continuing into modern elementary science programs, one has a spectrum of energy-releasing environmental arrangements which sometimes approach the miraculous in engaging the attention of young learners. When one takes into consideration as well studies of group and individual behavior indicating that students work better in an atmosphere which is task-oriented rather than person-oriented, where the teacher justifies requests in terms of their contribution to the behavioral objectives rather than their relationship to approval or disapproval of the teacher, one begins to feel that the tremendous emphasis on personal relationships and interpersonal contacts which has characterized much of education in the past has been perhaps overdone and has at times even interfered with the progress of communication of knowledge. Task-orientation can be coupled with warmth of relationships with groups and individuals to provide an environment wherein curiosity and other intrinsic motives can function.

If one accepts the thesis that discovery learning has advantages, then one must ask how this interacts with the effectiveness of error-free learning as discussed previously. It seems on the surface that discovery learning would result in errors, and thus that the two are antithetical.

Can they be resolved, or synthesized? Discovery implies a degree of autonomy in learning: generally speaking this also implies a higher probability of error. However, a false hypothesis may not appear to be an error if the student regards it only as information; thus the effect of the error is dependent on the previous learning (including classical conditioning of attitudes). One may reinforce a student for hypothesizing, even though the hypothesis is incorrect, and then reinforce him for restructuring the environment and coming up with a new hypothesis, which he also tests. If this is seen as the correct procedure, then there are no "errors" per se. Another factor that enters in is the number of possible hypotheses and their complexity: one can imagine a discovery situation where the problem is so simple and the logical alternatives so few that the probability of successful discovery of the answer is very low. This could lead to fewer errors, and in the extreme case, to errorless learning. Here the crucial matter would be the autonomy of the learner, that is, whether or not he felt he was free to choose his course of action—and in a sense, he would not be, since the alternatives left him would be very few. Whether he regarded this as a discovery situation or felt he was being "programmed" would depend on his view of the process, and this in turn would be dependent on his previous experience.

Discovery learning is sometimes made synonymous with inductive learning, that is, with learning from examples rather than through principles or rules. However, applying a rule can be a discovery process in a sense. One must interpret the words of the rule, form some hypothesis about its applicability to the existing problem, and then test that hypothesis. This is not entirely different from inductive thinking, either, because one may view the words of the rule simply as addresses by which one finds previous experiences in memory. In this case, one must again process, or reprocess, the previous experiences and come up with some relevant application or hypothesis concerning the current problem. Here again, the simplicity of the problem and of the rule affect the probability of error, and again the previous experience of the learner determines his attitude toward feedback, which tells him that his hypothesis was not appropriate or effective.

16–12 A Model for Achieving Change in People

A widely accepted conclusion that can be drawn from personality theories is that one cannot change the basic personality of adults, or even of adolescents. It has always been felt that the influence of early experience in combination with inherited potential is too great to overcome by any artificial means, at least after the person is past childhood. In this era, however, one has come to expect traditional views to be upset, and there is evidence that this view is no exception. There are groups who are engaged in bringing about changes in basic factors of people's personalities, through "workshops" and other experiences. One of the first factors of personality to be worked with in this way is one called the "need for achievement." This aspect of personality was identified and studied extensively before attempts were made to change it. Then, when it was decided to try, a many-sided model for bringing about change was derived from research in psychology, sociology, and education. It is this many-sided model that will be reviewed here, since it is one that can be used to bring about many different types of change; that is, it can be used as a many-sided approach to motivating students. The model was developed by David McClelland in an article entitled "Toward a Theory of Motive Acquisition," in the May 1965 issue of *American Psychologist*. This model has been applied to increasing the achievement need of businessmen. The examples that follow are taken from these "achievement motivation" workshops, but the principles can be applied to other factors of personality or areas of learning.

GOAL SETTING

One of the first steps in any training process or course is to bring the participants to expect it to "work," that is, to expect a change to occur in themselves. With this in mind, they are presented with information concerning the course and the teachers, information designed to lead them to think highly of the effectiveness of the approach and the personnel. This is essentially invoking the concept of prestige and its effects on learning and attitudes. Another preliminary step is to give the participants a preview of the kind of outcomes which they may expect from the course or experience. This both informs the participants that other courses of this type have been successful and raises expectations of positive outcomes.

This attempt to impress the participants and raise their expectations leads into another activity, that aimed at bringing the students to commit themselves in some way to following through with the course in order to experience the improvement that has been promised. This commitment can come in various ways—in making definite plans for oneself in terms of the promised behaviors; in structuring one's activities to enable one to keep a careful record of his successes and failures in the course; in choosing to play certain games which are part of the course and putting up a sort of "ante" in order to play.

TEACHING THOUGHTS AND BEHAVIORS

The activities discussed above have to do primarily with setting a goal for the learner and developing ways for him to keep track of progress toward it. Another phase of bringing people to change (motivating them) is to enrich the cognitive life of the participant in a way compatible with and productive of the behavior one wishes. In achievement workshops, which are based on this model of motivation, participants are taught the ideas and feelings that are typical of achievement-oriented people. The tool used for this is programmed instruction, which in itself requires some activity on the part of the learner (writing answers in spaces, where these answers are increasingly complete stories evidencing achievement orientation). Thus the participants are taught to "think achievement," just as they could be taught to "think French" or "think mathematics."

At the same time, realizing the inadequacy of verbal behavior alone in effecting actual behavior in all its variety, we lead participants to play certain particular types of games where achieving behaviors pay off. These games emphasize independent and autonomous action and the element of choice, and the payoff in these games is a function mainly of the ability of the player to match his aspirations to his past performance. The player must risk a certain amount to play, must choose the level of performance to which he aspires, and must pay penalties for overestimating his performance. He is also given profits for good performance. The achievement-oriented person, it is noted, plays more for the challenge of the game than for the concrete rewards, although they too are important. Furthermore, he aspires to a performance of medium difficulty or a little above that on the basis of his past performance, rather than shooting too high or too low. A similar behavioral approach, using games, could be designed to bring students to act like physicists or economists.

Knowing thoughts and actions connected with a way of behaving is not enough to guarantee a change in that direction. One must also *relate* the verbal associative network and the game activity to "real life." This is done through examples of applications, through discussions related to the individual's own environment and life style, and through suggestions for application from various members of the group. This leads naturally into another phase of the course, that having to do with the relation of the new way of behavior to various referent groups of each individual participant and to his culture in general.

GROUP SUPPORTS

As one source of group support, the course itself is seen as a particular reference group and its "groupy" characteristics are emphasized. One way of doing this is to hold it in a setting where no other people interfere; such a setting is often called a "retreat" setting. If the group is the only one around, then there is greater probability of topic-oriented thought and action and less probability of outside distraction; this increases the intensity of the experience.

Another source of group support is a series of group and individual discussions emphasizing a confrontation with codes of other groups that tend to inhibit achievement-oriented behavior, plus attempts to reason these through in such a way that they are no longer barriers. For instance, some religions reject the attitudes and behaviors of achievement-oriented activity: they lead the individual to be satisfied with what he has and not to aspire to something better, although within his grasp (the "opiate of the people" aspect of religion). In the achievement workshops these taboos are discussed and the resulting problems are thought through. Some societies have codes and beliefs that inhibit achievement behavior: the most obvious of these is the "evil-eye" concept of certain African tribes, where individuals do not want to risk achievement (involving accumulation of wealth or property) because they will be seen as having taken it from someone else and thus invite others to give them the "evil eye," that is, to wish them ill and thus make them actually ill or make some accidents come about. Similar religious and cultural barriers exist in respect to other areas of learning and change: for example, the reader may experience some such reactions to a science of human behavior.

INDIVIDUAL SUPPORTS

The type of leadership given the group itself has important implications for the motivation of the individuals in the group. Achievement motivation research has identified a type or style of leadership that seems to be typical of parents, particularly fathers, of high achievement-motivated boys, and which is used in these workshops to further encourage or shape achievement motivation. This treatment features an accepting response to behaviors of the participants, combined with personal warmth; this is essentially nondirective therapy, combined with a supportive attitude toward achievement-oriented behavior, including both suggestions for achievement lying within the capability of the student (but permissiveness in letting the person choose his goals) and a reinforcing type of behavior following achievement. This treatment is interesting in its similarity to teaching styles discussed in a later chapter.

One additional aspect of this model for motivating changes which is interesting in its own right and also in relation to concepts of motivation covered previously has to do with the individual and his view of himself and his environment. Individuals are brought to confront themselves and their own attitudes toward the desired change; this is done in small groups, as described previously, and in individual counseling sessions. These are designed to allow the person to work through associational and experiential blocks to the new behavior so that he may pursue the acquisition of such behaviors without being threatened by his superego.

These individual and group sessions thus invoke the type of therapy that has been discussed previously as nondirective therapy and T-Groups, and further synthesize aspects of subject-matter oriented behavior and concerns for the emotional components of learning. They seem to imply generally that one is in either case attempting to communicate concepts and processes. In T-Group work, one is trying to communicate concepts of group interaction and affective responses accompanying it and uses the actual group present to generate exemplars that can be used in the discovery process. In nondirective therapy, one is providing an accepting environment in which the patient can bring up experiential data to examine and thereby reformulate his concept of himself in relation to others. In teaching subject matter, one is trying to provide an environment in which the student can deal with exemplars of concepts and processes, furnish hypotheses which explain them, test these hypotheses, and react accordingly—a concept formation or identification process that is facilitated by an accepting atmosphere where hypothesis-forming is not punished if it diverges from the accepted "correct" formulation and where the ideal learning *process* is reinforced as well as the correct convergent responses that are derived from the principles so established.

Bibliography

BRUNER, JEROME S. *Toward A Theory of Instruction.* New York: W. W. Norton, 1966.

KRUMBOLTZ, J. D. *Revolution in Counseling.* Boston: Houghton Mifflin Co., 1966.

ULRICH, R., STACHNICK, T., and MABRY, J. *Control of Human Behavior.* Glenview, Illinois: Scott, Foresman & Co., 1966.

17 Teaching: Some Strategies and Modes

17-1 The Relationship of Teaching to Learning

Teaching is a process of arranging the environment so that certain behaviors become more probable. This requires preparation of the environment and also interaction between students and teachers. There is assumedly an initial and a final state of the learner, and these states can be compared by observing the behavior of the student to judge whether a change has occurred. This in turn implies evaluation. The evaluating agent may be a hungry tiger waiting for a caveman who has not learned that the tiger waits in a certain place at a certain time, or a teacher who informs a student about tigers and admonishes him when he starts out at the wrong time, or a computer which presents a simulated search problem and informs the student that he may consider himself to have been eaten because he took the wrong path at the wrong time.

Teaching as arrangement of the environment has to do with the question of whether learning comes from without or within the learner. One can imagine a student who is being taught about tigers and finds it extremely dull; he feels that this useless information is being forced on him and that he really ought to be allowed to study something relevant. One can imagine another who is hungry and needs to get food but wants to avoid being attacked; to him the learning is meaningful. If there *is* real danger from tigers, both students need to learn about it; however, if tigers have become extinct, the first student may be justified in his opinion.

In either case, the learning is imposed from outside the learner. John Locke viewed learning as coming from without when he said,

Let us then suppose the mind to be . . . white paper, void of all characters without any ideas; how comes it to be furnished? Whence comes it by that vast store which the busy and boundless fancy of man has painted on it with an almost endless variety? . . . To this I answer, in one word, from experience; in that all our knowledge is founded, and from that it ultimately derives itself.

John Dewey reflected a similar view in one of his later books, *Experience and Education*. On the other hand, Socrates felt that the elements of knowledge were in some sense inherent *in* the student, and that teaching involved bringing these latent concepts into useful expression or existence. Plato's views of early education, however, imply that he would not depend entirely on these inherent ideas, but would impose basic skills at the elementary level. Rousseau, in his *Emile*, asserted that education comes to us from three sources, namely, nature, men, and things. In his view, nature determined the make-up and capacity of "natural man," and "natural man" was subject to shaping or warping by his environment, by men and things. There is a modern view which treats learning as neural networks formed in the brain of the very young child in response to stimuli from his environment. The nature of the networks, and thus the nature of future learning to an extent, is determined by the nature of the experiences to which the child is exposed. In this sense the world impresses itself upon the child's brain, determining what he will and will not learn easily and quickly later on.

Another modern view of learning, that of Piaget, implies that children's minds unfold naturally through hereditarily determined mechanisms, and that some things are possible at one stage, more advanced things at another. The question of whether one can speed up this process is called by Piaget, "the American question"; he does not consider it to be a crucial question.

A balanced view of learning must reflect this nature-nurture duality. One way is to regard learning as an interaction between environment and learner, mediated by a teacher. Whether learning comes primarily from within or without, there is a practical need for environmental arrangements (contingencies) that harness the ability of the student and bring him to learn things that he might not otherwise learn. Arranging the environment is not the limited thing one might assume at first: it includes not only the physical surroundings, but the behavior of the teacher, use of texts and other such media, alteration of the social environment, and consideration of the point of view or frame of reference of the learner himself. One way of arranging the environment is by changing the physical location of the learner. Another way is to alter it by oral or visual presentations. Another way it can be changed, more subtle and not always recognized, is by directing the attention of the learner to different facets of it, to make him more *aware* of certain elements of the varied and complex array of stimuli that impinge upon him from without (and from within, incidentally). Thus one may "arrange" or change the subjective environment without altering physical conditions. The learner himself may direct attention to different components or aspects of the environment, calling up memories of past experiences that apply. This may be part of what is meant by "learning from within," as compared to learning "imposed from without."

Learning takes place regardless of teaching: the environment applies its contingencies in the absence of any purposeful arrangement. Teaching is the purposeful arranging of the environment, implying that effort or work has been put into it to make it more orderly, in a broad sense, while perhaps making it more disorderly from the immediate point of view. This in turn implies that there is some set of principles by which the teacher acts upon the environment, although he may act intuitively or imitatively without being aware of the principles.

17–2 Assessing Learning

Since one doesn't know what actually goes on in the mind of a student during learning, he must look for indirect evidence of change to show that learning has taken place. This can be gained by observing the behavior of the student under certain conditions. Now when one observes the behavior of another person, he calls portions of that behavior *responses* and calls portions of the environment accompanying and preceding the responses *stimuli*. The responses can be emotional or attitudinal in origin, or motor, or primarily cognitive. If one's objective is to elicit responses that demonstrate interest in the subject and enthusiasm for studying, then such responses become the criterion behavior and should be evaluated. If the teacher's objective includes acceptance of himself by the students, then some behavior on the part of the students which indicates acceptance should be the criterion. Such outcomes are relevant to teaching, just as is the process by which the student comes to respond correctly to a stimulus like, "The main mass of the nucleus of the atom is accounted for by nuclear particles called _____" or "Discuss some of the causes of the Russian Revolution of 1917."

While a student may have learned but may not respond in a certain situation designed to evaluate his learning, it is dangerous to talk about a student's "knowing" something but not showing it. The absence of a response in a given situation is important evidence that learning may not have been sufficient or that other responses are interfering. Unless these interfering responses can be identified and their controlling stimuli identified also, one should be very hesitant to conclude that the student has learned if he has not demonstrated it.

Some people involved in teaching feel that to require behavioral demonstration of learning mechanizes a process that is otherwise eminently human and creative. There is no more complex, delicate, and essentially human a task than that involving the attempt to arrange the infinitely complex environment of human beings in such a way that certain sophisticated and meaningful behaviors become more probable and come more under the conscious control of the learner. It also seems likely that there is no term which includes more complex and sophisticated human processes and activities than *behavior*. One should not be put off, then, by the oversimplifying of this behavior which is done in order to analyze and study it. One aspect of scientific endeavor which is little understood is the power of oversimplified models to assist men in coping with subtle and complex phenomena. There is admittedly no more difficult a set of behaviors to understand than those of humans in coping with their culture, and there may well be a limit to our ability to understand them. However, this does not mean we should not try, and to make progress we must submit our cherished uniqueness to close scrutiny in order to build models that help us cope with educational and social difficulties. Thus, while teaching will always be an art, it can simultaneously become more of a science. Such a science can enable the art to function on a higher plane.

17–3 Teaching and Stimulus Modes

Teaching is conventionally accomplished through the symbolic mode, by text or lecture or discussion. There is, however, increasing interest in the use of iconic and concrete modes for teaching at all levels and about use of selection rather than reception strategies to make learning more rewarding. As there are different stimulus modes, so there are different types of environmental arrangements and different strategies of teaching in respect to these modes. One can arrange the physical environment so that events combine to reinforce certain types of responses: such an arrangement is exemplified by the use of Cuisenaire rods, Montessori tasks for preschool children, and blocking and tackling drills in football. One can also arrange iconic stimuli to produce certain behaviors: examples are coloring books, graphical presentations calling for certain responses in mathematics, and illustrations in reading books that contribute to the meaning of the words. Symbolic arrangements obviously include both texts and spoken words, in various combinations and types of presentations.

Words are used to refer to common experiences and to simulate new experiences by bringing the old ones into new relationships with each other, as in the formal operational stage of cognitive processing described by Piaget. Problems inherent in this use of words stem from lack of clarity in the words themselves, which in turn implies a lack of experience with their referents on the part of students and/or general weaknesses in using such symbols to form new relationships from the old ones. For example, if a student is given the description "blue circle" or "under the table or beside it," he visualizes exemplars of these concepts in conjunction or disjunction and thus arrives at a hypothesis concerning the relationship described. This hypothesis can be tested by identifying some exemplar of the concept (relationship), or by describing one and receiving feedback concerning that response. If a student is receiving a continuous discourse on some topic, his hypothesis about the meaning of one sentence may be checked against subsequent ideas or relationships or descriptions given by the speaker. If these confirm the student's hypothesis, then he "understands" the speaker (teacher); if they do not, then *he* does not. If he does not, it may be difficult for him to shift his hypothesis to another one and examine it in the light of the new information, since the speaker continues on to related ideas and outcomes. Thus a student may "lose the thread" of the presentation.

One way to avoid the difficulty mentioned above is for the speaker or teacher to provide numerous exemplars of the concepts he is communicating, thus allowing more time for hypothesis forming, testing, and reforming on the part of the students. This gives more room for error and recovery from the error, as it were. Another way to avoid the difficulty is to provide opportunity for students to test hypotheses through questions put to the speaker. Since they have to form a hypothesis before they can test it through a question, the encouragement of questions also reinforces hypothesis formation and testing, a form of "learning to learn."

In another approach, the speaker puts forth a very limited presentation, perhaps a sentence or two, then encourages responses from the students and reacts to them so as to provide feedback and simultaneously reinforce the responding. He may shape the responses in the direction of more intelligent, thoughtful, insightful hypotheses over a period of time; shaping implies beginning at a level that is easily handled by the student and proceeding through gradual steps of successive discrimination between good and not-so-good questions.

One can go beyond this to a true discussion, where the teacher acts as a leader but where the feedback for one student is provided by other students, and where the interaction is among the students as much as it is between teacher and students. A small group such as this can become a society all in itself, with its own special language and relationships. It can become a T-Group, with the primary objective to explore verbal and nonverbal relationships among the members of the group, the data (information) being generated within the group in the form of verbal intercourse. Here, information does not need to come from "outside" the group, at least not for long periods of time. There is, however, some question about the effects of such experience on subsequent behavior, a transfer problem. Utilizations of the concepts and attitudes acquired through such a group process is affected by group dynamics existing in other settings that reinforce other behaviors and extinguish those conditioned in the special group setting.

This matter of the interrelationships of students and teacher varies from a simple presentation strategy, with all students receiving the stimuli generated by the teacher, to the case where the students are communicating with each other rather than the teacher. This is usually described in terms of verbal communication alone. However, the interaction concepts also apply the use of iconic and concrete stimuli in teaching. One may base a presentation on iconic stimuli, although it is customary to use words along with it, as in describing a graph or talking about a picture; one may also base it on concrete stimuli, usually with word accompaniments *but not necessarily*, as in giving a demonstration in science. This can be done with no overt response from students, or to encourage questions, or in a discussion mode with the students reacting to the iconic or concrete stimuli by communicating with each other primarily. On the other hand, one can have nearly pure iconic stimuli used, as in the *direct method* of foreign language teaching, where vocabulary words are acted out by the teacher rather than simply translated for students. Interaction involving enactive and concrete stimuli are also possible, although pure forms of the latter are rare. Sequences of learning tasks in these last two modes hold promise for interesting and productive approaches to teaching in many standard and special settings.

17–4 Teaching Strategies

There are several dimensions along which one may vary his instructional strategy. There are the stimulus or response modes—concrete, iconic, symbolic. There is the matter of exemplar, title, and rule: one may give exemplars in any mode, but the title must be iconic or symbolic, and the rule is obviously symbolic. This brings up the question of sequence: should the rule be given first, or the exemplar, or the title, or does the optimal sequence vary with the subject matter or perhaps with the student? Some of these questions will be discussed below. Then there is the dimension of teacher dominance or centeredness. This in turn determines in part whether the strategy is reception or selection by the student, where the latter implies emphasis on *overt* hypothesis formation and testing by the student, rather than the covert variety which assumedly is used in the pure reception case. Finally, there is the matter of the criterion behavior, that is, what behaviors are to represent "understanding": will it be sufficient for the student to state the rule, or does he have to describe exemplars of the concepts and processes in words, or should he identify exemplars in iconic or symbolic modes? Does he have to solve a "problem," thus going through a chain of behaviors and arriving at some convergent response or "answer," or does he have to give a number of appropriate but, to some degree, unique responses to the stimulus situation, thus being reinforced for "creative" behavior or "divergent" thinking? Whatever the stimulus mode, does the student have to give his responses in the symbolic mode, or in the iconic or enactive? If the symbolic, what form does it take—

one-word responses, essay, short sentence, or choice of one of several possible statements or answers? And what of the scheduling of such criterion requirements, or tests: do they come on an interval or ratio schedule, and are they regular or variable? All of these are affected by contingencies of the environment, including the number of students involved per teacher and the availability of technological resources for carrying out the desired strategies.

17–5 Pure Reception Strategy—the Lecture

If the teacher is presenting information through a lecture, and if the lecture has been well constructed and used a number of times with a similar audience, with revisions each time, it is quite possible that it includes frequent review of topics taken up earlier in the lecture, questions that are posed and then answered by the lecturer (which the student may also answer himself and then receive feedback), and helpful summaries of sections of the lecture, as well as previews and overviews of the topics that are to be treated next in lecture. Such devices serve to overcome the over-all serial position effect whereby one loses track of material presented in the middle of the lecture, and also overcome in part the problem of providing for formation and testing of hypotheses by the members of the audience. As B. F. Skinner has observed, the most interesting lecture is the one in which the lecturer says things that the listener was almost but not quite ready to say himself.

In such a situation, asking questions may be premature, and one can imagine a student insisting on this privilege and thereby holding up the rest of the class and interfering with learning as a result. Such a student might be one who has not learned to follow such a lecture, or take notes on it for later reference, or both. In this respect, familiarity with the teacher's strategies is an important factor in learning, and points up the importance of adapting to the behavior of the teacher so that one may learn.

Why is it that the lecture is so widely maligned? A number of possibilities offer themselves. The first is that the lecturers aren't what they used to be. The great effort formerly devoted to preparation of materials, illustrations, and demonstrations is no longer accorded this art. The revision of lectures and re-presentation of them is no longer a matter of interest; the lecture as an "art form" has died out. Another possible reason is that text presentations have improved greatly, and as a result students are better able to learn material on their own through the aid of texts. Another possible explanation is that students generally do not have the motivation necessary to concentrate as closely, to work as diligently on note-taking and rewriting, and generally to adapt themselves to the lecture form of communication. This may be partly because general academic motivation is less than it was, and partly because there is competition from other sources of information such as texts and, more recently, films, programmed texts, and paperbound treatises on special subjects. It may be, on the other hand, that familiarity with these other media and better understanding of their functions and limitations will result in a return to the lecture as one of many viable forms for instruction. One indication of this was observed by the author in a research study involving a multimedia system: here, where lectures were carefully held to a minimum (roughly four in the given unit), and where the concepts and processes were introduced initially through observation of concrete phenomena and iconic and symbolic translations of these via programmed texts and films, students rated lectures as being high in effectiveness and interest in relation to other media.

The feasibility and potential effectiveness of a lecture approach to learning, where students "learn to learn" and in some cases derive optimal benefits for the time involved, does not preclude interest in and attention to other forms of communication and student–teacher interaction, as suggested by the last part of the paragraph above. The taking of notes during a lecture is one device for handling the more difficult aspects of learning through a presentation–reception strategy. Another teacher-dominated type of interaction, one where frequent provision is made for student response relevant to the concepts and processes and facts being treated, is one in which the teacher asks questions of the students or provides opportunities of them to ask them, and responds to these so as to clarify and emphasize and generally improve the understanding of the student. Sometimes it is less realistic to ask students to *formulate* questions than to *ask* them pointed questions, since the processing of information required for asking questions is sometimes of a higher order than they are capable of providing. It requires relating the current information to other information that one may not be able to recall (due to retroactive interference) and a shift in learning set from following the speaker to processing the information and forming questions. This last can be viewed as a shift from a reception to a selection strategy.

With these difficulties in mind, one may predict the need for the teacher to shape question-asking. This requires a degree of analysis of student and teacher behaviors that is not often found in teaching, so that the teacher will have clearly in mind which behaviors he wishes to maintain and enhance and which to extinguish. Teachers are often inclined to be more conscious of what they do *not* want than of what they *do* want. However, if one corrects a student on the basis of sophisticated criteria when he is just beginning to show the general type of behavior wanted, one can extinguish responding altogether. Thus when the student asks a question that evidences formulation of some model of the relationships involved in the subject matter, the teacher should reinforce this, even though it is a long way from what the teacher wants. Of course, the shaping process needs to be continued to its ultimate conclusion; the teacher should not leave the student part way and assume he can do the rest on his own!

17–6 Teacher Dominance and Learning Through Verbal Communication

Teacher dominance should be differentiated from teacher-centeredness. A teacher who dominates the communication in the class can still do so with the student's needs in mind and can be successful in communicating concepts and processes to the students. However, there are some reasons to believe that dominance interferes with certain types of learning. In any discussion involving more than three or four students, some will be observing and learning vicariously or indirectly rather than taking part actively, so the basic variables are not only those of active participation of the student per se. The more fundamental question is that of a selection versus reception strategy in concept attainment, which in turn involves the formulation of hypotheses as discussed previously. Since one can carry only so much information in short-term storage, one must categorize and structure what one hears or sees, and one does this according to previously learned concepts. To determine the nature of the concepts involved, one must formulate these hypotheses and have them confirmed or contradicted by subsequent events. If the student employs correct concepts, and if his previous experience is relevant and applicable so that he receives confirming stimuli subsequently, he feels that he "understands." However, this implies he was very close to understanding already. For those not that close, the process requires shifting hypotheses on the basis of negative feedback, and implies a need for time for this shifting and retesting, with new feedback for each trial. Also relevant here is the social interference–facilitation effect discussed in Chapter 15, where the evaluative function of an audience is seen to interfere with learning in the early stages while promoting it in later stages. Thus there are two simultaneous requirements of the teacher: to arrange for an accepting and encouraging audience for each student (to prevent social interference) and to reinforce hypothesis formation and testing on the part of each individual or, if that is not possible, on the part of a large percentage of students in the class. It was pointed out before that this hypothesis forming and testing does not always require overt expression, but if one is to condition it and maintain it then one must bring it out. These considerations imply that a teacher-dominated classroom will not account for these needs as well as one where the teacher–student communication and interaction is more balanced.

17–7 Some Techniques of Interaction

The most obvious approach to encouraging the kind of interaction suggested by discussions above is through asking questions of the students. The response of the teacher to the students' answers is then, of course, crucial: both the content of the feedback that he or she gives, and also the attitudes conveyed by manner and tone of voice, will affect the future responding of the students. The teacher may say something that is designed to reinforce some behavior, but his tone of voice or manner may punish it at the same time, leading to avoidance of this behavior later on. The amount of *time* one waits for the student to ask a question and the *way* in which one waits for it affects the students' view of the teacher's feeling about such behavior; a teacher who is impatient punishes honest thought and sets up avoidance contingencies.

The influence of good examples should not be ignored. Identification with the model is still a powerful form of teaching, since it provides exemplars of the concept, "what works in this situation," and students are looking for behaviors that are effective. Once one has set a pattern for the kind of behavior one wants, one can then break the class into small groups and arrange for members of the groups to demonstrate the same behavior to others, receiving feedback from the groups: this gives wider opportunity for shaping of these behaviors since more students will be responding and receiving feedback, and those not responding will be more likely to be discriminating between correct and incorrect behaviors in order to respond to the other members of the group.

A corollary for this group process is to set up a "game," which is a set of contingencies where there is success and failure that can be anticipated and recognized by the players, and where there is some differential pay-off for degrees of approximation to the desired behavior. Through such contingencies of the environment one may bring about desired changes in the students' behaviors that are observable, and not dependent entirely on the assumed relationship between expressed verbal behavior and the appropriate physical behavior that it is supposed to motivate.

17–8 Factors That Interfere with Teaching

There is a problem which interferes with setting up contingencies that are best designed to shape desired behaviors, yet are not teacher-dominated and do allow for and encourage a high degree of student participation. It relates to the nature of satisfactions and rewards that people receive from teaching. It is that some teachers behave in such a way that it becomes evident they are reinforced by conforming student behavior; this is probably negative reinforcement since it avoids the negative consequences of deviant student behavior (misbehavior, noise, attention from authorities), at least in the mind of the teacher. However, it is often true that such motivation leads to treatment of students that brings on more, rather than less, deviant behavior, due to frustration, boredom, and lack of autonomy on the part of the students. Such insistence on conformity and submission evidences the desire of the teacher for power; at the same time, it enables him (in his mind) to avoid the aversive contingencies of student rebellion and aggressiveness. This is not to imply that teachers are more this way than other people, but rather that the organizational climate of schools brings out such behaviors in teachers and actually shapes them while extinguishing others that are more student-interest-oriented. Often when the climate of the school reinforces authoritarian behavior in this way, the teacher will rationalize it by attributing his behavior to the authority of the principal.

The analysis undertaken above does not imply that a teacher who lectures to his class is authoritarian and scared and not interested in the concerns of his students: a lecture may be the most appropriate and effective tool for the particular topic and situation, and the students may find it much more rewarding than some other form of instruction. It does imply, however, that a teacher should have a variety of strategies available, and that he should apply or use them flexibly and with variation. It is the range and appropriateness of instructional strategies that is most important, not the value of any particular one.

17–9 Verbal Interaction

If one assumes that a class has some ideal level and variety of verbal interaction, that students are encouraged to form hypotheses about problems and test them verbally, and that the resulting achievement on the verbal level approaches some ideal, then one must go further and ask what the relevance and applicability of this learning is. That is, does the achievement of the student on well-designed sets of criterion tasks imply that he is able to use the subject matter for whatever its purposes? Can he, for instance, apply historical concepts and facts to a current problem, or can he use his theorems and other mathematical tools to learn more mathematics or to solve some problem in physics or engineering? Do the concepts of logic and philosophic interpretations affect his behavior in life?

These questions are not the only and final questions that must be asked concerning the importance of learning, but they do indicate that verbal learning is not the be-all and end-all of education. Thus we must turn also to concrete and iconic stimulus modes and to enactive responses as criteria for learning, and examine the learning process in relation to them. Before coming to this, it first seems appropriate to examine one representative analysis of verbal behavior in the classroom that is compatible with the views of desirable strategies already presented.

There are several approaches to the analysis of verbal interaction in the classroom, one of which will be described briefly below. Analysis can be a research tool, and can also be the basis for initial or remedial teacher education. In Chapter 12, teaching was discussed as problem solving; analysis of verbal interaction is one method of giving feedback to the teacher regarding his problem-solving process in relation to teaching. The approach to be described is often termed the "Flanders System" or just plain "Interaction Analysis" (see reference at end of chapter).

The categories of teacher behaviors noted by the observer who analyzes classroom interaction according to this system are given below*:

1. Accepts feelings: accepts and clarifies the feeling tone of the students in a nonthreatening manner. Feelings may be positive or negative. Predicting and recalling feelings are included.
2. Praises or encourages: praises or encourages student action or behavior. Jokes that release tension, not at the expense of another individual, nodding head or saying "uh, huh?" or "go on" are included.
3. Accepts or uses ideas of student: clarifying, building, or developing ideas or suggestions by a student. As teacher brings more of his own ideas into play, shift to category five.
4. Asks questions: asking a question about content or procedure with the intent that a student answer.

5. Lectures: giving facts or opinions about content or procedure; expressing his own idea; asking rhetorical questions.
6. Gives directions: directions, commands, or orders with which a student is expected to comply.
7. Criticizes or justifies authority: statements intended to change student behavior from nonacceptable to acceptable pattern; bawling someone out; stating why the teacher is doing what he is doing, extreme self-reference.

8. Student talk—response: talk by students in response to teacher. Teacher initiates the contact or solicits student statement.
9. Student talk—initiation: talk by students, which they initiate. If "calling on" student is only to indicate who may talk next, observer must decide whether student wanted to talk. If he did, use this category.

10. Silence or confusion: pauses, short periods of silence, and periods of confusion in which communication cannot be understood by the observer.

Categories 1 through 4 are classified as *indirect*; implicitly they are

*Edmund J. Amidon and Ned A. Flanders, *The Role of the Teacher in the Classroom: A Manual for Understanding and Improving Teachers' Classroom Behavior* (Minneapolis, Minnesota: Paul S. Amidon & Associates, Inc., 1963), p. 12. Reprinted by permission of the authors and publisher.

more student-centered or less teacher-dominated than categories 5 through 7 which are titled *direct*. This refers to teacher behavior; student behavior is accounted for in categories 8 through 10. To analyze class behavior, an observer notes down the category into which behavior falls; he does this at intervals of three seconds. Thus the observer records a list of numbers representing the sequence of behaviors observed in a given time period: if the period of time is five minutes, obviously he will have recorded about one hundred numbers. One way to process this is through a simple frequency count, that is, by making a table showing how many instances there were of category 1, how many of category 2, and so on.

One statistic employed to advantage in such an analysis is the number obtained by dividing the total of indirect tallies by the total of direct tallies. This "I/D ratio" can be related to a number of variables that are potentially dependent on the statistic, that is, on the indirectness or directness of the teacher's behavior. Among these might be classroom climate, achievement, interest in subject, liking for teacher. Some research in this area indicates that there is indeed a relationship between I/D and achievement, where classes with a higher I/D ratio demonstrated better performance on achievement tests. There are also indications that the better teachers are those who have higher I/D ratios and demonstrate a wider range and flexibility of teaching strategies. One hypothesis that might be formed on the basis of such facts is that some teachers avoid many of the more warm and human elements of interpersonal behavior, perhaps out of anxiety over authoritarian and punitive influences in the environment, and thereby sacrifice both student rapport and to some degree communication with their students. This in turn may interfere with interest in and concentration on the content of the course.

The particular classification system described above can also be used to diagnose the behavior of the teacher and class and to suggest shifts in behavioral emphasis. One interesting mathematical tool adapted to this analysis is a graphic portrayal of the nature of the classroom atmosphere in respect to these variables. The list of numbers recorded by the observer might be as follows:

$$5, 4, 8, 4, 8, 3, 5, 5, 4.$$

To graph this sequence, one pairs the first with the second, the second with the third, and so on.

$$(5, 4), (4, 8), (8, 4), (4, 8), (8, 3), (3, 5), (5, 5), (5, 4), \ldots.$$

These ordered pairs are plotted on a graph or grid: the first pair (5, 4) would be plotted by placing a tally in the fifth row and the fourth column of the grid, that is, in the cell or square formed by the intersection of the fifth row and fourth column, as in Figure 17.1.

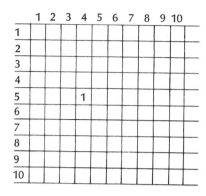

FIGURE 17.1

This type of analysis is based primarily on verbal interaction and implies the type of classroom where the teacher employs a presentation strategy with perhaps more emphasis than is conventionally given to questions by the students, both solicited by the teacher and initiated by the students themselves. In one investigation using interaction analysis, for example, the use of lecturing was between twenty-five and fifty per-cent of the behavior of the teachers in the sample, whether they were classified as high or low in indirect behavior. The difference between the two groups, low and high indirect, was not primarily found in the amount of time they spent lecturing, but in their behaviors during periods devoted to other activities. While the analysis system does allow for the kinds of behaviors involved in selection strategies for learning as long as the teacher–class relationship is maintained, it does not cover models of classroom interaction that emphasizes small group discussions, individual interaction with phenomena or programmed sequences, laboratory experiments, laboratory stations where small groups observe phenomena (demonstrations) and react to them in a qualitative rather than quantitative way, and other instructional strate-gies. Thus, while it is a convenient tool for analyzing one approach to teaching and to shaping teacher behavior in directions considered help-ful and productive, it also can be taken to imply that this conventional strategy of instruction (teacher–class verbal interaction) is the best or most effective one—something that one should not assume without some examination of the subject matter and the kinds of behaviors one wants to teach.

17–10 Interactions via Iconic Stimuli

Stimuli in the iconic mode, that is, diagrammatic and pictorial stimuli, have been presented as different from other modes in the degree of abstractness that they represent. Implicit in this has been the concept of sequencing of teaching experiences, with iconic exemplars assumedly being used to precede symbolic ones in the learning, just as in the case of children, who evidently develop abilities at the iconic level before they achieve the symbolic stage of cognitive processing. This recapitulation type of theory is but a first approximation to empirically derived principles for sequencing learning according to different modes. It does, however, suggest certain approaches to teaching that are not always followed at present.

If one analyzes verbal behavior from the standpoint of operant conditioning, defining verbal behavior as that reinforced through the mediation or intervention or response of another person, then iconic stimuli can be classified as "verbal." That is, one achieves certain responses in others through the use of iconic stimuli such as graphs and drawings of things or clock faces, just as one does through the use of symbolic (verbal) stimuli. This puts iconic stimuli in an interesting position in respect to instructional strategies, in that they are verbal and thus assumedly are handled in a manner similar to that used for verbal stimuli, and yet they are less abstract and therefore are appropriate to an earlier stage of the learning process. Thus one can use them initially to shape behavior through the use of simple versions of the task involving redundancy (perhaps using some irrelevant cues), then one could fade these cues and make the task more complex as learning proceeds. This would not necessarily involve any words, although words might be used to express certain things for which iconic stimuli are not available, or where they would be too convenient or difficult to provide. The important point here is that sequences of learning tasks can be designed which use iconic stimuli primarily or solely. The design of such sequences involves problems basically similar to those one finds in writing conventional text materials.

A more complex problem presents itself when one begins to examine the problem of compound stimuli, that is, stimuli in more than one mode, in this case combinations of iconic and symbolic. The interaction of the two is more properly a concern of instructional technology than instructional theory at present and involves also matters of student–medium interactions as well as student–teacher interactions. Generally speaking, the use of words with pictures and diagrams can clarify and improve the meaning of the total experience. However, there are cases where the use of diagrams or pictures has been shown to *confuse* the meaning of the words, and others where the use of words has been shown to interfere with the understanding of the diagrams. Research on this type of interaction is just beginning, and so it is difficult to prescribe or give general principles. Early indications are that in cases where the criterion behavior is primarily symbolic, diagrammatic and pictorial adjuncts to the symbolic presentation (words) are helpful and clarify the meaning. However, the engineering of the interaction of the two, so that they complement each other rather than cause confusion, is a matter that has received little attention. Where the criterion behaviors are primarily based on diagrammatic or pictorial stimuli, there seems to be reason to believe that iconic presentations (with brief word descriptions or explanations initially but more purely iconic tasks, ultimately) are most appropriate. This may seem obvious, yet present emphasis by text writers and publishers on verbal (word) presentations, that is, on prose as the vehicle for explanations, results in overuse and over-dependence on words. The conditioning of verbal responses, either individual or chain, is still the primary goal of many tests and teaching approaches, regardless of their relevance to the kind of behavior required later of the student.

17–11 Concrete–Enactive Interactions

In discussing the concrete–enactive aspect of learning one must distinguish between (a) enactive behaviors of the teacher designed to convey meaning, (b) enactive behaviors of the student, which are designed to give him resulting experience with concepts and processes leading to learning (Cuisenaire rods, for example), and (c) concrete stimuli arranged or presented by the teacher, or already existing to be observed, or both, which are exemplars or which may be acted upon to produce exemplars for learning. An example of (a) is found in a compound stimulus presentation in French, where the teacher is attempting to convey the meaning of a simple French phrase through his actions, while he is speaking it also, that is, he (alone or with another) is acting out the meaning. One may view this as a concept formation process where the concept is the meaning of the French phrase, and the exemplars are the situations or relationships or processes acted out by the teacher. Here the redundancy is relevant, in that it is more realistic and closer to the ultimate criterion behavior to have actions and situations accompanying the conversation than to present the conversation in conventional classroom fashion without such dimensions. Thus we have a case, and will see more such cases, where the adding of dimensions increases the redundancy rather than decreases it and where "realism" and increased complexity of the stimulus result in better learning. However, one should observe that it is quite possible to find that such a learning experience is more difficult than the conventional classroom approach, and that some teachers abandon attempts at such "direct" teaching because it *is* more difficult for the students. One should *also* observe that the "difficulty" experienced may be a function of the unfamiliarity and insecurity of the situation, and that if students had been "brought up" (previously conditioned) to learn this direct way, they would find *it* the easier approach.

The involvement of enactive responses and concrete stimuli has received much attention from science and mathematics educators. The use of concrete manipulanda in teaching basic concepts of mathematics is familiar to many: examples of this are found in the Cuisenaire rods for mathematics and the so-called Attribute Blocks of the Elementary Science Study group, among others. Enactive responses are also involved, in more sophisticated forms, in many games designed for use in training programs and in schools. Enactive responses are of course an integral part but not a primary objective of learning that goes on in physics, chemistry, and biology laboratories. Needless to say, physical education concentrates on the enactive aspects of behavior to a high degree and has developed methods of shaping complex behaviors to a high level of sophistication.

Also dependent on complex and sophisticated enactive responses are matters of personality and life style. One projects his image, his personality, his view of the world through behaviors that are observed and interpreted by others. These behaviors are to a large extent learned, although obviously controlled by attitudes and emotions as well as by environmental contingencies and patterns. The question of the relationship between verbal (symbolic) behaviors or responses and the actual physical behaviors they are supposed to affect has already been discussed. Communication through nonverbal behavior is just beginning to receive adequate attention.

The discovery or inquiry approach to a physical system involves enactive responses (on the part of the student) that affect the system in some way, causing it to react. The reaction of the system becomes the datum for problem solving. In a way, the student is "speaking to" his system through enactive responses, but these are not symbolic communications. Again, too, one has the possibility of shaping the behavior, of using redundancy, by providing the student with simple systems initially and then increasing their complexity little by little.

17–12 Interactions Generally

One general statement which may be made on the basis of discussions above is that the symbolic mode is used extensively, perhaps at the expense of the others in many cases where the others would be preferable. Combinations of modes are used and should be investigated for their relative effectiveness, rather than accepted in their common forms and relationships with each other. Perhaps most important, the relative effectiveness of various types of presentation should be investigated regardless of the present expense of these. There is reason to believe that the use of the symbolic mode almost exclusively in most educational presentations is attributable more to the economic advantages than the instructional ones: words are cheaper to produce than pictures and diagrams, which in turn are cheaper to produce than concrete exemplars, for large-scale use. They are also easier for the teacher to produce and easier to present, which accounts for some part of the predilection of teachers for getting up in front of the class and lecturing instead of adopting other strategies.

17-13 Preparation for Instruction

Learning as a process of hypothesis formation and testing requires problems or tasks to stimulate such behavior. To put it another way, one cannot formulate hypotheses if there is no problem situation to face, nor can one test them if one receives no feedback. If one is dealing with a physical system, one can stimulate it and observe the reaction; if, on the other hand, one is dealing with iconic or symbolic presentations, perhaps some describing a system, then the input will have to be simulated and the reaction of the system must be simulated also, through more symbolic or iconic stimuli. The student must give some response and then receive feedback simulating that reaction, or he must observe the simulated reaction and then respond to it in some way, receiving additional feedback concerning that response. Now the student's responses can be made by selecting some test to make on the system, in which case the feedback will tell him what came out of the system in return, and he will make further tests based on this. On the other hand, his response can be a prediction of how the system will react to some input determined or suggested by the teacher: in this case, the feedback will be information as to whether he is right or wrong. What this amounts to in practice, in iconic or symbolic presentations, is a sequence of tasks for the student, that is, problems or situations which he recognizes as requiring some response from him. After each response, no matter what its nature, the student will receive some feedback. This implies that the teacher has sequenced these tasks ahead of time and has determined the nature of the feedback; it also means that the student's responses are in some way predictable, so that feedback can be provided for them in advance. To some degree, then, this implies restraints on the possibilities of responding so that this feedback can be provided.

Bibliography

AMIDON, E. and HOUGH, A., eds. *Interaction Analysis: Theory, Research, and Application.* Reading, Mass.: Addison-Wesley, 1967.

DEWEY, J. *Experience and Education.* New York: Collier Books, 1963.

18 Programming for Learning

18–1 Programmed Instruction

In arranging the environment for learning, a great number of relationships and factors must be considered and utilized. Among these are conditioning paradigms, the concept of feedback, concept formation, interference factors as covered in verbal learning, and the success–failure dimension in relation to aspiration level as well as in relation to understanding. Given conventional approaches to teaching, it is not very easy to control these factors, since much of what is done in the classroom has been handed down through the years and has no particular rationale or theory behind it. A relatively new approach to teaching, developed fairly recently as an outgrowth of research in operant conditioning, does lend itself to well-controlled learning sequences. Its use has shed light upon the teaching process in general as well. This approach has been called *programmed instruction*. It emphasizes the control of limited responses through verbal stimuli and the breaking down of subject matter into many simple tasks so that the student is successful in answering correctly.

In programmed instruction one presents a task or question or statement that requires some response of the student, usually a verbal response and usually limited to one or a few words; the student writes his answer in a space provided for it. Then he is given the correct answer, or finds it, and compares with his own. Then another such task or question or statement is presented, and so on. A high level of success in responding or answering is maintained by developing the tasks so that the probability of success is great; this development involves trying out the questions or tasks on a student, then revising them on the basis of that student's responses, then trying them out on another student, and so on, until a high level of communication is achieved.

The combination of requirements put on programming, first that it permit the student to respond actively, second that it make it possible for him to be successful in responding, and third that it give him the correct answer or other information to allow him to judge his own responses, all of these place a great burden on the programmer. Thus programs are very hard to write well and also take a great deal of time and effort to produce. In spite of this, this approach to teaching has attracted many advocates and a considerable amount of research and development involving them has been generated. Some of this research uses "teaching machines," mechanical contrivances built to present the questions or statements or tasks of the program in sequence, to provide for student response, and then to enable the student to call for the correct answer when he is ready. "Programmed texts" are more frequently used; in these the correct answer is placed just below or beside the question, with a mask to hide it, or else it is placed on the next page, with the student turning to it after he answers himself.

Two major differences between programmed texts and conventional texts, aside from the very different appearances they give, are the large amount of preparation that goes into a very little material in the programmed version and the great expansion of space and print that the programs often require: what a conventional text might cover in four pages could fill a programmed text of forty or more.

One major requirement for programming is the breaking down of subject matter into small "steps." This is done so that the student will learn without making many errors. Another major requirement is the provision of statements or questions that require a response of the student: this is not always as easy to provide as it might seem. Where a conventional text will go through many sections and pages before presenting a number of questions, a programmed text asks questions of the student—and gives him the answer—every one or two sentences, or every paragraph at the most. There is some reason to believe now that in early programs this breaking down of subject matter was somewhat overdone, and that while active response and feedback are important factors in learning, more active response was required than was good for the learning process. It also turned out that students showed a reaction to this kind of learning not entirely different from that of athletic teams to calisthenics; that is, while they recognized the value of the practice, they preferred to scrimmage. To put this more elegantly, the programs often required generally too much responding, gave more feedback than was necessary, and partly as a result of this, brought on a negative reaction in students. In other cases, where the response requirements were more sensible and helpful and where the programs led to real learning, students reacted as if the degree and duration of concentration required were more than they could tolerate initially. Also, in many programs, the structure of the subject matter was poor and the learning process it required was not the best. Basically, however, programmed instruction has very solid theoretical foundations, and there is a great deal of empirical evidence indicating that it is an effective model for instruction. More needs to be done in developing new types of programs and adapting to other modes of presentation (beyond the purely verbal) before they will realize their potential.

All teaching represents a degree and type of programming. "Programmed instruction" has come to mean a certain type of presentation, perhaps unfortunately, since this promising approach has become stereotyped and rigid early in its development. Following concept identification procedures, it seems appropriate to present exemplars of tasks that might appear in a "program"; these tasks can be presented by programmed text, by teaching machine, or by computer-assisted instruction. In each case, one must assume that the correct answer or other appropriate feedback is presented after the student responds: it may be on the next page of the text, or it may be concealed by the machine until after the student responds, or it may be withheld by the computer until the student types his response.

> *Exemplar 1:* A stimulus is an input to a person in the form of some change in sensation. A response is some output from the person, often coming soon after the stimulus. For example, if a doctor taps the tendon just below your kneecap with a rubber hammer, and if your knee jerks, then the tap can be regarded as a s_____ and the knee jerk may be viewed as a _____e.

The redundancy of relevant and irrelevant dimensions here takes the form of verbal chains which suggest the order and nature of the answer, also the irrelevant dimensions of the first letter of the first response (a "cue") and the last letter of the second response (which may be seen as a "cue" as well as a confirmation of the correct response when given). Another irrelevant property which has been used extensively in such programming is the underlining of the key words in the paragraph before they are called for: for example, *stimulus* and *response* might have been underlined in the first sentence. Such irrelevant redundancy or "cuing" contributes greatly to the probability of the correct response, but at the expense of appropriate stimulus control, that is, the student answers correctly but may not learn what he needs to know because the controlling stimulus is largely irrelevant. Thus the exemplar above is negative in respect to *good* programming.

One basic question in programming, as in all teaching, is the relative value of irrelevant or extrinsic cues or prompts or hints in bringing out the correct response. In some cases a lower probability of correct response may be preferable if it invokes only stimulus properties which are *relevant* to the subject matter. Redundancy through repetition of the task in another form (varying irrelevant dimensions) can then be used to bring the student to criterion on the task. That is, one can give more difficult exemplars or tasks and give several versions of them until the student responds correctly.

The next exemplar illustrates the use of relevant and irrelevant dimensions in presenting a *model* for the student to use to respond correctly. There are other ways in which the programmer could bring about the correct response, but he might do so at the expense of the subject matter if he used verbal cues or directions, that is, if the redundancy of *irrelevant* dimensions was employed to simplify the task.

Exemplar 2:

(1) $3x + 2 = 14$ (1) $4 + 5@ = 19$
(2) $3x + 2 - 2 = 14 - 2$ (2) $4 + 5@ - 4 = 19 + -4$
(3) $3x = 12$ (3) $5@ + 4 + -4 = 15 + 4 + -4$
(4) $3x/3 = 12/3$ (4) $5@ = 15$
(5) $1x = 4$ (5) $5@/5 = 15/5$
     (6) $@ = 3$

(1) $6\# + 3 = 27$ Using the two examples above, find a simple statement about #, that is, $(6)\# = \underline{\quad\quad}$.

Here the redundancy is achieved through limitation of the number of exemplars presented, but not through the use of irrelevant dimensions. That is to say, examples of equations are limited to one of several possible patterns, and thus that pattern becomes a cue for the correct answer; for example, $25 = 7 + 6x$ is a similar equation, but has a slightly different pattern which was not used in this presentation. Such redundancy or cuing (remember, *redundancy* is diminishing the total population of possible exemplars) must be decreased to bring each student to a higher state of understanding, of course; thus, eventually, the variety of types of equations must be increased in subsequent tasks. There is some question at present as to the optimal degree of repetition of one type of task at a given level before going on to another, and as to the amount of change to make from exemplar to exemplar at one given level. Some data indicate that if one repeats fewer different examples a number of times, one will make transfer to other more complex tasks easier, while other data indicate that if one repeats too few patterns (gives too little variety), such transfer is made more difficult. Thus old-fashioned drill may come back into style, but in limited and modified fashions representing better understanding of the concept formation theory underlying it. The necessary research in this area has yet to be done.

Exemplar 2 also illustrates a group of symbolic patterns which do not employ words. The previous learning of the student conditions him to recognize the possibility of using examples to develop hypotheses concerning the solution of the incomplete equation (inductive learning). He may have had some previous training in this strategy of learning, and assumedly he would have learned the solution of the simpler equations involved in the hierarchy; that is, he would have learned to solve

$3x = 6$ and $x + 5 = 9$. It is interesting to speculate whether or not he would be able to learn the more complex task given previously if he had only learned *one* of the simpler ones which it is based on. Some research indicates that he would, but that the success rate would be much lower, given a heterogeneous group of students. One might even teach the two simpler forms of the equation by teaching the complex or synthesized one first: this would be whole-to-part (or difficult-to-easy) learning, where the full capabilities of the student would be harnessed to the more complex task, and the subtasks would "fall out" of the learning, so to speak. However, there is also research indicating that if one applies the two different strategies, whole to part and part to whole, to two heterogeneous similar groups, the part-to-whole strategy results in quicker learning of the entire task. This may imply that there is a transfer problem in going from the more difficult to the easier tasks, just as there is in going from the easier to the more difficult. Whether these matters depend on the ability of the student, however, is not clear at this point. It might be that for the more able students, those who have shown greater achievement in the subject previously, the whole-part method is advantageous; that is, they could and would accomplish more using it.

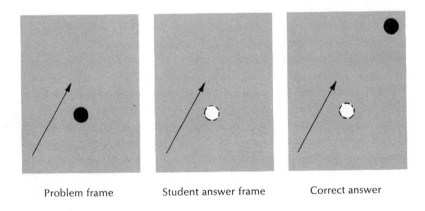

Problem frame   Student answer frame   Correct answer

FIGURE 18.1

The next exemplar (see Figure 18.1) is given to illustrate the feasibility of a purely iconic presentation: the student comes through experience with the program to recognize the first frame as presenting a task, the second as calling for his response, and the third as giving him feedback concerning his response. This also exemplifies reduction to a minimum of irrelevant stimulus control (redundancy of irrelevant dimensions). The few irrelevant dimensions (absolute direction, absolute length) are varied from task to task. There is also redundancy of relevant dimensions, achieved through repeating the task in various forms at the given level of difficulty. This repetition continues until the student is able to respond correctly. He responds to a number of different tasks of this type until he reaches some criterion, say two consecutive correct responses, then goes to the next stage. The concept involves a conjunction (length and direction), a relation (length and direction compared to the standard vector), and a before–after dimension. The strategy of teaching is reception, in that the sequences of exemplars is determined for the student and given him one at a time. This is also a discovery task in a sense, however, in that the student must form a hypothesis about the response, indicate it to test the hypothesis, and receive feedback as to its correctness. Verbal coaching can of course be given in the form of directions to "move the dot the same distance and direction as that of the arrow." If, however, the student learns without verbal directions he may learn to learn in a different way, one in which he operates from the iconic evidence rather than from symbolic stimuli (words). In this sense one is shaping inductive learning behavior. In one study using such a program the inclusion of verbal directions was found to interfere with the learning process to a degree. Thus there is some evidence that the discovery approach results in better transfer in this case, but it is not as yet convincing.

A final exemplar of programming exists in the concrete mode and involves enactive responses. Thus it can only be described here. It consists of a puzzle that one is to put together from a number of pieces of plastic of various shapes (triangles, trapezoids, squares, and others) to form a square: one must use all the pieces provided. This is quite difficult. The designers of the game have furnished a number of simpler tasks of this type using cardboard pieces; by going through the simple versions one arrives at a facility with this kind of task which enables him to do the final one. Here is programming again, the simplification of the task and gradual increasing of the difficulty until the student comes to some criterion behavior. It requires, as all programs do, a careful development process, that is, trials with students, revision, and more trials. It also involves feedback, in this case the kind whereby the student arrives at the previously set pattern and knows without being told that he has succeeded—this in turn sets up an "insight" situation, which was discussed in terms of reinforcement in a previous chapter.

18–2 Some Technical Aspects of Programming

Programmed instruction, as has been said, involves frequent student response, a high degree of success, and feedback concerning the correctness of response. It requires specification of the behaviors which the student is to exhibit, in terms of the tasks to which he is to respond and the kinds of responses that are to be acceptable (are to be rein-forced or confirmed). This in turn requires a degree of specificity not common in instruction, which in turn requires a degree of analysis of subject matter and teaching processes which is even more unique. It is not hard to satisfy some of the requirements superficially, that is, fre-quent response, high degree of success, feedback, although these re-quirements do often result in rather extensive analysis of subject matter. It *is* hard to satisfy the requirement of attaining a criterion behavior at the end of the program, a behavior that was not demonstrated by the student in a pretest. When taken together, the requirements of suc-cess in learning and success in achieving criterion are rather rigorous. They imply in turn that one must "develop" a program, which means trying it out on students while one is writing it, and revising it on the basis of each trial. One could try it out on many students simultane-ously, but then one gets so much data on each frame that he cannot process it effectively. Once one has tried it out on several students, one may want to try it out on small groups and then on large groups to see if they reach criterion adequately.

This development aspect of programmed instruction is probably its most powerful factor. When one has gone to this trouble, the result is bound to be more effective than an ordinary text that has not been so tried out and revised. Indeed, some experiments have indicated that if one takes a program that has been carefully developed this way, fills in the answers, and asks students to read it like an ordinary text, they still learn more than from the ordinary text that covers the same mate-rial, and almost as much as from the programmed text without the an-swers filled in.

A great deal has been said in the past about types of programs. Some are called *linear* because the student covers one frame at a time, respond-ing to each, getting feedback, and going on, in a "straight-line" fashion, and every student goes through the same series of tasks. Obviously this series of tasks will be too hard for some and too easy for others: for most students, it will be about right.

Other programs have points at which the student is told to skip sev-eral tasks if he has done well on a particular one that sums them up, or if they are special review for students who have been having a difficult time: this is a simple type of "branching."

Other programs present a few sentences or a paragraph and then ask the student to answer a multiple-choice question. After each possible choice, there is a page number, to which the student refers if he selects that number. Some of these pages, those referred to in a *wrong* answer, may say something like "No, you are wrong. Go back and make an-other selection." These programs are sometimes called *branching pro-grams*, sometimes *scrambled programs* or *scrambled books*.

Where content requirements deal with discriminations and where the possible alternatives can be displayed, a multiple-choice type of question is appropriate; after all, a simultaneous presentation in concept formation is a type of multiple choice also. Where the alternatives cannot be adequately specified, one may want to use a *constructed response* type of program. Here the student selects from his personal store of possible or relevant answers, that is, he fills in a blank. In this sense it too is a "multiple choice," but not overtly or obviously so. There are other variants of these basic types of programs, including that demonstrated previously where a given type of task is repeated a number of times, with feedback, until the student reaches a certain criterion, then another set of tasks (requiring the understanding of the earlier one) is presented. The variant or form of program chosen should of course be a function of the objectives and content of the program, and a given program could use a number of different approaches as needed. The particular format (linear versus branching in particular) has been an over-argued matter: the real source of power in programs comes from the development process as described above. It is not inconceivable that programming might benefit from a trial of several alternative approaches before settling on a final one.

The following is an example of the multiple-choice type of programmed instruction.*

(In this program we will describe a series of experiments, you will be asked to examine the experimental results and to answer questions regarding these results.)

1. Let us suspend a very light, graphite-covered sphere by a dry nylon thread as shown in the diagram.

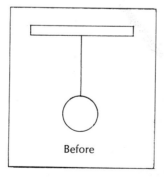

Before

FRAME 1a

---

*W. E. Hunter, M. D. Smith, and O. T. Benfey, *Electrostatics and Electric Potential Energy* (Richmond, Indiana: Earlham College Press, 1963), pp. 1-2.

We now rub a hard rubber rod with cat fur and bring it close to the sphere.

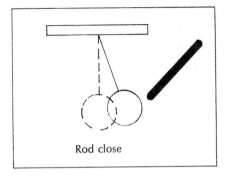

Rod close

FRAME 1b

According to the drawing, the sphere moves (toward) (away from) the rubber rod.
_____
                         toward
_____
2. The rod seems to (repel) (attract) the light sphere.
_____
                         attract
_____
3. By moving the rod closer to the sphere we allow the sphere to touch the rod. Note what happens in the next two drawings.

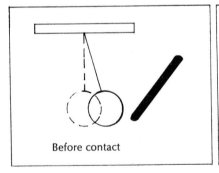
Before contact

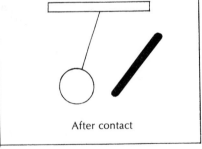
After contact

FRAME 3a   FRAME 3b

After making contact with the rubber rod the sphere moves (toward) (away from) the rubber rod; in other words, the rubber rod now seems to (repel) (attract) the light sphere.
_____
                away from   *repel*
_____
4. Let us suspend two spheres as shown in the diagram. We now touch *both* spheres with the fur-rubbed rod.

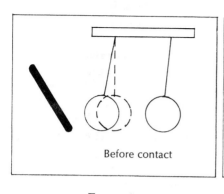
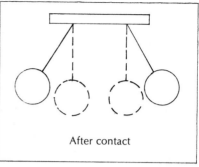

Before contact

After contact

FRAME 4a   FRAME 4b

After *both* spheres have contacted the rubber rod, they (attract) (repel) one another.

_____
repel
_____

5. Let us do another experiment, using two different uncharged spheres. The rod is rubbed with the cat fur. However, the cat fur (not the rod) is used to contact the two uncharged spheres.

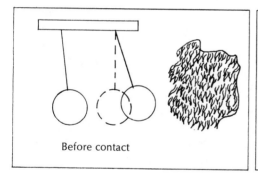
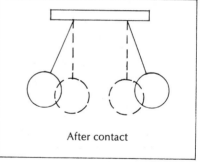

Before contact

After contact

FRAME 5a   FRAME 5b

After the spheres have contacted the *cat fur*, they _____ one another.

_____
repel
_____

18–3 Specifying Terminal Behaviors

One important effect of interest in programmed instruction has been an increased awareness of the need for accurate specification of behaviors which a student is to exhibit. Such terms as *meaning* and *understanding*, so common in statements of objectives, are slowly giving way to operational definitions in terms of classes of stimuli and responses.

While we have only begun to analyze the behaviors involved in learning, and must recognize the crudeness and incompleteness of current
behavioral specifications, attempts in this direction are reasonable first
approximations. One must take care, however, lest he presume too much
in his enthusiasm over the beginning of a scientific approach to teaching.

It has frequently been stated that one should specify the *terminal
behavior*, which is the objective of a programmed sequence, before he
begins to program. While it is true that one should have an idea of
his objective in teaching of any kind, particularly programming, it is
also true that the process of development of a program, through testing
and revision, often leads to a revised concept of what the terminal behavior is or should be. From another point of view, no behavior can
be considered *terminal*, since it represents only one example of a population of similar behaviors that might be considered the objective;
that is, any one task is only a representative of a number of similar
tasks that one wants the student to be able to perform.

As a result, one danger of overemphasis on terminal behaviors is
that the instructor, or programmer, is distracted from attention to the
crucial observing, mediating, and other learning behaviors or strategies that are required of the student. That is to say, if one sees a particular task as the final criterion, one is perhaps more likely to be
satisfied with a more superficial understanding of the material, one
sufficient to perform that task but perhaps not other similar or somewhat more complex tasks.

On the other hand, a response to the criticism given in the preceding
paragraph is as follows. If a particular criterion task does *not* require
demonstration of the kinds of behaviors that represent true understanding and that generalize to other tasks, then the criterion task is not well
chosen. Then there are two alternatives generally, one to choose a
more rigorous or searching task, another to present several tasks of
the former type rather than one; perhaps both would be ideal.

Projects devoted to revision of curricula view subject matter as a
vehicle for shaping general responses and response chains related to
what they call "good physics" or "good mathematics" or "good chemistry." These behaviors are hard to specify, and are made up of a
variety of tasks; subject matter experts work with them intuitively—
but this does not mean that they do not "understand" them empirically.
On the other hand, programmed instruction projects have taken their
subject matter as it appears in traditional texts for the most part, and
attempted to bring students to criteria specified in these texts. They
have been content with a somewhat more limited view of "understanding." While their ability to achieve these criteria through programmed
self-instruction is significant, one cannot be surprised when the subject
matter people show some lack of enthusiasm; they have been turning
away from such criteria and seeking more encompassing and deeper ones.

How might one combine the two views? This calls for a careful consideration of criteria and objectives of learning, specification of the learning strategies one wishes to teach in terms of the behaviors they involve. It will also call for a turning away from strictly textual presentations and extension of the programming concept to include all media (the teacher among them) in the sequence of learning experiences. It will also require some reduction of the babel of jargon and pseudo-jargon which has been developed to the point that it is a barrier to communication. Current taxonomies are an improvement but far from ideal.

To summarize, while one may specify terminal behavior before constructing a sequence to condition such behaviors, the construction and development of such a sequence is likely to change one's concept of the terminal behaviors that he began with. Furthermore, if one attends only to the terminal behaviors themselves, he may be distracted from consideration of more important outcomes, observing and mediating behaviors and strategies of learning which are conditioned along with the content. Finally, while subject matter experts have set down what they consider "good physics" and such, in the form of new curricula, and while psychologists have been attending to problems of programming technique and general learning theory paradigms via programmed instruction, there is an important place for research that attempts to define the nature of the observing and mediating behaviors involved in the former in terms of programs which need specifications set down by the latter. Such research will produce data in the form of superior programs.

18–4 Step-Size

In requiring a response of a student in programmed instruction, one does so in a way that calls for desirable learning behavior in order to respond correctly. Thus it is not the response itself, but what it implies concerning the student's behavior that is important. The complexity of the behavior of the student in performing a given task on a program, as compared with that required on the previous task, is involved in what is vaguely referred to in programming jargon as *step-size*. This includes a large variety of unidentified behaviors, which could be classified in many ways, each involving its own hierarchy.

Basically a program which has a large step-size is one which requires a large amount of or a much more complex form of cognitive behavior on the part of the student on a given frame as compared with that required on the preceding frame. In terms of a previous discussion of initial and final states and steepness of the learning process or curve by which one goes from one to the other, a large step-size program would differ from a small step-size program in the number of tasks required of the student to go from a given initial state to a given final state. The large step-size program would have fewer tasks or frames or steps than the small step-size program: in another sense, it would probably be considered more difficult.

In a certain sense, this situation is like receiving directions from a stranger. Some people give a brief description that may include all the necessary information but is hard to follow or decipher; others give long drawn-out step-by-step directions that are hard to remember although easy to follow. Others fall somewhere in between, giving the necessary detail but nothing extra. This is also like matching the input of a radio message to the channel capacity or ability of the receiver: one can put in too much, or one can put in too little.

As a result of this, a given program (with a given inherent step-size) will be just right for some students, too fast for others, and too slow for still others. Thus, through programming, one enables a student to "go at his own pace" in one sense, in that he doesn't have to wait for the others to complete a given task, but in another sense one offers a pace and sequence that may not be the correct one for the given student.

18–5 An Uncertainty Principle

In programming, one requires a response in order to make sure that the student observes relevant stimulus properties and engages in the desired (covert) mediating behavior. In physics, when one attempts to determine the momentum of such a small particle as an electron, he changes that momentum in the attempt. Paralleling the case of the electron and its momentum, we may postulate that the response requirement in a program alters the nature of the very behaviors it is designed to ensure. The change may or may not be a desirable one. It seems worthwhile to speculate concerning the situation generally considered ideal among members of the programming fraternity, in which the student responds correctly (and for the correct reason) and thus progresses successfully toward the terminal behavior.

Let us assume, then, that the probability of correct response is greater than some arbitrarily high value, say ninety-five percent. This is to say that ninety-five out of a hundred responses by a given student will be correct, and if the sample is fairly *homogeneous*, ninety-five out of a hundred students will be correct on a given frame. These two definitions are not identical, of course, but have not been differentiated so far since program development utilizes extremely small populations. This assumes, then, that the response given belongs to a set of correct responses, where this set is usually rather limited. Now we ask the question, "What is the effect of 'filling in' the response, or, how does the behavior of the student differ in overt as compared to covert responding?" In some research into this question it has been concluded that overt responding does not contribute significantly to understanding; in other research, the conclusion has been that overt responding is important in more "difficulty" programmed sequences, but makes little difference where the response requirements are simple. This problem is not entirely unrelated to the question of how some students learn better than others, both on programs and from conventional text presentations. One wonders as to the nature of the covert mediating and observing behaviors involved in their "studying." The nature of this behavior is largely unspecified at present, but it probably does not occur entirely through processes of maturation: it must be conditioned, or "shaped," if you will. This shaping process must take place through the mediation of accidental contingencies of reinforcement.

There is another facet to the "uncertainty" principle. Consider a physicist who is seeking the position of an electron! The "uncertainty principle" states that one can never know where the electron is to an accuracy less than a certain margin, because when one gets that close to determining its position one will *change* its position in the process of locating it. That is, the act of finding it (through some kind of super-microscope using other electrons or light beams or the like) disturbs it. In a similar, but much cruder sense, one cannot assure learning in a student beyond a certain degree, because the more one makes certain that the student gives the correct response, the less certain one is that he has responded for the correct reason. To put this another way, there are many degrees of guidance one may furnish a student to bring him to give the correct response in a given situation: the greater the degree of guidance one gives, the greater the likelihood of the correct response —but the less one is sure that he could have given it by himself without any help, that is, that he "understands" what he is supposed to. Thus in programmed instruction, perhaps more than in other approaches to teaching, one has to be aware that one is cuing the response, and one has to risk some lower levels of certainty of a correct response in order to be sure that the student is "getting it." The level of difficulty one begins with, and the rate at which one increases the difficulty, are parameters which depend on the preparation and learning ability of the student.

18–6 Programmed Instruction in the Schools

This discussion of a rationale for programming leads to consideration of the important aspects of program selection and evaluation. We have been told that programming may replace teachers; this is a little bit as if a chemist doing research in drugs predicted that doctors would be obsolete within ten years. This would be possible only if people did not care about the health of their children: replacement of teachers, by the same token, would be possible only if people ceased to care greatly about their mental health and capacity to learn. That children learn more than facts and processes in schools is a truism; part of the theme

of this book is that in programs they also learn more than merely subject matter. This breadth, however, does not approach that of the many
roles of the teacher.

What then might one look for in a program? Since programs specify
subject matter in operational terms, one would look toward the end of
a program to determine whether content is traditional or modern, thorough or superficial. Since programs also determine the kind of learning behavior required of the student, and since the student learns this
kind of learning behavior as a result, it is also very important to examine sample sequences from the program to determine what kind of
behavior they require. Not only must the student provide the behavior
which is required by the program, be it simple or complex, the student
also learns through providing it that this behavior represents the way to
learn. Therefore, the processes one uses in teaching through programming should be those processes which will stand the student in good
stead in future learning situations of a nonprogrammed kind: where
the student does not possess desirable behaviors of this type, programs
should be available that build such repertoires through carefully staged
sequences. A program can be designed to condition complex chains of
unobservable mediating behaviors, those which we call generally *problem-solving* processes. A program can be designed to condition abstract
responses which apply to broad classes of stimulus situations, the kind
of behavior we call generally *concept formation*. Unfortunately, programs can also be designed to evoke correct responses through hidden
and visible cues which allow the student to respond correctly for irrelevant reasons: when such cues are used consciously, the programmer
must be careful to remove them as he proceeds toward final frames, and
thus set the learner on his own in the process. If programs do not do
this, they may leave him as he is or, worse, they may lead him to abandon complex learning behaviors developed through other situations.
While it is a difficult task, ideally a response should require the best
behavior a student can furnish at each step: anything less does him a
disservice.

Having taken a preliminary look at the appearance and content of
programs, what can one expect of them in action? In other words, how
well can they teach? Do they teach every student in the class no matter
what the class? No—this is not a miracle of that order. Not every student can learn from every program, and there are always some who
could but won't. Furthermore, we don't want students to learn from
programs exclusively, at least not until we have a better understanding
of all the implications of such experience. There is also another consideration, that of individual differences. It is possible to identify two
different strategies of teaching: one is a reception strategy where the
student has no control over the nature and order of the information he

receives, the other a selection strategy where the student is given all the information he needs to solve a problem and then told when he is getting hot or cold. Some students are trained to one strategy, some to another. Students who are strongly conditioned by previous learning experiences to search for the information they need to solve problems and who have been taught to be reinforced by answering such challenges, such students will not take to programming as we know it now. This does not mean there is not a best order of learning events; it simply means that some students want to do things for themselves; I believe all students should be encouraged to do this. Such learning is a challenge to the broader process which I have described as *behavioral analysis*; programs will eventually be developed which condition this type of behavior.

What does research in teaching through programming, and increased effectiveness in teaching procedures, imply for the immediate future? A brief look at this problem may occasion some discussion. The programmed material available today, impressive as it is in its volume and variety, is but a drop in the educational bucket. Concentrated in a few fields, with few programs covering full courses, it can hardly claim to affect educational practice significantly. However, we have enough experience to risk certain predictions. We are not able to say with certainty whether programmed instruction is better than conventional teaching. Comparisons are difficult to make well, and then it is risky to generalize on them. However, there is one thing that is quite certain: programming reveals more problems in teaching and supervision than it solves, at least so far. Problems of individual differences in ability, best ways of teaching, handling students going at different paces, dealing with the motivational problems which programs make so obvious— each experiment brings up a dozen new leads for the researcher and often as not leaves him in the dark about the question he started with. However, the individualized aspects of programmed instruction and its potential effectiveness make it appear to be an instrument of change, an enabling tool, one which may enable the teacher to shift his function away from group instruction to the more professional one of individualized teaching and guidance. It seems to make more feasible such educational reforms as team teaching and nongraded schools.

The process of specifying and ordering student behaviors for greater effectiveness in the teaching process, with its accompanying procedure of trial and revision, makes up a larger unit which may be titled *behavioral analysis*. Such analysis, it can be seen, can be applied to all teaching, whether by text, film, slide, or through the most complex and sensitive medium of all, the teacher. While the process is not under the same degree of control in all of these, and while the requirements of active response are more difficult to satisfy in some, the role of analysis is just as important. Thus we may discuss programming for classroom presentation, or for film presentation, as well as for programmed text. Furthermore, if it should turn out that the requirement of active response can be satisfied effectively on a less frequent and variable schedule, the programmed text of the future will not look the same as that of the present; it may come to look more like conventional texts, but it will teach like no text yet written. A more likely development, however, will be the integrated program involving text, film, three-dimensional models, and audiolingual equipment under control of the student: here the use of graphical, symbolic, and diagrammatic portrayal (both in combination and also in separate presentations) will supplement and replace words to some extent. If programmed materials of various types are to be made available within the visible future, however, there must be a source of programs and funds for their production.

Psychologists who deal with research in learning will continue to contribute to the understanding of basic processes involved. Subject matter specialists, whether physicists, historians, or linguists, will have much to say concerning the nature of behaviors to be required, especially those less obvious mediating behaviors that make up "good physics" or "good writing." The task, however, requires someone whose primary interest is the specification of these understandings in terms of student behaviors, the ordering of them in increasingly complex sequences of tasks for the student, and finally the scientific development of these materials for presentation through texts, machines, films, and other media, under the coordinating direction of the teacher. Such a person might best be termed an instructional systems engineer or technologist. His work may affect the role of the teacher, who will need greater understanding of both subject matter and of the social and experimental psychology of education. If implications of present experience are heeded, it will require more, not fewer, teachers: for programming increases student differences and the need for individual guidance. Certainly we need a major investment by interested agencies in the analysis and development required. We also need individuals trained in the coordination of team approaches whereby these materials can be developed. The task is immense: it will be some time before we reach the point where results multiply and become significant.

18–7 Multimedia Approaches

The sequencing of learning tasks through what is commonly termed *programmed instruction* is conventionally accomplished by a book format or by materials designed to be presented by some machine or through a computer. Variations include tape–text systems for language teaching, slide–tape–text complexes for presenting lectures with pictures and also questions for the student to accompany them, and slide–tape–

computer station combinations that can perform a variety of functions. These technological adjuncts are not central to the programming process but do provide media for various types of learning tasks, as well as limiting what can be done through such sequences. A broader view of teaching can be taken as well, where the day-by-day and week-by-week sequencing of learning experiences is taken into account. Such longitudinal processes as putting the student more on his own as the course develops, or giving variety from day to day and week to week to maintain interest can be considered in such planning. This is also programming, but it can include programming of variations and options for the student. A truly individualized instructional system, if such is desirable, will require a tremendous amount of careful programming: the nonindividualized instructional systems prevailing now require comparatively little, although it is still enough to keep administrators more than busy.

One approach to such "programming" has been developed under the title of *multi-media systems*, or *multi-modal systems*. The concept here is the interaction of the various media in producing a more ideal learning system for a given unit or course. The assumption is that the text, commonly the "backbone" of the course, is only one of many media that can be used to assist the teacher and student in attaining learning objectives. Films, programs, overhead projections, loops, readers, laboratory materials and processes, group discussions—all can and should contribute to the experience. If these can be organized in such a way as to meet the requirements of individual differences, whatever they may be, all the better. At the least, their integrated use can provide a more varied and interesting instructional fare than is commonly experienced by students in schools at present.

It is not the purpose of this section to describe principles for such a system; that belongs in a treatise on instructional technology. However, it is appropriate to treat briefly the potential and possible roles of various media that might be used in such a system. Thus the following are first approximations to a definition of the relative functions of different media. Much more exploration of such systems needs to be done before one can view such formulas as valid and reliable, however.

18–8 The Instructional System

The utilization of a number of media in such a way as to achieve an optimal learning experience for as many students as possible is a challenge that few have attempted to meet as yet in education. Inherent in such a project are problems of interaction of students and media, students and teacher, teachers and media, and media and media. What media do students respond to best, and which do they learn from best? Or is this the correct question? Perhaps it is, "Which medium helps one understand a certain type of concept, or a certain skill, and which

Schedule for Unit One

(1) Film: Frames of Reference Small Group Discussions (SGD) on Film — Programmed	(2) Pretest 1 — Text; Reader	(3) Lab Stations 1 Uniform Motion — Text; Programmed Sequence	(4) Pretest 2 — Text; Quiz	(5) Lab Stations 2 Accelerated Motion — Quiz; Programmed Sequence	(6) Film: Straight Line Kinematics Small Group Discussions (SGD) — Text
(7) Experiments: Orbit of Sun; Naked Eye Astronomy Sequence Programmed — Text; Reader	(8) 17th Century Experiment — Text; Reader	(9) Programmed Instruction: Velocity and Acceleration — Text; Programmed Sequence	(10) Small Group Problem Solving — Programmed Sequence	(11) SGD on Reader — Reader Articles	(12) Teacher Presentation: Galileo Quiz — Reader
(13) Computer-Assisted Type Problem — Text; Orbit of Sun	(14) Lab Stations 3 — Text; Reader	(15) Lab Stations 4 — Text; Lab Write-Up	(16) Film: Inertia Programmed Sequence: Proportions — Programmed Sequence	(17) Small Group Problem Solving — Text; Programmed Sequence	(18) Film: Frames of Reference (Galilean Relativity) — Programmed Sequence
(19) Lab Stations 5 Projectile, Circular and Simple Harmonic Motions — Text	(20) — Text	(21) Student Presentations on Lab Outcomes — Reader	(22) Review — Reader	(23) Unit One Test	(24) Discussion of Unit One Outcomes and Observations for Unit II

*M. Daniel Smith. "Response to a Multi-Media System." *Journal of Research in Science Teaching 6* (1969) : 323.

communicates another type, and so on?" What are the relative roles of the media, and how do they combine to give the best sequence of learning experiences from both motivational and cognitive points of view? Perhaps, for example, one can achieve the most through variety, having different types of presentations from class to class. Perhaps the same concept needs to be presented a number of different ways, through a number of different media. And what is the role of the teacher, or how do such systems change the roles that the teacher plays?

As has been said, there is very little known about this field. Most development and research has involved one or a few media, rather than many used in integrated fashion. However, it seems clear that the learning system of the future will utilize a number of media in integrated form, and will call for a different pattern of teacher behavior and of teacher–student interaction. Some of this will result in greater individualization, while some outcomes will involve mass learning of common concepts and skills with an efficiency not yet realized.

The design and development of such learning systems is something beyond the capability of the local teacher team. It is a process which has not been experimented with by curriculum groups to a significant extent either. It will require teams of instructional technologists and theorists, working with volunteer experimental students, with many media and great varieties and amounts of materials at their disposal, as well as unlimited time to try sequences and try them again, both with experimental students and then in the field. Such systems, once developed, will be highly effective and worth exporting to classrooms around the world. They will combine the effectiveness attributed to programmed instruction and the motivation attributed to discovery learning; they will both provide empirical data for extension of our understanding of the interconnections of various aspects of instructional theory and enable us to design more complex systems for the future.

Bibliography

DeCecco, J. P., ed. *Education Technology*. New York: Holt, Rinehart, and Winston, 1964.

Markle, S. M. *Good Frames and Bad*. New York: John Wiley and Sons, Inc., 1964.

Skinner, B. F. *The Technology of Teaching*. New York: Appleton, Century, & Crofts, 1968.

19 Factors Contributing to Effective Teaching

19–1 What is a Good Teacher?

Everyone has some concept of a "good" teacher. One's point of view is affected by his personal interests in teaching. Some people associated with licensing and teacher certification believe good teaching is the result of the training acquired through formal education. Some who have dealt with teachers administratively, such as principals, feel that it is largely a matter of the personality of the individual: a dynamic personality is often described in very general terms, however. Some administrators—and some teachers—feel that the degree of discipline the teacher maintains in the classroom is a primary factor. Generally, a good teacher is one who favorably affects his students, and who helps them develop the necessary skills and understandings and work habits along with desirable attitudes and positive personal styles.

Some early research studies of good and poor teachers indicated that high academic achievement does not assure success in teaching; on the other hand, some more recent work has indicated that good teachers tend to have higher academic achievement than poor teachers. In one early study, students were asked to describe teachers they liked most, those they liked least, and those they felt were "best." A composite showed that the liked teacher was helpful, explained clearly, was cheerful and good-natured, was human, friendly, interested in students, and made the work interesting. The disliked teacher was cross, crabby, not helpful with school work, had pets and picked on others, was superior and aloof, and was unreasonable and ill-mannered. The *best* teacher was more exacting in standards, stricter in marking, better at explaining, knew the subject better, could put it over better, was stricter and more rigid in discipline, but made the work interesting. In eighty percent of the cases the teacher liked most was also the best teacher; this of course meant that in twenty percent they were *not* the same teacher.

In other relatively early research (since the 1930's), it was found that the correlation between personality and teaching success was higher than that between intelligence and teaching success. Some research looked for phrases that described effective teachers as compared with noneffective ones. Other research along this and similar lines has shown teaching effectiveness to be multidimensional. More recent research in teacher effectiveness has treated the teaching act as one analogous to giving therapy to individuals and groups. While the problem of synthesizing this with the communication of subject matter has not been adequately explored, some of the findings are suggestive for the personality and style of the teacher.

19–2 Personality and Teaching

The pattern or style of behavior demonstrated in a number of situations and contexts establishes one's personality; teaching personality is similarly conveyed as a concept to students by many exemplars acted out by the teacher. The relationship between teaching personality and personality outside of teaching has not been studied: there may be significant differences in many cases, or it may be that the basic elements are consistent throughout. It seems likely that a teacher's personality is brought to bear in the teaching situation, but that it is altered by the different contingencies of the class and school situations. On the other hand, sociopsychological research implies that certain behavior patterns bring predictable responses from groups, while others bring others, and that one's personality can be altered to achieve certain types of responses. Whether this can be done successfully over a long period of time, say, a semester or a year, is another matter.

19–3 Some Studies of Teacher Behavior

A more recent study along these same lines has come up with the following dichotomies*:

EFFECTIVE	INEFFECTIVE
Alert, enthusiastic.	Apathetic, dull, bored.
Appears interested in pupils, classroom activities.	Appears uninterested.
Cheerful, optimistic.	Depressed, pessimistic.
Self-controlled, not easily upset.	Loses temper, easily upset.
Likes fun, sense of humor.	Overly serious, too occupied for humor.
Recognizes, admits own mistakes.	Is unaware of or fails to admit own mistakes.
Fair, impartial, objective.	Unfair, partial.
Patient.	Impatient.
Shows understanding and sympathy in working with pupils.	Is short with pupils, shows lack of sympathy.

*David G. Ryans, *Characteristics of Teachers: Their Description, Comparison and Appraisal* (Washington, D.C.: American Council on Education, 1960). Reprinted by permission of the author and publisher.

Friendly, courteous.	Aloof, abrupt.
Helps pupils with personal problems.	Unaware of pupil's personal needs.
Accepts pupils' efforts as sincere.	Suspicious of pupils' motives.
Anticipates reactions of others in social situations.	Does not anticipate reactions of others in social situations.
Encourages pupils to try to do best.	Makes no effort to encourage pupils.
Procedure planned and organized.	Procedure without plan.
Original materials and techniques.	Uninteresting materials and techniques.
Clear and thorough in directions.	Directions incomplete, vague.
Disciplines in quiet, dignified, positive manner.	Reprimands at length, ridicules and resorts to cruel or meaningless forms of correction.
Gives help willingly.	Fails to give help, or gives it grudgingly.

These polarize behavior somewhat unrealistically, but serve as an introduction to such classifications. The redundancy involved has the effect of underlining the negative bias of an individual in one case and the positive bias in another. It is not too far from the findings about good and poor teachers in the studies just discussed. Another formulation, originally used by Anderson in research in teacher behaviors and resulting student attitudes, is the following:

> Dominative–aggressive–rejectant versus integrative–affiliative–nurturant.

While these emphasize the affective domain of behavior, they can also be related to learning strategies and instructional processes: *integrative*, for example, implies using student hypotheses and information in communicating concepts or processes. The three words in each category are probably not enough to describe adequately what was intended by Anderson in terms of actual behaviors, so the following amplification may be informative:

Integrative–Affiliative–Nurturant: Accepts, clarifies, and supports ideas and feelings of pupils. Praises and encourages. Asks questions to stimulate pupil participation in decision making. Asks questions to orient pupils to schoolwork.

Dominative–Aggressive–Rejectant: Expresses or lectures about own ideas or knowledge. Gives directions or orders. Criticizes or deprecates pupil behavior with intent to change it. Justifies his own position or authority.

This study was mainly oriented toward elementary schools. In studying teacher behavior and effectiveness, research at all levels will be considered, although the requirements at the different levels change in some respects. A classic study by Lewin, Lippit, and White also had to do with elementary students, but in clubs outside of the school situation. The variables in that study were defined as follows*:

Authoritarian: determination of policy, dictation of techniques and activities, dictation of particular work tasks and companions, personal praise and criticism of work of each member, disdain of group participation by leader, friendly but impersonal treatment of the club members.

Democratic: policy setting through group discussion and decision, suggestions of alternative procedures regarding techniques, choice of tasks left up to the group, choice of working partners left up to individual, objective and fact-minded praise and criticism by leader and participation by leader in group without undertaking to do the work.

Laissez faire: freedom for group or individual decisions regarding policy, complete autonomy in working by members, leader only supplies materials and information when asked, freedom to choose partners and tasks on the part of members, no attempts to interfere with or become part of group activities.

Important to considerations of teacher personality is the fact that in this study the group leaders took turns playing the various roles in different clubs. Thus it was possible to note whether any effects observed were a function of the actual personality of the leader or of the role itself. Since the effects were consistent across the different leaders, it implied that it was the role, not the "real" personality of the leader, that was coming through. The different roles did achieve different responses, as follows*:

Authoritarian: either (a) high aggression with much rebellion and persecution of scapegoats, or (b) docile, submissive, lifeless, apathetic behavior indicating too-complete submission.

Democratic: moderate aggression; a stable atmosphere not easily disrupted.

Laissez faire: high levels of aggression.

Production was highest in authoritarian groups, although the democratic groups showed better production in situations where the leader was absent. The productivity in laissez-faire groups was relatively low. Nineteen of twenty boys in the clubs liked the democratic leader better than the autocratic one.

---

*After Kurt Lewin, Ronald Lippit, and Ralph K. White, "Patterns of Aggressive Behavior in Experimentally Created Social Climates," in E. Amedon and J. Hough, *Interaction Analysis: Theory, Research, and Application* (Reading, Mass.: Addison-Wesley, 1967), p. 26.
*After Kurt Lewin, Ronald Lippit, and Ralph K. White, "Patterns of Aggressive Behavior."

19–4 Matching Teachers and Students

Consider the possibility that different students react differently to a given teacher, that there are interactions involving personality differences. One might hypothesize that if there is a matching of student personality to teacher personality one might have more productive learning situations. Some research has been conducted to examine this question. Generally it has not shown significant differences in outcomes when the matching was carried out. In one study students and teachers were matched on personality factors and interests, but achievement did not differ significantly from unmatched groups. In another study, students identified what to them was the ideal teaching style, and the styles of their teachers were observed and classified also. Students whose preferences indicated a match between them and their teachers did not show significantly better achievement or attitudes than students who did not. The investigator concluded that there should be some optimal level of difference between the student and the teacher for best performance or most positive reaction.

Another study of student–teacher congruence was carried out at the high school level by one investigator. After matching students and teachers on the Allport–Vernon–Lindzey Study of Values questionnaire, he found no significant correlations between pupil–teacher difference measures and achievement in the course. Given the results above, one must conclude for the time being that the major factor in classroom climate and learning environments is teacher personality and teacher behavior.

19–5 More Complex Analyses of Interaction

In analyzing classroom interactions, one needs behavioral definitions of teacher personality, student personality, teacher behaviors, and attitudes that result from teacher behaviors. Research that explores these areas has increased in recent years, although there is still much to be done before general conclusions can be drawn and theorems formulated. In the absence of general principles, it is still informative and useful to study the various traits of personality and types of attitudes that are used to detect differences among people and attitudes, and to observe the factors that emerge from such studies. The reader should remember that statistically speaking a *factor* is a group of test items which correlate highly with each other. For example, suppose that students are asked to respond to a number of questions regarding their feelings about various things. Among these are five which in previous administrations of the questionnaire have yielded results which correlated highly with each other, and thus which have been found to describe collectively some "factor" of the students' attitudes. Now, if a given student shows a similar pattern of response on these five items, one may conclude that he is demonstrating that attitude or feeling which the others demonstrated previously. One interesting thing about this approach to research is that groups of tests or questions may show high intercorrelation with each other, and thus form a "factor" without having any obvious logical connection between them—that is, they may reveal relationships which one has not anticipated, and which one would not logically believe, yet which empirical evidence indicates are there. This in turn inspires further hypothesis formation concerning what is actually going on in the classroom.

Before examining some of the research of this type, it may be well to describe some conventional measures of personality or attitude. One such test is called the *Thematic Apperception Test*. Pictures of situations are shown the teacher, and then the teacher is asked to write a story about each one. This story, or "protocol," is analyzed for various themes that might appear in it. The themes the analyst looks for are those which were previously distilled from many, many such stories by an investigator named Henry Murray.* Through these analyses, and through comparing themes which he noted along with other aspects of the personalities of the people involved, he arrived at a number of traits. Some of these are listed below; the n before each one stands for *need for*:

n Dominance: To control one's human environment, to influence or direct the behavior of others by suggestions, persuasion, or command. To dissuade, restrain, or prohibit. To induce another to act in a way which accords with one's sentiments or needs. To get others to cooperate. To convince another of the "rightness" of one's opinion.

n Achievement: To want to attain a goal for the sake of attaining a goal. To want to be the "best" at something. To want to do something different, something unique. To want to be better than others at something.

n Nurturance: To give sympathy and gratify the needs of a helpless other, an infant or any other that is weak, disabled, tired. . . . To assist another in danger. To feed, help, support. . . .

n Affiliation: To draw near and enjoyably cooperate or reciprocate with an allied person: another who resembles oneself or who likes one. To please and win the affection of such another person. To adhere and remain loyal to a friend.

n Rejection: To separate oneself from another with whom one doesn't want to affiliate. To exclude, abandon, expel, or remain indifferent to an inferior other person. To snub or jilt another.

n Order: Some persons function in a coherent, coordinated, and integrated fashion: others are confused, uncoordinated, and disorganized.

---

*From H. A. Murray, "The Variables of Personality," *Explorations in Personality* (New York: Oxford University Press, 1938), pp. 142–242.

Such dichotomies as authoritarian–democratic and dominative–integrative subsume a number of such factors, traits, or elements of personality. This in turn explains in part the different outcomes found in similar treatments in research, since teachers adopting roles like "authoritarian" or "integrative" will do so in different ways and thus achieve different results. Yet the lawfulness in outcomes of such simpler studies imply that further exploration of classroom behaviors and climates could be rewarding.

One application of the Thematic Apperception Test has been its use in comparing the personalities of successful and unsuccessful teachers, as defined by student reactions to them. In one such study successful teachers constantly mentioned the need for action to overcome failure, while the less successful ones tended to see success as something which comes easily or which does not come in spite of constructive activity. The successful ones foresaw difficulties and recognized the need for planning and preparation, while the others attributed failure to extraneous causes rather than their own inadequacies. The better teachers tended to be active, hard-working people who recognized their own limitations and the requirements of achievement, while the poorer teachers visualized success as coming without working for it and were less able to face difficulties or failures. They (the poorer teachers) failed to see the relationships between events of life and their own initiation of behaviors or reactions to them.

A recent study of teacher personality and classroom climate in classes in high school physics by H. J. Walberg* has revealed some data which indicate the complexity of the interactions involved. These results also imply that our models of classroom interactions are as yet rather crude and insufficient for understanding what is going on. They may also appear to an experienced teacher to be a more adequate expression of relationships which he has observed. Walberg analyzed personality by factor-analyzing data from the Allport–Vernon–Lindzey Study of Values, the Edwards Personal Preference Schedule, and the Minnesota Teachers Attitude Inventory. These were related to classroom climate as measured by a special questionnaire designed for that purpose. Teacher personality and classroom climate were found to be highly correlated. There were several dimensions along which this correlation existed. These will be described in some detail here because they have interesting implications for those who wish to improve their understanding of relationships between teacher personality and classroom interaction.

Walberg's analysis, carried on through a type of processing called *canonical correlation*, revealed several patterns of personalities and behaviors or climates that were relatively distinct from one another.

---

*H. J. Walberg, "Teacher personality and classroom climate," *Psychology in the Schools 5* (1968): 163–69.

The first of these showed the following results for the two aspects of the study, personality (of the teacher) and climate (of the classroom):

Personality: Succorance, order, change, political.

Climate: Organizational formality, group subservience, social heterogeneity, strict control, internal friction.

This seems to imply that a teacher who values power and is dependent on other power figures needs both order and change. His personality is reflected in a formal, subservient class where the students perceive some friction and social difference among themselves but where they do not feel controlled. Walberg feels that subservience in the teacher implies willingness to be controlled by an outside group, perhaps the school administration. He also speculates that such teachers invoke the authority of others to achieve order and thus the students do not feel "controlled" as in a more direct, obviously authoritarian situation. Another set of correlates formed the second pattern, as follows:

Personality: Abasement, affiliation, nurturance, aggression, endurance, deference.

Climate: Strict control, personal intimacy, goal directedness, responsibility, stratification, group status, classroom intimacy (negative).

Here again is an ambivalence in the teacher personality which is reflected in a class where the students feel controlled, goal directed, and unstratified. The members may feel less intimate with one another in class because the teacher monopolizes the affective interpersonal relations. The third pattern was as follows:

Personality: Nurturance, intraception, order, aggression, exhibitionism, change, affiliation, nonabasement.

Climate: Goal directed, socially homogeneous, nonsubservient, informal, common interests, nonegalitarian.

The teacher shows opposite feelings of need for order versus need for change; aggressiveness yet need for nurturance and affiliation; exhibitionism and introspection and analysis of motives of others. Such teachers feel less guilty. The fourth pattern was:

Personality: Achieving, heterosexual, abasing, expressive, non-pupil-centered.

Climate: Disorganized, egalitarian, constraints on speech, socially homogeneous, little control, low group status.

This seems to resemble somewhat the laissez-faire atmosphere of the Lippitt-Lewin study, and the key may be the self-centeredness of the teacher in terms of high needs for achievement and expressiveness, interest in the opposite sex, and less pupil-centeredness. Pupils feel homogeneous and less closely supervised, and the class is somewhat disorganized.

This analysis contrasts markedly in its sophistication and complexity with scales presented previously and to be presented below. It affords some confusion in the reader, but that is good, because the matter of classroom interaction is a difficult one to analyze, and we should expect surprises, contradictions, and need for replications. It is revealing, however, in pointing out the simultaneous existence of good and bad aspects of personality, and of good and bad aspects of climate—good and bad in the conventional sense, that is.

19–6 Some Evidence from College Teaching

Teacher–student interaction studies and evidence have been derived from all levels. Obviously, they do not have enough in common to allow one to apply easily results from one to another, and yet they all study a common situation, that in which a teacher is attempting to communicate to students, and thus all are relevant. One group of studies of teacher effectiveness has emerged from the work of McKeachie and his colleagues at the University of Michigan.* Most of these are based on classes of college students, yet they have points in common with studies at other levels. In a review of previous studies in this area, McKeachie and his colleagues found two general aspects of teacher behavior to have been reported frequently. The first involved sympathetic attitude toward students and fairness in grading; the second included self-reliance and confidence, good presentation of subject matter, and interest in it. They also reviewed a paper by Gibb, who had previously reviewed the literature and found the following to have been important:

1. Friendly democratic behaviors,
2. Communication behaviors,
3. Organization behavior,
4. Academic emphasis.

McKeachie presented the results of some of the Michigan work in which several factors had emerged from analysis of questionnaire results. These factors were as follows:

1. All-around teaching ability or skill, including putting the subject across, stimulating intellectual curiosity, skill in observing student reactions.
2. Assigned difficult reading, asked for more than the students could get done, assigned a great deal of reading.
3. Organization and planning of the course.

---

*R. I. Isaacson, W. J. McKeachie, J. E. Milholland, Y. G. Lin, M. Hofeller, J. W. Baerwaldt, and K. L. Zinn, "The Dimensions of Student Evaluations of Teaching," in W. J. McKeachie, R. I. Isaacson, and J. E. Milholland, *Research on the Characteristics of Effective College Teaching*, Cooperative Research Project No. OE 850 (Ann Arbor: University of Michigan, 1964).

4. Feedback to students.

5. Group interaction—students were friendly, free to express opinions, argued with one another without hostility.

6. Student-teacher rapport—listened attentively to whatever class members had to say, was permissive and flexible, explained reasons for criticisms.

In a later study at the same institution, Isaacson identified the following factors from data gathered from classes in beginning economics:

1. Skill: organization, application of theory to real world problems, preparation.

2. Value of course: relevance.

3. Change in beliefs: some students seem to want to have their attitudes changed.

4. Overload: degree to which the student finds the work excessive.

5. Structure: degree of organization exhibited in presenting material, for example, too complicated, strayed from the topic.

The Michigan group also conducted some studies in student–teacher personality relationships, finding that men high in power motive tend to be more highly motivated in sections where there is a good deal of opportunity to volunteer opinions, and men high in affiliation need are able to achieve better grades when working under friendly teachers. This relates to the personality-matching research discussed previously.

Studies of public school teachers by Cogan* in 1958 and Ryans in 1960 have also indicated that a dimension characterized by friendly, integrative, affiliative, nurturant behavior is important in public school teaching. Teachers high in these dimensions produced more student self-initiated work than teachers low in them. Taba,† on the other hand, has emphasized teaching behaviors which encourage the use of higher mental processes instead of recall–retrieval types of requirements. She describes behaviors which "lift" a discussion from one level to another; they relate to concept formation, making inferences and generalizations from specific data, applications of generalizations to explain new phenomena and predict consequences of events and conditions. Through analysis of taped discussions she has made it evident that the teacher's behavior has enormous influence on the thinking of students. Bruner* has emphasized a need for arranging situations in which students play the part of scientists, or historians, or other appropriate figures, and actually act in an appropriate way. He feels that this is the way to learn these subjects because the student is getting more different aspects

---

*Morris S. Cogan, "Theory and Design of a Study of Teacher–Pupil Interaction," *Harvard Educational Review* 26 (1956) : 315–42.

†Hilda Taba, "Teaching Strategies and Thought Processes," *Teachers College Record* 65 (1964) : 524–34.

*Jerome Bruner, *Toward a Theory of Instruction* (New York: W. W. Norton, 1966).

of the content and process simultaneously than if one breaks it down into conventional types of learning experiences. This is obviously a whole–part approach which emphasizes the ability of students to cope with complex situations, if they are presented in the right way. These two views of teaching behavior, one emphasizing warm accepting human relationships with students, the other emphasizing confrontation of students with relatively complex and rich learning tasks to take advantage of their natural capacities and abilities, are not incompatible but rather complement each other. They both call for a great deal of faith on the part of the teacher in the ability of the student to cope with his environment and in the basic desire of the student to behave in a productive and appropriate way socially, so long as the behavior is relatively compatible with his own personal needs, interests, and desires. The studies reported previously of teacher effectiveness, some coming from college courses, are based on conventional structures and teaching processes, but they neither contradict this point of view nor are entirely incompatible with it. For instance, the "skill" or "expertness" factor described in some of these is a general one having to do with both the way the material is presented and the personality of the teacher who presents it. Previous discussions of modes and styles of teaching have emphasized the interaction of teacher personality with hypothesis-forming and testing behavior on the part of the student.

Another factor that enters into this discussion is the subject matter. Some subjects, such as science, can best take their data from physical systems, which are initially rather impersonal unless the teacher participates in the interaction and lends a personal, accepting, encouraging attitude to the process. Other subjects, such as history, are so personal in the basic nature of their presentation (that is, the situations and facts must be presented before discussion can begin) and their subsequent processing through comment by the teacher and discussion, that one can easily overdo the personal aspect at the expense of rigorous analysis of the happenings and generalization and application to current problems and events. This in turn brings out the problem of the duality of the teacher's task, which is to shape behavior effectively and productively (thus requiring increasingly high levels of sophistication and accuracy and rigor) and at the same time present a warm, accepting audience to student responses so that they are not extinguished or punished.

Some of the complexity of this task is taken into account in a model of teaching at the college level by Richard Mann,* another of the University of Michigan group. He produced a questionnaire that classified teacher behavior into six components and asserted that each of these

---

*Richard D. Mann, A Report on the Student Evaluation Forms (Term I, 1966–1967). Mimeograph copy sent to author.

must be demonstrated by the teacher at some minimum level if he is to be at all successful. The categories that Mann considered important were:

a. Expert: Knowledge of subject matter.
b. Formal Authority: Grading, judging, setting standards.
c. Socializing Agent: Representative of community of specialists in this area —mathematicians, historians, etc.
d. Facilitator: Organizer, guide, tutor, programmer of content and learning process.
e. Ego Ideal: Someone with whom students identify, their ideal.
f. Person: Someone with whom they can talk, who relates to them as a person.

These categories were formed subjectively, through experience supervising a group of graduate assistants teaching introductory courses in psychology; the questionnaire was designed to return data on these categories. In order to assess the responses to the questionnaires more objectively, a factor analysis was done which revealed the following factors:

a. Teacher halo: an over-all positive rating factor across all aspects of teaching.
b. Structure: a high score indicates a high-structure classroom style.
c. Rapport: as it implies.
d. Relevance: of the course for the student, something which turned out to be important in the reaction of the student to the course.
e. Overpersonal: a factor which indicates that the students feel that the teacher is too interested in closeness, personal matters.
f. Teacher investment.
g. Difficulty.

One particular result found by Mann in relating responses to the questionnaire items to the various factors was that over-all teaching ability reflected not only the main halo factor, (a) just above, but also the extent to which the student sees the course as relevant; that is, if the course is relevant to his objectives, the student is more likely to see the teacher in a positive light. He found that the judgment by the student of the over-all value of the course was primarily a function of the *relevance* of the course to the student, but also reflected the "good teacher" factor.

19–7 Teaching Effective Teaching Behaviors

Since effective behaviors are responses, they can be conditioned under appropriate contingencies. This is being done increasingly as a part of teacher education. Some examples of behaviors taught this way may be of interest. They are derived from teacher education techniques developed by Dwight Allen and colleagues at Stanford University.*

One such behavior is that of reinforcing responses of students who evidence participation in the ongoing learning process. The teacher can do this through such phrases as, "Good," "Fine," "That's the right idea" following student participation, or he can nod or smile or write the responses on the blackboard. He may differentially reinforce the responses by picking out particularly relevant or desirable aspects of them. He could, on the other hand, announce that students who do not participate will receive a poor grade, or frown at those who respond minimally, or berate them. The task of shaping the more desirable of these behaviors requires close observation of the teacher's behavior in a representative class of students with differential reinforcement of that behavior. One way an observer might operate is to stand at the back of the room and look happy when the teacher does the right thing, or look unhappy or stern when he does not do it. Another way is to have a small transmitter that makes a tone sound in a small receiver in the teacher's ear, and to use it as a secondary reinforcer for the correct behaviors. Another way is to make a video tape of the teacher's performance and to discuss it afterwards with the teacher while observing it. Another is to have the students in the class comment on the performance.

Another behavior which has been shaped in such a manner consists of requiring students to go beyond a first-answer response to a question or problem. It is designed for lessons where pupil participation is a prerequisite to the goals of instruction. Some techniques for shaping such behavior include clarification of the student's response by the teacher, prompting the student to go further, encouraging alternative hypotheses, and redirection of the students' thoughts. A somewhat more sophisticated behavior calls for the teacher to withhold an immediate answer to the pupil's question, instead of reinforcing it as in shaping simple participation, and then to give cues which lead him to "go beyond" the information given and to differentially reinforce pupil responses that demonstrate increased critical awareness. The behaviors by which the teacher brings out this behavior include clarification of the question or response, redirection of the response, prompting through incomplete statements, encouraging alternative answers, assuming certain possibilities and proceeding as if they were true, and requiring the pupil to summarize at some point in the discussion.

Another behavior important to teachers is establishing a positive attitude toward the topic at hand, as well as establishing appropriate frames of reference for learning the topic. This involves reinforcing

---

*After *Micro-Teaching: A Description*, Stanford University, School of Education, Secondary Education Program (Summer, 1966).

teacher behaviors that result in an introduction both germane to the topic and related to students' past experiences and interests. Still another behavior to be encouraged in teachers is the relatively frequent summation of topics and concepts that have been introduced: this allows for proactive and retroactive inhibition, setting up discrimination learning contingencies between various topics where necessary, and furnishing mediating links that encourage facilitation rather than interference from one topic to another. Such frequent summaries or reviews also result in a distributed type of practice or learning session schedule which is conducive to clarity and retention.

19–8 Teacher Roles

One useful set of categories of teacher behavior, complex and many-faceted as in the Mann model, has been offered by Redl and Wattenberg in a book entitled *Mental Hygiene in Teaching.** The following are their categories, with brief descriptions of each; they form a good introduction to the more subjective observations on teacher behavior which follow:

Representative of society: By precept and example . . . try to develop the moral attitudes, the thinking patterns, the life goals which . . . make for good citizens. . . .

Judges and screeners: In many neighborhoods, school is considered the stairway which can lead a child upward into a social class above his parents. Teachers, so to speak, stand on each landing and determine who may enter the next flight of stairs.

Source of knowledge: An instructor is expected to be a living textbook from which one can get information.

Helper in the learning process: The teacher is expected to help students overcome obstacles to their learning, both collectively *and* individually.

Referee: The instructor is valued for the fairness of his verdict in a conflict between students, and for his skill in reconciling differences.

Detective: Prestige may occasionally rest on success in restoring stolen property to its rightful owners or in reassuring a group that law and order are being preserved; blundering in this role may lead to unwise use of third degree methods or mass punishment, or the class may be made too conscious of this role by over-elaborate measures to prevent cheating.

Object of identification: Through values expressed in punishment or voiced in words or illustrated in actions, teachers serve as models after whom some class members pattern themselves.

Limiter of Anxiety: By setting limits to permissible behavior, by acting with a confident and competent air, by dealing with "bad" behavior in an

---

*F. Redl and W. Wattenberg, *Mental Hygiene in Teaching* (New York: Harcourt, Brace, and World, 1951), pp. 299–304. Copyright, 1951 © 1959 by Harcourt Brace Jovanovich, Inc. and reprinted with their permission.

understanding way, teachers can meet the expectations and needs of students for support and limitations to their many anxieties.

Ego-supporter: Teachers who arrange to see that each child tastes success and that each feels sure of the teacher's confidence perform this role well: however . . . traditions of some school systems encourage teachers to stand by while slower children destroy themselves in futile efforts to meet unrelenting academic standards, and that some educators even add to the damage by expression of suspicion, hostility, or contempt.

Group leader: Teachers are expected to provide guidance so that groups achieve harmony in functioning and efficiency in reaching group goals: this may be done consciously, as for instance, by preserving an air of solemnity during the discussion which might follow serious infraction of an important rule, or by establishing a confidential informality in preparation for group counseling.

Parent surrogate: A sizable number of youngsters are unable to react objectively to instructors because their thinking processes are distorted by their feelings toward their parents, which they generalize toward all adults in authority.

Target for hostility feelings: Young people develop hostility feelings toward grownups . . . for many . . . they have been deepened by rejection at home, by parental overdomination, or by community pressure . . . One outlet . . . is to vent them against teachers. . . . This outlet is psychologically attractive because it does not involve the perilous conflicts with feelings of the love one should bear parents. Therefore . . . many teachers must cope with . . . ill-will that has nothing whatever to do with the teacher's personality or procedures. Because it may be undeserved it often hurts badly. There is no escaping this role; the best we can do is to play it in such a way that children learn how to express hostility feelings in more socially acceptable and conflicting ways.

Individual friend and confidante: Although there is a danger that a child's social development may be stunted if he substitutes friendships with grownups for the more typical relationships with his age-mates, warm personal ties with a teacher may have a definite place in rounding out children's worlds. A good teacher is almost always a good friend to many children.

Object of affection and crushes: Just as most adults need to have someone to love, so also do young people. Consequently, . . . sometimes ordinary friendly feelings in a class will take on special force for some youngsters . . . these express psychological needs that are as real and may have as little to do with the teacher's personality as the hostility discussed above. Here too the task is to deal with matters so that the children learn to handle their feelings in an appropriate manner.

Here again we have a many-variable model of teaching behavior, and the implication is that the better teacher is the one who can handle a number of these adequately, while being stronger in some than in others.

19–9 Further Discussion of Teacher Behavior

Foregoing discussions have concentrated on matters pertaining primarily to structuring, arranging, and sequencing environmental situations to make learning more probable. When this has been done, or while this is being done, there is another aspect of the teaching function that is equally important. It has to do with the personal interactions between student and teacher, between student and student, and the interactions between student and instructional medium—film, text, program, and the like.

Teaching is a complex behavior, part art, part science. Early socio-psychological studies of the effects of types of leader behavior on groups, for example, implied that there might be dependable response patterns to various teacher behavior patterns. A classic study by Lewin, Lippit, and White indicated that if one acted the part of an authoritarian leader in a group, he could expect greater conformity but also greater potential for aggression and disruption than if one acted the part of a democratic leader. The "democratic" model elicited or evoked somewhat more confusion and a higher level of over-all aggression but less susceptibility to disruption and more stability when the class was left to itself, as when the teacher left the room. Other studies have not consistently replicated these results, however, and while there are general principles that can be followed, one cannot make himself an ideal teacher by following a set of precepts derived from research. Nor can one attain such an ideal from following tradition or conventional precepts such as, "Start out tough and then get easier" or "If you really like the kids, you will make out all right." The relationships between such advice and different teacher personalities is too complex, and what works well for one teacher often seems to be just the wrong approach for another. However, there seem to be some guidelines for instruction emerging from research which make sense in terms of experience in the classroom.

An example of a helpful approach is an analysis of student–teacher relations in respect to aggression, by Horwitz.* He asserts that uncooperative behavior and aggression result from a discrepancy between expectation of the student concerning the amount of consideration shown his desires and the actual amount of consideration given as evidenced by the behavior of the teacher. This can be viewed as a special case of the optimal discrepancy model of motivation discussed previously, as well as of a frustration-leading-to-aggression model derived originally from Freudian analysis. By this model, if the students expect

---

*Murray Horwitz, "Hostility and its Management in Classroom Groups," from W. W. Charters and N. L. Gage, eds., *Readings in the Social Psychology of Education* (Boston: Allyn and Bacon, 1963), pp. 196–212.

to have their views on amount of homework considered, and if the teacher then pays no attention to these views, their expectations will not have been realized and frustration (thus aggression) will result. (If, on the other hand, they did not expect to have their views considered, then the behavior of the teacher would elicit no such response). The result will be some degree of uncooperative behavior or, in extreme cases, outright aggression. Such behavior will probably be interpreted by the teacher as reflecting on his or her personality or looks or other personal attributes; this may result in negative reactions from the teacher that make matters worse. However, the basic cause has nothing to do with the teacher personally. Another example of this is a class that expects very little in the way of consideration of their desires; an authoritarian, autocratic teacher may be just what they are looking for, while a democratic teacher may find frustration and aggression because he or she is taking their views into account to too great a degree, and the responsibility or lack of structure threatens them. Another common situation occurs when a democratic teacher sets too high a level of consideration for students' views in relation to the degrees of freedom open to the teacher: ultimately this means that the teacher will run into situations where he or she cannot grant the students as much consideration, perhaps because of prevailing school policy or because of expectations of other teachers concerning the amount of freedom to be given students. In such cases, the teacher may try to establish a lower level of considerateness, and show by his behavior that the desires and expectations of the students in particular matters are not to be considered as before. This can raise a great deal of frustration in the students, where there would be no such reaction if they had not originally been conditioned to this expectation. This sort of reaction can come also when a class of students is conditioned to expect one level of treatment by one teacher, and then in another class or another semester or another year receives much less from another teacher. However, if the second teacher has established a reputation for this level of consideration, then the students will have been forewarned and may not be frustrated since they have come to expect it in advance. Furthermore, students can adjust to quite wide discrepancies in expectation from class to class.

This model is suggestive for teacher behavior. It does not spell out details by which a given teacher may follow an ideal path in setting standards and expectations, of course. Generally speaking, students are no different from their adult models in their desire to maintain a well-ordered environment, although the level or order may be somewhat different for them. Some optimum level of deviant behavior is to be expected and is probably healthy, when all factors are taken into consideration. It may be regarded, for example, as that part of human group behavior which tests the limits and makes sure (a) that there *are* limits (for security reasons), and (b) that they are not too confining. The limits are set by the teacher, and within them he can operate without violating the expectancies of students.

The main intent of the Horwitz model is to deal with the pervasive and often threatening problem of student discipline and control as related to the establishment of expectancies by the teacher. One can, of course, establish the norms or expectancies through group consensus, involving student voice and vote, keeping in mind school rules generally, in which case there would be less problem of student acceptance of them initially. However, when the rules are set down, one must remember that they are verbal descriptions of a set of concepts of behavior, and these concepts must eventually be clarified by example. The students then may be regarded as problem solvers or concept attainers, and their behaviors as hypotheses that test whether their concept of the rule is correct. If incorrect, information must be communicated to them immediately and consistently, perhaps ultimately through some mild punishment, so that the feedback will be unmistakable: the reaction need not be punitive in *tone*, however. In this way, the class will establish by example the concepts of the limits which are in force, and thus will understand these concepts better than by the rule alone. Of course, the class may be relatively sophisticated and understand all implications of the rule through *past* experience: in this case, the deviant behavior that is demonstrated will be more for the purpose of testing the *teacher's* "understanding" of the rule (and of the game that is being played) than to test the rules or limits themselves.

Another situation where the students form concepts regarding the teacher's behavior is in the area of grading and testing. It is customary in studying testing and measurement to discuss the concept of validity at some length, where validity refers to the degree to which the behaviors required on a test correlate with behaviors emphasized or demonstrated or learned in the classroom and in independent study prior to the test. For example, it is not unusual to see a teacher describing the important points of a unit to a class, and stressing certain types of thinking and understanding, and then giving a test that either omits some of the points or requires a different type of understanding (or little understanding), or both. The students form a concept of what the teacher wants from the test, and they may subsequently ignore the teacher's invalid verbal exhortations or lectures, or they may become aggressive or disruptive due to the lack of correspondence between the class activities and the criterion behaviors. This kind of discrepancy can go deeper than this test-class activity difference. Analyses of the verbal behavior of teachers often show that they give mutually contradictory messages to their students, unknowingly, and behave in other ways to make their communications quite unclear and full of "noise."

19-10 Teacher-Centered Versus Learner-Centered Behavior

Most investigations of teacher behavior or personality have utilized two categories described as *teacher centered* and *learner centered*. In psychotherapy, in counseling, and in management, one finds similar dichotomies regarding the treatment of others. Directive versus nondirective counseling is an example. These in turn are related to the choice between use of avoidance contingencies and using positive reinforcement, or between guidance and discovery. Leadership is often described in terms of the authoritarian-democratic dimensions, or dominative-integrative, or employer-centered versus employee-centered. In classroom practice, this interacts with teaching strategies, in that the personality of the teacher helps determine the particular approach used (that is, lecture, discussion, demonstration), although these should actually be chosen according to their relative contributions to learning and their interactions in respect to the learning process, rather than by the preference of the individual teacher, stemming from personality and previous experience as a student. Thus democratic behavior is often associated with discussion approaches or strategies while lecturing is considered authoritarian or direct; yet discussions can be other than learner centered, and lectures can take individual and collective needs into account, and each has its place in the well-designed instructional system.

In a resumé of studies related to the variables discussed above, Richard Anderson* concluded that democratic leadership is associated with high morale when a primary group objective is social, while morale is higher under authoritarian leadership in groups that are primarily committed to some task goal. Anderson concluded that the evidence available failed to demonstrate that either has been associated consistently with higher productivity. Furthermore, he concluded that the authoritarian-democratic construct provided an inadequate conceptualization of leadership behavior. Implicit also in many of the studies conducted has been a moralistic implication regarding the two polar adjectives. Lewin, for example, was a German concerned with the terrible internal events in Germany during the Second World War in relation to minority groups; Skinner, in developing analysis of behavior through reinforcement paradigms, has as one objective the development of a Utopian society, as witness his formulation of such a society in *Walden Two*.

---

*Richard C. Anderson, "Learning in Discussions: A Resumé of the Authoritarian-Democratic Studies," in W. W. Charters and N. L. Gage, eds., *Readings in the Social Psychology of Education* (Boston: Allyn and Bacon, 1963), pp. 153-62.

19–11 Tone and Clarity of Teacher Behavior

One component of teacher behavior, which is seldom taken into account sufficiently, is the tone of the teacher's voice and behavior. If the teacher communicates with the students in a tone that implies interest in the subject and that has no overtones of threat, compliance with the teacher's leadership or directions will generally be good. If there is roughness in the voice or behavior of the teacher, on the other hand, there is, potentially, resentment and overt deviance from the behavior desired. Now this roughness may be used on purpose, to indicate the nature of the relationship desired by the teacher, but it must be understood in its effects on student behavior and allowed for by the teacher: if the teacher is ready to cope with the outcomes, then it may be a valid approach for certain purposes.

19–12 Grades as Contingencies for Learning

One source of extrinsic motivation which is ever the subject of debate is the use of grades. Current feelings about grades include espousal of their complete abandonment, the use of pass–fail options, and the use of comments and exhortations along with the grades to give them a personal touch. The grade is in a way similar to the food at the end of the maze; however, it is far enough away from most sections of the course that, as the goal-gradient concept implies, motivational effects will be low. This can be changed through the use of frequent interim tests and quizzes, that is, giving grades more frequently. This can lead to an adaptation effect and is thus to some degree self-defeating. On the other hand, more frequent grades can be viewed as feedback: as such it is reinforcing to some, punishing to others. Constant punishment in the form of low grades obviously implies avoidance behavior; the situation to be avoided can be the particular course or teacher or, in the case of consistent failure in many courses, avoidance of school altogether. The drop-out problem is partly a function of this, although the rationalizations of this behavior probably avoid specification of the real cause and mention instead such matters as irrelevancy and boredom. If the concept of shaping could be applied, this would be less of a problem. However, grades are used to select the better students for college and for better jobs, so obviously one cannot give a high grade to a student who is performing very poorly in relation to the rest of the class, no matter how great his progress! Or can one?

There is a facet of motivation, as presented previously, which implies some amelioration of this seemingly impossible impasse of grading practice. Students establish a level of performance which determines to some degree their expectations if there is not too heavy interference from outside influences such as parents or teachers or administrators. They will often work very hard to maintain their accustomed level but may be content with it as long as they achieve it. Thus the D student is not punished by the D as long as it is not less than he expected, unless of course he is made very anxious about it by other parties concerned with him. One should be careful about pushing such a student to achieve a higher grade, since such behavior requires the teacher to be consistent in his pushing and in his aid over a long period of time: if one should succeed in bringing the student up, and then deserts him and lets him drop back down, he inflicts unnecessary punishment. On the other hand, if one can analyze basic learning difficulties and do something to eliminate them and to maintain the new behavior, then there is every reason to intervene in a special way, beyond the regular activities of teaching. However, the problem can be that the student is avoiding improvement as a means of coping with an environmental situation that punishes academic success. Here the task is a dual one, to change the conditions that bring this about and to arrange for the student to acquire necessary fundamental concepts and processes that he has failed to learn.

Accepting these requisites, the teacher should also be alert to individual differences in the course of his or her regular behavior. Since dependent-prone persons are reinforced for compliance with authority, while creative ones are likely to exhibit unique though appropriate behaviors that may be interpreted as somewhat threatening to authority, the teacher must recognize and accept both types and not attempt to enforce completely consistent reactions across all students. The students accept each other much as they are and make allowances for differential treatment on the part of the teacher, as long as it does not violate basic expectations that are not related to individual differences. Thus one can tolerate independence of thought and action on the part of one student, and even view it as nonthreatening in most cases, so long as it is not intended to test the teacher, in spite of the fact that another student would not think of doing anything like that. Actually, if the teacher wishes to benefit his students the most, he will encourage them to show independence and curiosity and to choose tasks that enable them to be successful, since such behaviors seem to lead not only to success but to increases in ability to learn and gain success later, even to the point of increasing the score on general achievement tests ordinarily entitled "IQ" tests. There are teacher behaviors that can encourage this: some have been mentioned, including emphasis on expansion and amplification of ideas, giving alternatives and possibilities rather than straight statements of fact, and listening to the students' responses attentively and responding to them in such a way as to encourage the best aspects of them. There is also some evidence that if one encourages students to reflect upon problems at greater length than is their wont, one can contribute to their cognitive success and as a result improve their concept of themselves—thus improving their personalities in general.

19–13 Teaching Processes

Personality is best defined as a consistent pattern of behavior in general: teaching personality (as differentiated from teacher personality) is the pattern or style of behaviors exhibited in teaching. An analysis of the processes available for teaching might be expected to be related to both teacher personality and learning strategies. Thus processes are very much under discussion in this age of interest in teaching and its variations and ramifications. One such process is inquiry. Dewey referred to it as the scientific process of inquiry. Bruner calls it the "heart of education—disciplined inquiry." This gathering and processing experience strengthens the faith of the student in the regularity of the universe; it also in his opinion builds self-confidence and strengthens inductive ability. It is related to reflective thinking, productive thinking, analytic thinking, and intuitive thinking, and involves curiosity, self-motivated learning, exploring the environment, finding out how things work, becoming interested in subject matter, analyzing problems, looking for causes, defining problems, planning before acting, and such. It is also related to a selection strategy for concept attainment.

The problems of arrangement of the environment and, more particularly, of giving feedback to each student (and assisting him in interpreting it) is often a major barrier to this as a teaching strategy. In addition, one must consider the effect of discovery learning on teacher self-concept and anxiety: if students are free to think for themselves, they can threaten the teacher by their ability to note things that have been ignored by the teacher and to ask questions that the teacher cannot answer. The teacher does not have the reinforcement of completing a given lesson in a predetermined time, of wrapping concepts up in neat packages, of being able to identify the stage or level of achievement of each student through a diagnostic test, and is not able to punish recalcitrant learners with a low grade (for their own good, of course).

On the other hand, one must observe that the process of learning through deduction, given certain principles or verbal rules whose intersections or unions produce new relationships, and applying these relationships to the identification of exemplars or solution of problems, is equally important and should not be overlooked. As in the analysis of selection strategies, if the student cannot form hypotheses to apply to the situation, the opportunity to hypothesize is wasted. (One can, however, shape a nascent ability to hypothesize through providing carefully graded opportunities for such cognitive behavior).

Another process in teaching and learning which has received some attention is sometimes referred to as *self-initiated learning*. This is often regarded as one criterion for interest in the subject generated by other teaching strategies. Related to this is self-evaluation. Both of these student behaviors need to be conditioned through contingencies of the environment that result in positive affective responses to the students (i.e. positive attitudes toward them), as well as in positive outcomes in the form of satisfaction, encouragement by others, and generally feelings of competence and achievement, as well as a feeling of independence and autonomy. The latter are often punished rather than rewarded, as when a student takes off on his own only to have the teacher reprimand him for taking the wrong track or for making a mistake. This is not an easy matter, however, for to bring about self-initiated learning implies creation of environmental conditions in which it is highly probable and in which it will be reinforced, and to bring about self-evaluation means teaching the self-evaluation procedures or behaviors that make this possible—neither process is ordinarily well understood by teachers, and where it is, there are often routine barriers to their implementation. The mass education scene is generally not conducive to such differentiation and individualization, and the teacher often pays a price for attempting to encourage such things. This is not to discourage teachers from them, but to point out realistically some of the problems involved with them, and thus explain why they are not more widespread. At present then, skill in taking examinations, in following instructions, and finding solutions to problems set by others are the predominant ones encouraged and rewarded in our educational system, partly because they are the ones that can be measured easily and reliably at present. This implies that what is taught tends to be limited to that which can be evaluated—an unfortunate thing for education.

19–14 Self-as-Process

There is another process that is more subtle, more abstract, and more closely related to matters of personality than the processes above. This is sometimes referred to as *self-as-process*. It implies that, to the degree that the learner has mastered conventional learning processes and can perform them reasonably accurately without devoting full attention to each phase of them, he can turn attention to himself as a learner, a thinker, a perceiver, concept-attainer, and the like. This ability to observe oneself in the act or process of learning implies an ability to monitor one's learning in the light of previous experience and theories of learning and instruction. This is not different from the uses of concepts and processes, but is merely another step in the addition of levels of complexity and sophistication to the basic paradigms of learning.

Generally, this monitoring of one's own behavior, including cognitive behavior, and modifying it accordingly is an area which has received very little attention. It reflects human capacities at a high level of sophistication, however, and one can hope that ultimately a science of instruction will be able to cope with this phenomenon as well as others of the same level.

Bibliography

SCHULMAN, L. and KEISLAR, E. *Learning by Discovery: A Critical Appraisal.* Chicago: Rand McNally, 1966.

STEPHENS, I. M. *The Process of Schooling: A Psychological Examination.* New York: Holt, Rinehart, and Winston, 1967.

Index

Piaget, Jean, 54, 219; and developmental aspects of problem-solving, 143–46; problem-solving views of, 146–47; and research in problem-solving, 133–34

Plato, 219

Practice, distribution of, 67, 121; in form of drill, 78–79; function of, 77–79; negative, 196

Problem (defined), 125–26

Problem-solving, computer-related analyses of, 139–41; computer simulation of, 157–60; defined, 126; developmental aspects of, 143–44; developmental stages after Piaget, 145–46; Dewey analysis of, 138–39; exemplars of, 127–37; Gestalt analyses of, 141–43; by groups, 155–56; habit or set for, 155; as heuristics, 153–54; implications of Piaget's view of, 146–47; learner-system interaction in, 148–51; teacher's role in, 156–57; teaching strategies in, 152–53; wholistic vs. partistic, 154–55

Programmed instruction, 236–40; and the instructional system, 253–54; multimedia approaches to, 252–53; in schools, 249–252; and step-size, 247–48; technical aspects of, 241–47; and uncertainty principle, 248–49

Programs, 242–43

Projection, 166

Psycholinguistics, 51–52

Psychosexual development, 173–74

Punishment, and conditioning, 9–10; effects of, 30–31

Quizzes, 210–11; *see also* Tests

Rationalization, 166

Reaction formation, 166

Redl, Fritz, 176–77, 269

Redundancy, 112–16

Regression, 166

Reinforcement, of desirable behavior, 38–39; in drive theory, 183–84; implicit, 25–26; intermittent, 13; interval, 13; and management of student behavior, 26–29; and motivation maintenance, 26; negative, 17–18; ratio, 13; scheduling of, 13, 210–11; scheduling to maintain motivation, 27–29; variable, 29–30

Reinforcer, 1, 5, 6; intrinsic vs. extrinsic, 43; necessity of, 8; secondary, 2, 8–9; transituational, 42

Releasing mechanism, 43

Remembering (teaching of), 73–74

Repetition, 58; *see also* Practice

Response, chains of, 20; classical, 2; classical vs. operant, 9–10; conditional, 1; controlled by common subset, 83–84; elimination of, *see* Desensitization; forgetting of, 9–10; iconic, 40; imitative, 8, 47; involuntary, 3; latency of, 20; operant, 3; probability of, 5; problem-solving, 129; recovery of, 6; spontaneous recovery of, 1; as stimulus, 41; suppression of, 9; symbolic, 40–41; unconditioned, 1; and verbal stimulus, 40; voluntary, 3; *see also* specific responses

Response chains, 43–44

Reversal shifts, 100–102

Rousseau, Jean-Jacques, 219

Rowe, Mary Badd, 151*n*.

Ryans, David G., 257, 265–66

Scheduling (of reinforcement), 210–11

Self-as-Process, 278–79

Self-concept, 102–103

Sensitivity training, 194–95

Sequencing (by programming), *see* Programmed instruction

Serial learning, applications of, 62–63; retention in, 62; serial position curve used in, 60–61; speed in, 62

Shaping, 15–16, 199–201

Sharpeners, 22

Sign learning (signal learning), 19

Social behavior, 42

Social facilitation, 26, 189–90

Socrates, 218–19

Step-size, 247–48

Stimulus (i), aversive, 17; conditioned, 1; discriminative, 5; expanded concept of, 82–83; figure in, 82; generalization, 21–22; ground in, 82; nature of, 10–11; neutral, 1; pairing of, 7; reinforcing, 5; and response control, 36; response-produced, 165–66; secondary reinforcing, 8–9; sequences of, 19–20, 38; substitution, 7; unconditioned, 1, 7; verbal, 40–41

Stimulus equivalence, 68

Stimulus modes, 53–54, 221–23

Stimulus sampling, 108–10

Sublimation, 167

Substitution, 7

Success, 192–93

Successive approximation learning, 15–17

Supergo, 172

Support, group, 215–16; individual, 216–17

Suppression (of response), 9–10

Symbolic stage (in child development), 146

Systems (multimedia or multimodal), 252–53

T-Group, 193, 194–95, 211

Teacher, congruence with students, 260; "good", 256–57

Teacher behavior, discussed expansively, 271–74; effective, 257–60; Mann model of, 266–67; recent studies of, 257–60; Redl-Wattenberg model of, 269–70; teaching of effective, 267–69; tone and clarity of, 275

Teaching, analysis of, 161–62; of concepts, *see* Concept teaching; of effective teaching behaviors, 267–69; factors interfering with, 227–29; as problem solving, 160–61; of processes, 277–78; relation to learning, 218–20; and stimulus modes, 221–23; and teacher behavior, 228–30; and teacher's personality, 257

Teaching strategy(ies), 223–24; in problem solving, 152–53; pure reception as, 224–26

Terminal behavior, 245–47

Test anxiety, 32; treatment of, 196–97

Tests (and reinforcement scheduling), 29

Thematic Apperception Test, 261–62

Therapy, behavioral, 195–98; group vs. individual, 216–17; motivation, 193–94

Thinking, convergent, vs. divergent, 178–79; deductive, 56–57; inductive, 56; symbolic, 55

Thought, symbolic 55; symbolic mode of, 123; teaching to effect change in, 214–15

Three-term contingency, 6

Transcription, 46

Transfer, 65–66

Translation, 45

Trial and error, 101–102

Uncertainty principle, 248–49

Understanding, 111–12

Verbal behavior, conditioned economically, 50–51; conditioned environmentally, 53; conditioning of, 43–44; defining, 41–42; development of, 49–50; early, 50–51; learning sets in, 68–69; psycholinguistic approach to, 51–52; reinforcement of, 42–43

Verbal learning, 76–77

Walberg, H. J., 262–63

Wattenberg, William, 269

A B C D E F G H I J   9 8 7 6 5 4 3 2 1

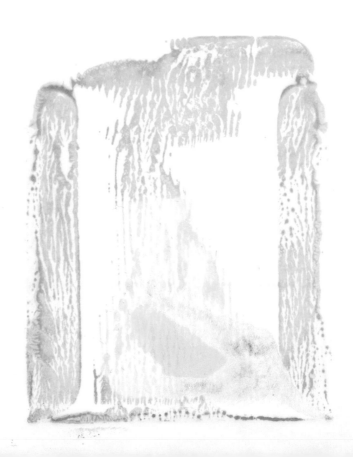